Singers and the Song II

Singers
and the Song II

Gene Lees

New York   Oxford

OXFORD UNIVERSITY PRESS

1998

Oxford University Press

Oxford   New York

Athens   Auckland   Bangkok   Bogotá   Bombay
Buenos Aires   Calcutta   Cape Town   Dar es Salaam
Delhi   Florence   Hong Kong   Istanbul   Karachi
Kuala Lumpur   Madras   Madrid   Melbourne
Mexico City   Nairobi   Paris   Singapore
Taipei   Tokyo   Toronto   Warsaw

and associated companies
Berlin   Ibadan

Published by Oxford University Press, Inc.
198 Madison Avenue, New York, New York 10016

Oxford is a registered trademark of Oxford University Press

Library of Congress Cataloging-in-Publication Data

Lees, Gene.
Singers and the Song: II / Gene Lees.
p.   cm.
ISBN 0-19-511556-2
1. Popular music–United States–History and criticism.
2. Singers–United States.   I. Title.
ML3477.L43   1998   782.42164'092'273–dc21   97–29823

1 3 5 7 9 8 6 4 2

Printed in the United States of America
on acid-free paper

Credits

To Philip Lees
My son, friend, and fellow songwriter

Contents

Foreword

Singers and the Song explores an art that originated in a time when to say "good popular music" was not to utter an oxymoron. It is one of two books that are indispensable to a deep appreciation of the vocal music that America has contributed to the world's fund of lasting cultural achievements.

In *American Popular Song*, published in 1972, Alec Wilder used his formidable learning, analytical ability, wit, and strong opinions to treat his subject with a seriousness it had never before received. At once scholarly and entertaining, Wilder scrutinized the work of songwriters from Jerome Kern to Frank Loesser. He discussed more than 900 songs and provided annotated analyses of 384 of them. Erudite and acerbic, a wonderful songwriter himself, Wilder imposed a minimum level of acceptable quality. He explained his criteria with clarity and elegance, lashed the best writers for mediocrity, and praised brilliance in genius and journeymen alike. His book, it is safe to say, is on the shelf of every songwriter, singer, and critic who reveres the popular song tradition.

Next to it, or nearby, is almost certain to be Gene Lees' *Singers and the Song*, first published in 1987, now polished and expanded into an even more valuable volume. Wilder achieved insight through his composer's formal knowledge and craftsman's sense as one of the last great songwriters of the classic period that ended in the mid-1950s. Lees brings to his consideration of popular song a creator's involvement, a performing artist's knowledge of what works, and a journalist's clear-eyed powers of observation.

Gene Lees the singer has performed and recorded with some of the best jazz artists of our time. He has a compendious knowledge of singing and songwriting, among a staggering variety of other subjects. He is a perpetual student with an omnivorous need to know why and how people do what they do. He wrote an unorthodox rhyming dictionary patterned after not English but French rhyming dictionaries. An important lyricist, he fashioned English words for several of the songs of Antonio Carlos Jobim. *This Happy Madness* is one of the finest sets of lyrics to grace a Jobim song in any language. Lees' words to *Corcovado* are a part of the cultural atmosphere of the second half of the century. His work has been recorded by Frank Sinatra, Tony Bennett, Peggy Lee, Ella Fitzgerald, Shirley Horn, Sarah Vaughan, Carmen McRae, Nancy Wilson, Joe Williams, and indeed just about every important singer of recent decades.

Most writing about jazz and popular music, as sophisticated readers recognize with a wince, is done by fans who have become writers. Most are cheer leaders, press agents without portfolio who leave in their printed wakes evaluations and pronouncements supported by raw opinion and nerve endings. Some go to the trouble of learning about the music beyond personalities and trends. The best of them transcend their star worship and their proclivities to promotion and advocacy. A few gain critical skills and faculties that allow them to produce work helpful to listeners who want a better understanding of the music. The late Willis Conover, titan of the *Voice of America*, often described himself as a "professional fan" and was the best of that breed, but he transformed himself into a superb writer about jazz and a respected critic, although he would have shrunk in horror from that denomination.

Gene Lees brings to jazz writing the skills of a trained and experienced journalist. He was born in Hamilton, Ontario, and grew up forty miles from there in St. Catharines on the Lake Ontario shore, near where Canada and the United States share Niagara Falls. He and trumpeter Kenny Wheeler were high school friends. His first job at a newspaper was on the *Hamilton Spectator*, covering city hall, school-board meetings, ribbon cuttings, political speeches, crime and fires and accidents. At the *Toronto Telegram*, he reported on the courts. He was beaten into the shape of a newspaperman by tough editors who demanded accuracy and clear story-telling. At the *Montreal Star*, he covered labor, then became an assistant city editor and a correspondent in Europe. The *Louisville Times* lured him to Kentucky and made him music and drama editor. He thought he should have a better understanding of what he was writing about, joined a drama group, and resumed the formal study of music, a pursuit he continues today. Awarded a John Ogden Reid Fellowship of $5000, a substantial windfall for a newspaperman in 1958, he returned to Europe and spent a year studying music, film, and drama festivals and arts funding.

Lees had long been captivated by jazz and insisted, in his writing for the *Times*, in treating it with the same respect that he applied to his writings about classical music. In his youth, the big bands were years away from foundering. He absorbed their music and was permanently affected by the bands, their musicians, and the culture that swirled around them.

Throughout *Singers and the Song*, he melds with his thoroughgoing research the sense of wonder and pleasure that grew in the boy listening to good bands that stopped near St. Catharines and played by the lake.

The beginning of the second piece in this book, the remarkable *Pavilion in the Rain*, is a masterpiece of writing that is evocative without succumbing to sentiment. The first two paragraphs capture a time and a thousand places that shared a cultural mood. *Pavilion in the Rain* goes on to defy the conventional thought about why an era passed. It makes a case so sound that the reader wonders why it took thirty years to emerge. It is Lees at the top of his game, which is illumination.

When in 1959 the opportunity came for Lees to become editor of *Down Beat*, he was mature in journalism and music. He brought to *Down Beat* a professionalism in coverage, editing, and style that elevated it significantly above its decades as a fan magazine. In his own writing, he honed his ability to find the center of a performance, a trend, a style, a person, as in his 1962 article about Brazilian musicians who found themselves culturally stranded and bewildered in New York during the first wave of the bossa nova phenomenon. It was one of the best things ever to appear in *Down Beat*, and Lees wonderfully expands its essence in *Um Abraço No Tom*, his essay on Jobim.

Lees founded his *Jazzletter* in 1981. He has written, edited, and published it with the rigor of an old-fashioned managing editor who enforces high standards of accuracy, clarity, and fairness—he once threw out one of his own pieces at press time on grounds of lack of objectivity—and with the passion of an editorial page editor who cares about his community. Lees' community may seem to be that of jazz musicians, but the 1500 or so subscribers to the *Jazzletter* include a sophisticated mix of players, composers, arrangers, prominent writers about the arts, and a fair percentage of listeners who are physicians, lawyers, computer professionals, airline pilots, professors, and actors. Like all good editors, he knows his readers and the community they comprise. He knows that his community is part of the world, and he knows how the two interact.

When he devotes an issue to a topic that seems apart from music and subscribers complain, he refunds their money and sends them on their way. That happened when a few readers grumbled about his examination of U.S. health care reform and the Canadian health system. Lees thought that musicians and jazz listeners would be concerned about one of the most pressing economic and social issues of the 1990s. They were; his mail responding to the essay was heavy and largely positive. The letters he printed reflected a wide and intelligent range of thought about a troubling societal problem.

When writing about music and musicians, Lees is not reluctant to move out of the tight little categories on which so many jazz devotees insist. The pieces on Julius La Rosa and Edith Piaf may have seemed out of context to some *Jazzletter* readers, but they illuminate (there's that essential word again) the condition of the artist, indeed the human condition. I showed the La Rosa story to a friend of mine who is an anesthesiologist. He is from a close Italian family that gave him support and encouragement, a family quite unlike La Rosa's. Reading the piece, he recognized his life and his family, and the difference, and wept.

In the foreword to the first edition of *Singers and the Song*, Grover Sales wrote that only *I.F. Stone's Weekly* compared to Gene Lees' *Jazzletter*. Izzy Stone's meticulously researched hell-raising is gone. Lees comes from the tradition that produced Stone. He applies its values to a division of the arts that gets little of the loving, stern, journalistic attention it needs. The *Jazzletter* has been his demanding taskmaster for nearly two decades. From time to time he tells his readers that he is thinking about giving it up. Let us hope that they continue to dissuade him, because the *Jazzletter* is the source of books like *Singers and the Song*.

—Doug Ramsey

Doug Ramsey has a distinguished history as a newspaper reporter in Seattle and television reporter and anchorman in San Francisco, New Orleans, and New York City. He has been writing about music for forty years. He is the author of Jazz Matters: Reflections on the Music and Some of Its Makers.

Singers and the Song II

William and Harold
and How to Write Lyrics

In the autumn of 911, the Frankish king Charles III, known as Charles the Simple, unable to halt the bloody Viking incursions on his northwestern coast—indeed, the longships had gone up the Seine as far as Paris—made the best of a bad situation by coming to an agreement with the marauders. This was the so-called treaty of St. Clair-sur-Epte. Charles allowed them to settle permanently in an area to which in due course they lent their name. They were, in their own language, *nortmanni*, northmen. Nearly a thousand years later some of their far-distant descendants would come from places as yet not dreamed of, such as Quebec and Winnipeg, Wichita and Chicago, Rimouski and Hoboken and San Diego, to land once more on these shores, young men bearing names derived from the *nortmanni*, such as Beaudry and Dupuis, Plumber and Draper, and Fitzgerald. They called the beaches here by new and alien names—Utah and Omaha, Sword and Gold—and many of them would die in the surf or flinging their grappling hooks up the cliffs or climbing the ropes with rifles on their backs, die in their struggle to come home to their ancestral Normandy.

In return for his undoubtedly grudging generosity, Charles got an agreement from the *nortmanni*, whose leaders became the dukes of Normandy: they were to keep the other Vikings off his neck, support his monarchy, and speak the language of the country, which was already recognizable as French, a dialect of the soldier Latin left behind by the long-vanished Roman garrisons. He thereby initiated the chain of historical events that determined how people who speak English as their primary language actually think, tell jokes, express anger, make love, and write songs.

Charles the Simple might be called the grandfather or possibly the midwife of the English language. But whatever we call him, had he not allowed the Vikings to settle in Normandy, the Franco-Germanic hybrid we call English would not exist.

The Normans were a ruthless, energetic, bellicose people with a taste and a talent for power. One of their dukes had by his mistress a son, a boy who was called William the Bastard. This is not a flattering name, and so after he defeated the army of King Harold near Hastings in September of 1066 and had himself crowned King of England, he saw to it that he was henceforth known as William the Conqueror. This is called public relations.

Conquerors are notably disinclined to learn the language of their subjects. We may surmise that this is because they are so busy with more important things, such as appropriating land, giving themselves titles, selecting the best of the local girls, and dispensing justice to those who object. In time the conqueror's language is perceived as that of the successful—the rich and the powerful who evolve into an emplaced aristocracy. To this day names like Beaumont and Clairmont and those with the prefix "de" seem to people who speak English to have more class than those of Anglo-Saxon origin. Traces of the social strata extant under the Normans are preserved in surnames. Those of craftsmen are English, for example Baker, Fisher, Hedger, Shepherd, Shoemaker, Wainwright, Weaver, Webber. But those of skilled artisans are French—Carpenter, Draper, Mason, Plumber, Tailor. And of course Irish names beginning with Fitz, corrupted from *fils de*, son of, are all Norman French.

Legal proceedings were conducted in French. This continued until the Plague killed so many people that there were not enough French-speaking judges to go around and English at last became the language of the courts. But by then the very vocabulary of the law was almost entirely French, excepting Latin technical terms such as *sine die* and *nollo contendere*, and thus it remains: *tort, appeal, justice, jurisprudence, arraignment, verdict, illegal.* For nearly three hundred years, until 1362, Parliament (itself a French term) spoke French.

But though the common people learned a certain amount of French, they did not forget their own language, which in our time is referred to inaccurately as Anglo-Saxon. The Angles and Saxons were only two of the Germanic peoples who had brought their languages to England. The Danes had been there, and they left their mark in place names ending in *-by*, such as Rigby. Old Norse also made up part of the language which, by the time Harold caught an arrow at Hastings, was already known as English.

Once the flow of French into English was begun, it never ceased. And whereas the first influence was Norman French, Central French later penetrated the language. Thus we find in English a whole series of separate but related words imported from those two forms of old French—*catch* from Norman French, *chase* from Central French, the *w* of the former replaced by a *g* in the latter: *warden* and *guardian, warranty* and *guarantee, wage* and *gage, reward* and *regard.* Indeed, English preserves many traces of the evolution of the French language that French itself does not. These include any number of words imported twice, both before and after French dropped an *s* and replaced it with a circumflex accent over the vowel—*hostel* and *hotel,* for example.

Because the French were the aristocracy, to this day things in French seem so, well, *chic,* that we continue to import French terminology insatiably, adding to the English vocabulary such words as *couturier, coiffeur, chemise, culotte, chef, maître d'hôtel* (now assimilated to the point of the truncated "mater dee"), *hors d'oeuvre, cuisine, à la mode, à la carte, au gratin, au jus,* and *table d'hôte,* reflecting a profound admiration for French food and fashions. So great was French pioneering in the field of flight that its vocabulary is still extensively French—*aviation, aviator, aileron, fusillage, nacelle, dirigible.*

Latin remained the language of the scholars. For three centuries England's literature was not just bilingual but trilingual. There is a "pop" song of the period that contains these lines in French, English and Latin:

> Ma très duce et très amé,
> night and day for love of thee,
> supiro.

English continued to borrow from Latin words that had already entered it in their French forms, giving us such pairs as *blame* and *blaspheme, chance* and *cadence, count* and *compute, dainty* and *dignity, fealty* and *fidelity, frail* and *fragile, poor* and *pauper, ray* and *radius, spice* and *species, strait* and *strict, sure* and *secure.*

With their pride of language broken, the English became wanton in their importations from other languages, eventually taking in *shampoo, bungalow,* and *pajama* from Hindi, *typhoon* from Chinese, and *tycoon* from Japanese. An enormous amount of Spanish has come into English through the American Southwest, and the process is accelerating.

But of all the languages to which English is indebted for the richness of its vocabulary, none compares to French. Roughly half the language is French or else derives from Latin words that are also used in French. The other half derives from Anglo-Saxon or Old Norse. The result is that English seems to have two words, or more, for almost everything. Those that derive from Anglo-Saxon seem earthier and more immediate than those from French, as in the pairs *freedom-liberty, friendship-amity, hatred-*

enmity, truth-verity, lying-mendacity, domicile-home. Consider your own response to those two French words *hostel* and *hotel* and that Anglo-Saxon word *inn.* An inn seems older, more intimate, cozier, than a hotel, with good plain food and a fire. The words for basic things and concepts tend to derive from Anglo-Saxon: *heaven, earth, hell, love, hate, life, death, beginning, end, morning, night, day, month, year, heat, cold, way, path, meadow, stream.* But we use French or Latin or sometimes Greek words to cope with and express abstractions. When we use a French word instead of the Anglo-Saxon, it has an effect of intellectuality and detachment. English contains the word French word *crepuscule* but it does not have the emotional heat and evocative power of *dusk, twilight, sunset,* and *sundown.*

I have often wondered whether a language shapes the people who speak it or a people develop their language in accord with their own tendencies of temperament. A language is always in harmony with the broad general character of the people. The Spanish language, with its formality, seems like the Spanish people. The German language, with its relentless consistency and inflexible structure, is like the German people in their passion for *Ordnung,* order. And the French language, with its clarity and transparency and lightness, is so like the people who speak it. Only a people who spoke such a tongue could have invented the *soufflé.* Or *meringue.*

In the case of English, one can see various important ways in which the language has shaped the people. Of course, all history shapes us, but English has some peculiar and powerful emotional effects on those who speak it as their native tongue.

Let us return to the Anglo-Saxon peasants laboring in the fields for the Normans. At their work they spoke English. When they surrendered the product of that work to the master, they spoke French. They raised pigs and cows and sheep and lambs, but when they turned the meat over to the Normans it became *porc* or *boeuf* or *mouton* or *veal.* In many French words the *l* has fallen silent, replaced by *u,* which is how *veal* became *veau.* English uses the older form of the French word. A French word containing *u* after another vowel often yields up its meaning if you replace it with *l.* The acute *é* at the start of a French word, like the circumflex in *bâtard,* usually indicates a vanished *s.*

The use of French words instead of the available Anglo-Saxon equivalents is one of the ways reality is masked in the thought processes of English-speaking people. I have yet to encounter a psychiatrist or psychoanalyst who had a grasp of this fact.

The horse escaped double-naming. The only thing you can call horse meat is horse meat. And we won't eat it. But the French, Swiss, and Italians will and do. How would you feel about ordering swine flesh in a restaurant? That is what pork is called in German—*Schweinfleisch.* Would we eat horse if the meat were known as *cheval?* I think we might. Calling it *cheval* would permit us to avoid the awareness of where it came from.

Polite ladies and teachers caution the young not to use certain words because they are "not nice" without having any idea why they are not nice. They are "not nice" for no other reason than that they are, or sound like, or seem like, Anglo-Saxon words, still perceived as the language of the coarse and lowly. For example, to avoid the use of the word *belly,* which derives from Anglo-Saxon *belg,* polite people say *stomach,* which is grossly inaccurate since the stomach is an internal organ of digestion. But *stomach* derives from the French name for that organ, *estomac,* and therefore seems more genteel (from French *gentil,* meaning kind). A promenade seems to have more "class" than a mere walk. And in English the verb *to promenade* carries a connotation of conspicuous display and self-conscious posturing. Nice people don't sweat, they perspire. An odor (*odeur*) is less offensive than a smell. It is far more elegant to recline than to lie down, to retire rather than go to bed, to dine than eat.

This psychological bifurcation reaches its extreme in words pertaining to the body. Those Anglo-Saxon words denoting the body and its parts and functions have not only been barred from polite conversation for centuries, they have been literally outlawed until recent times. People could and did go to jail for using them.

The most suppressed word in the English language is a verb for the act essential to the survival of our own and every other species on this fragile sphere. There are more than four billion human beings on it, not to mention dogs, cats, lions, armadillos, dolphins, dugongs, lemurs, ladybugs, and fireflies. And we all got here the same way. The word in question is the only transitive verb we have for this action. And we are not supposed to use it. Mind you, the French cognate for it is used only in a coy and evasive way in slang expressions such as *fous le camp* and *je m'en fous.* The French use their word for *kiss* to replace it and then, having thoroughly confused the issue, use their word for *embrace*—demonstrably something done with *les bras,* the arms—to replace *kiss.* But the French cognate of our condemned word has nowhere near the power of shock of the English, which to the day she died my mother referred to as "That Word." That Word is not, despite a popular theory, an acronym for an old British navy charge, *For Unlawful Carnal Knowledge.* Nor can it be defined as slang. Besides the French cognate, it has another in German, *ficken,* and still others in other languages. It traces back to Sanskrit.

Although French too has its evasions, they are nowhere near as extensive as those of English, and the French do not have the same fear of words that the English do, or the same need to conjure euphemisms from the vocabularies of other languages. The result is that many words that are quite "strong" in English from suppression have become weak from casual use in French. A classic example is *con*. It surely is not necessary to explain the cognate in English. Add the word *pauvre*. When the French call someone a *pauvre con*, the expression not only does not have the force of its English equivalent, it does not even have the same meaning. It means merely poor guy, poor jerk, and there is even a certain compassion in it. A film advertised and exhibited all over Paris was entitled *P'tit Con*. Even today, long after the death of Lenny Bruce, it is difficult to imagine a title utilizing the English cognate on billboards and movie marquees in Canada, Australia, the United States, or England.

The discomfort with Anglo-Saxon words, and even words that sounded as if they might be Anglo-Saxon, lasted so long that eventually any direct mention of the body became difficult if not impossible for many people. In some, even an indirect symbolic illusion became distasteful. During the reign of Queen Victoria, the polite English person would avoid use of the word *leg*, from Old Norse *leggr*, substituting the word *limb*, which is in fact Anglo-Saxon but looks French, perhaps because of a resemblance to *jambe*. This idiocy went so far that gentlefolk would even speak of the "limbs" of a table, and in time came to find even the sight of them so suggestive that they took to hiding them under long tablecloths. One can only shake one's head in wonder at the neurasthenia of people afraid of being turned on by a table.

It is but a short step from finding the word for something dirty to finding the thing itself dirty. The Protestant Reformation did not originate in England, but the structure of the language assuredly made its people particularly susceptible to the Manichaean austerities of the sects we refer to collectively as Protestantism.

Finally, with the rise of Puritanism, at first in England and later in America, certain Anglo-Saxon words were driven altogether underground, and it became illegal to print them. This remained so well into the twentieth century. During the time of its banishment, That Word, as if in retaliation, took on a quality of anger that eventually made it extremely useful in expressing insult or contempt. In French, its cognate can be used for similar purpose but has nowhere near the intensity, because the taboo is lighter.

In any culture, there is a strong relationship between taboo and humor. What one should not talk about is precisely what is funny to talk about since it surprises, and surprise is a critical element in causing laughter. Religious jokes seem to be fairly common in many Spanish-speaking countries, sexual jokes less so. The latter are probably the predominant form of joking in English, because of the capacity of both the subject and the Anglo-Saxon vocabulary for it to induce shock. The two are inextricably linked, which one can see by taking any such joke and replacing its Anglo-Saxon terms with French or Latin synonyms.

If Anglo-Saxon provides the vocabulary with which we express anger and induce laughter, it is also the vocabulary that induces sexual arousal, as an examination of a piece of contemporary pornography reveals. And it is also the most effective vocabulary to use in poetry or lyrics. It is then, at any level and for any purpose, the most emotional part of the language. We use the French half of our language to express our abstract thoughts, the Anglo-Saxon for our most concrete feelings.

Editors and teachers commonly urge writers and students to use small words, as if there were some special virtue in their length alone. The reason these words are so effective is not that they are small but that they are Anglo-Saxon. Lo these nine centuries after William the Conqueror crossed the Channel and left poor Harold, as an old Lancashire-accent music-hall rhyme puts it, "with an eye full of arrow, on 'is 'orse with 'is 'awk in 'is 'and," the old language still has an extraordinary hold over us.

It has been said that we whose primary language is English speak Anglo-Saxon until the age of three and then begin learning French. Ever afterwards we will by some deep intuition use the old language for matters of the heart and things of the earth and things close to home, and French to soar into imaginative abstraction. A child first learns words like *hand, foot, arm, leg, mouth, smoke, burn, feel, touch, rain, sun, moon, sleep, wake, love, fish, kiss, sky, stars.*

Cole Porter uses French in the light and sardonic phrase in such songs as *I've Got You Under My Skin*, urging the recipient of the attentions to use her mentality and wake up to reality. But when he wants to evoke strong images and emotions, he turns to Anglo-Saxon, as in his magnificent song *In the Still of the Night*, using such words as *flight* and *thoughts* (with their vanished *gh* gutterals), *gaze* and *stray*.

Johnny Mercer, the archetype of the modern troubadour and perhaps the best lyricist in the whole field of American song, does the same thing constantly.

Mercer's work unceasingly illustrates a principle stated by T.S. Eliot: that poetry can communicate before it is even understood. It is haunting because of the evocative power of the language he uses and the resultant instantaneous imagery.

Yet for all this vividness of imagery, English has drawbacks as a language in which to write lyrics. For one thing it is poor in rhyme. There are only four words in English that rhyme with *love–above, dove, glove*, and *shove*, with *of* forming, at least in North American usage, a fifth. (In proper British English, *of* rhymes with *suave*.) Since the overwhelming majority of our songs are love songs, this presents a problem, and leads to endlessly recurring references to the stars or moon or sky above and to things one is dreaming of. In French, however, there are fifty-one rhymes that I know of for *amour*, including the words for *suburb, deaf, day, work, drum, tower,* and *around.* Thus it would be child's play in French to knock out a quatrain or two about being deaf to all else when I come home after a long day's work with a heart beating like a drum to my true love in our ivory tower in our suburb, all of it in rhyme. Try it in English.

The rhythmic character of the French language further enriches its rhymes. There are scores of words that rhyme with *nuage*, meaning cloud, including *verbiage, mariage, visage, voyage, pillage, cage, bandage, village, plumage,* and *image.* All these words exist in both languages. They rhyme in French but not in English. The stress in French is even, balanced, which tends to determine the character of French music. Consider the music of Debussy, so like the French language in its elegant equanimity. Because of this balance, all the aforementioned words can function as one-syllable or masculine rhymes: mari*age*, pil*lage*, ban*dage*. But English is a strongly stressed language, and most of those words have what is called a feminine stress, with emphasis on the penultimate syllable. Thus in English only two words on that list rhyme with each other, *pillage* and *village.*

Rhyming in French has been further expanded by the gradual dropping of terminal consonants. Going back to the words that rhyme with *amour*, we find that it is correct to use *faubourg*, meaning suburb, because the final *g* is silent, or *sourd*, meaning deaf, because the *d* is silent. Furthermore, you can rhyme singular words with plurals in French because the *s* is mute except before a vowel, in which case you should not be at a rhyme point anyway.

Finally, the option of putting the adjective before or after a noun further opens up the rhyming of French. To be sure, whether you put it before or after the noun subtly and sometimes profoundly alters the meaning. But this alternative has almost disappeared from English. At one time it was quite acceptable to put the adjective after the noun, particularly in poetry, and the practice was unobjectionable as recently as 1937, when Oscar Hammerstein could without qualm write of building a home "on a hilltop high."

But I would hesitate to do that today. For better or worse, lyrics have tended toward the natural sequence of normal speech, and in English the now almost infrangible rule is that the adjective precedes the noun.

Some years ago in Paris, I told Charles Aznavour that I envied him and other French lyricists the richness of the language's rhyming. "It's true," he said, "but in practice we end up using the same rhymes over and over again, just as you do in English. It is what comes before them that gives a lyric freshness." This is quite correct. It takes dogged patience to find a new approach to an old rhyme.

Another advantage of French over English is the device of liaison, the technique of linking syllables in a fluid manner. You pronounce *très* as *treh* (but not *tray!*), as in *très tard* (very late), but *très agréable* as *treh zagrayabl.* In either instance, the flow of sound is elegant and smooth. This and other rules of pronunciation render almost non-existent the collisions of consonants that the better lyricists in English, such as Mercer and Alan Jay Lerner, seek so consciously and constantly to avoid. And that avoidance further restricts the writer's choice of words.

For all these reasons, French flows better, and it is my impression that the devices of the language's pronunciation make it possible to sing it faster than English. The magnificent songs of Charles Trenet have, sad to say, fallen from fashion. Back in the 1930s, the years between the wars, as the French think of them, when Jerome Kern, Harold Arlen, Howard Dietz and Arthur Schwartz, Irving Berlin, and Cole Porter were at the peak of their productivity in America, Trenet in France turned out a body of songs (both lyrics and music) that are among the best of this century, including *La Mer*, which has a magnificent lyric, a hymn to the sea that was turned in an American incarnation into the pedestrian love song *Beyond the Sea.* Another of his songs, *Que reste-t'il de nos amours?* (What's left of our loves?) fared rather better as *I Wish You Love,* although the English lyric has little to do with the original. In any case, I don't think certain of Trenet's songs—songs such as *Je chante, Pigeon vole,* and *Fleur bleue*—could have been sung as fast as he was wont to do them had their lyrics been in English.

Much of the better American popular music created before the rise of rock and roll is being seen as an art music, and perhaps rightly so. During the period between 1900 and 1955—when, as Alec Wilder said, the amateurs took over—these two languages, French and English, produced an astonishing body of exquisite songs. No other language, not Italian, not German, not Portuguese, not Spanish, raised the popular song to such heights. Support for this view comes from colleagues in other countries in explaining their fascination with American songs. The brilliant Portuguese lyrics that played as important a role in the bossa nova movement as the music itself, the work of such poetic writers as Newton Mendonça and Vinicius de Moraes, were something new to Brazil, and in part inspired by the work of such Americans as Cole Porter. In the case of de Moraes, there was undoubtedly a French influence as well, since he had lived in Paris and spoke French.

What American songs and French songs of that golden age had in common was excellence. In style, subject matter, and content, however, they were quite different. Most of the best American songs came out of musical theater and, to a lesser extent, movies. The songs were at first little interpolations into negligible stories, but later, as musical comedy became more sophisticated in structure and content, each song was expected to advance the drama or illuminate the characters and situations. The composers usually tried to design several of the songs in a play so that they could stand on their own, be recorded and played on the radio. This ambivalent function was never more brilliantly fulfilled than by Lerner and Loewe in *My Fair Lady* and by Frank Loesser in *Guys and Dolls*.

The great French songs came from a different tradition, one growing out of the old music halls and for which there has never really been an American equivalent. This is the individual song written for an individual singer—Mistinguette, Maurice Chevalier, Edith Piaf, Jean Sablon, Juliette Greco, Charles Trenet, Gilbert Bécaud, Charles Aznavour, Yves Montand, and the Belgian Jacques Brel. Sometimes the performers were, as in the cases of Bécaud, Brel, Trenet, and Aznavour, themselves the composers of their material. But sometimes, as in the instances of Chevalier and Piaf, the singer was dependent on the output of certain favored composers, with whom they would often work in close collaboration. Piaf's songs were *designed* for her. They were not songs she picked up from song-pluggers or musical comedies.

Because these songs were meant to be heard in recitals, referred to as *tours de chant* (one-man or one-woman shows that far predate the *Evening with So-and-so* format that emerged later in the United States), they had to have a powerful and unique dramatic character, each of them a free-standing entity, a sort of short story in a setting of rhyme and music. Thus while the best American songs were fragments of dramatic monologue, often written in the second person and addressed to some unseen "you," the French song might be a first-person narrative, or, not infrequently, an observation in the third person. This use of the third person, which one encounters in Hoagy Carmichael's *The Lamplighter's Serenade* and Mercer's humorous *The Girlfriend of the Whirling Dervish*, is comparatively rare in American popular music. Usually the narrator of the song is himself or herself a participant in the tale. The strong tradition of the objective external observer, which you find in some of the wonderful French lyrics of Boris Vian and in Piaf songs such as *Les Forains*, hardly exists in American popular music, except, interestingly, country-and-western music.

The American song tended to be thirty-two bars long, with an AABA or ABAB melodic structure. The French song was much more likely to be long form, to accommodate the subject material. The chanson evolved into a complex tale-unto-itself, such as Brel's *Zangra*, often exploring complex and difficult subjects, as opposed to the almost incessant love songs of the United States. Not that the French don't love love songs. But the character of them is very different and the view of the subject has always inclined to be more realistic, a consequence of the comparative lack of taboo about language.

Most country-and-western music is commercial trash, but some of the songs—those of Mickey Newberry among them—are excellent indeed, every bit as good as what the Nashville people call "uptown music." Good country-and-western songs not infrequently explore subject matter much like what you encounter in French chansons. In the 1940s, Edith Piaf recorded *Jean et Martine*, which is about the worried wife of a truck driver waiting for him to come home. There is a country-and-western song on the same subject. The important difference between them is that in the latter song, the wife prays, God intercedes, and the husband comes safely home through the storm. In the Piaf song he is killed. The American song caters to the religious primitives who form so large a part of the country-and-western audience, but it also illustrates the sentimentality of much American popular art, movies included, in its maudlin happy ending.

If Trenet's songs were exuberant celebrations of life, alternated with occasional wistful and gentle explorations of sadder subjects, Piaf's songs were almost universally tragic, and unblinkingly objective. She was singing her tough narratives about prostitutes when Cole Porter's comparatively pallid *Love for Sale* was barred from American and Canadian radio stations.

In older American movies, women manage the miracle of becoming mothers with no detectable abdominal enlargement. Florescence apparently occurs by parthenogenesis, although sometimes it seems to be the consequence of kissing, and the condition is announced without use of the word *pregnant*, the husband saying something like, "You mean ... you mean we're going to ... to have a ..." to which the lady may reply with shyly lowered eyes, "Yes, dear." It seems unlikely that this bowdlerization of movies did anything to protect the morals of children, most of whom were bright enough to notice for themselves the changes that overtook a woman who really was, in one of the euphemisms of the time, in a family way. What is more, farm children even knew how she got that way.

It is the lack of suppression of either language or fact in French movies, novels, plays, and songs that doubtless inspired the strange British and American belief that the French are a "sexy" people, casual in dalliance. A people who had to cover the legs of tables and even put frilly ruffles on the legs of pianos were bound to find any people sexy. The French happened to be the closest—and reading the works of Zola and Hugo while Victoria was imposing her vision of virtue on England and, later, lamenting her Albert to Disraeli. No wonder her son Edward was always popping off to France.

The strange vision of love that never seems to have a physical fulfillment, embodied in the songs and movies of a recent American yesteryear, goes far back in history to the Manichaean heresy that is also the root of Protestantism.

Manichaeus was born in Persia in 215 or 216, the son of a father who belonged to a sect that believed in sexual abstinence. After the dreams and visitations from angels that customarily attend religious conversions, Manichaeus formed his own sect and set forth a cosmogony whose complexity is exceeded only by its lack of accord with reality. In its essentials, it was a dualism, good versus evil, light at war with darkness.

The Manichaean religion died out in China around the fourteenth century, but its influence is still with us, because it affected Aurelius Augustinus, who was born in Roman Africa in 354 and is known to us now as St. Augustine of Hippo. Augustine is considered the greatest thinker of Christian antiquity. Significantly, he was a Manichaean for nine years before his conversion to Christianity. Augustine's views were so uncompromisingly severe that he made even other churchmen uncomfortable, and one of them accused him of lapsing into Manichaeism. Augustine believed that mankind is involved in Adam's guilt and punishment through dependency on the sexual passion for reproduction. Retaining the Manichaean hostility to sex, he saw spirit as good, matter as bad. Therefore physical life is bad. And the act that makes life is particularly evil. It apparently did not occur to him to blame God for setting things up that way, nor did it to those whom he influenced, including Calvin, Jansen, and the New England Puritans. In a park near downtown Geneva, Switzerland, the city of Calvin's birth, there is a row of heroic statues celebrating Calvin and his disciples. And there, larger than life, stands Roger Williams.

But there is another way that the Manichaean heresy came to shape our lives. By a direct lineage, it gave rise to a later heresy, that of the Cathars in northern Italy and southern France, which flourished in the twelfth and fourteenth centuries. The Cathars—also known as the Albigenses—continued the doctrine that life was evil. They had a passionate belief in celibacy, did not favor reproduction, and pushed the whole thing to its logical extreme by looking favorably on suicide. Marriage was considered particularly odious, a sort of institutionalized vice. The highest state was that of being "perfect," which one attained through a ceremony called the *consolamentum*. Such were the rigors of this condition, including sexual abstinence, that most believers put it off until they neared the ends of their lives, when they gave up, with appropriate repentance, that for which they had probably lost the capacity.

The hotbed of this religion was Provence, that haunted and haunting part of southern France whose vision is burned into our minds by Cézanne. And it continued there until it was bloodily eradicated by the Church in actions that evolved into the Inquisition.

Now, it was in Provence that our love songs were born.

The vision of romantic love to which most of us in this era are addicted was more or less unknown to the Greeks and Romans. Love was not unknown, as witness the story of Ruth and Naomi, the devotion of Damon and Pythias. Nor was uncontrolled passion, as witness David's deadly compulsion for Bathsheba, the poetry of Sappho, and the dalliances of Greek gods. But a single helpless lifelong devotion was considered an aberration, even perhaps a form of insanity.

The troubadours of Provence changed that.

Scholars debate the meaning of the poetry that these songwriters produced. One author claims that they were "eager to clothe the caprices of their senses with mystical grace." Others have held the opposite, contending that the troubadours were Cathars whose love poems were coded celebrations of their own religious experiences.

It is a poetry that talks of conspiracy and secrecy and guarded nocturnal meetings and fear of discovery and a yearning for some sort of initiation. Into what? Into the perfect state of the Cathar religion?

Whatever the true meaning of the songs of the Provence troubadours, it is wise to remember that they came into being where that intensely anti-sexual religion had flowered. The songs are full of longings for kisses that never come. The passions are never consummated, and this very fruitlessness is idealized. Jauffre Rudel wrote these lines:

> *Car nuls autres joys tan nom play*
> *come jauzimens d'amor de lonh.*

Let us note in passing that the words *joy* and *play* came into English unchanged from that period, while their spellings became *joie* and *plait* in French. The lines translate:

> For no other joys so much me please
> as the pleasure of love from afar.

This reminds us immediately of the lyric to *My Silent Love*:

> I reach for you as I reach for a star,
> worshipping you from afar . . .

One of the troubadours wrote of a man who all his life loves a princess he has never met. He meets her in the end only to die in her arms. Was the poet describing the final Cathar initiation at the end of life? Whatever it was, its tradition finds an echo in a Richard Whiting–Leo Robin song:

> Will I ever find
> the girl in my mind,
> the one who is my ideal?
> Maybe she's a dream
> and yet she might be
> just around the corner,
> waiting for me.
>
> Will I recognize
> the light in her eyes,
> that no other eyes reveal?
> Or will I pass her by
> and never even know
> that she was my ideal?

This is an idealized and essentially asexual vision of love. Since the only possible excuse for doing "it" was that you were *in love with* the object of your ardor, and the only thing you could do about *that* was to marry her or him, that song actually hints at an entire life lived in celibacy.

The idealized asexual vision of love took its deepest hold not in Catholic France but in largely Protestant America. Protestantism, echoing the anti-sexuality of Manichaeus, took root in England, partly, I suggest, because the suppression of the Anglo-Saxon language eventuated in an array of unconscious assumptions that made her people particularly susceptible to its guilt infliction and denial of the physical self. And the most extreme Puritans emigrated to America. Little wonder, then, that the vision of love first put forth by troubadours of Provence should spring up again west of the Atlantic.

It is impossible to estimate how deeply the songs of the 1930s, '40s, and '50s, saturating the North American society through radio and records and movies to an extent never before possible, influenced the life outlook of the people consuming them. And song after song told them love would solve everything, once you found Mr. or Miss Right.

Love doesn't solve everything, of course. It isn't even a very good cure for loneliness. But generations of Americans grew up with expectations inculcated by an all-pervasive popular music and by movies that ended with a comparatively chaste kiss whose duration was limited by the film industry's censorship system. Because the songs and movies celebrated the heady emotion of *falling* in love, millions of people though that this temporary exhilaration was love itself, and so, when it ended, many of them moved on to the next marriage. And possibly the next, in a process that became so universal that a sociologist named it "sequential polygamy."

That era is ended. Many factors contributed to its fading. Rock-and-roll was a major one. While women's liberation asserted a woman's right to sexual freedom, rock lyrics proclaimed man's right to use these liberated woman without gratitude or responsibility or even feeling, and the girls who were its fans became the disposable instruments of male gratification, leading inevitably to a song called *You Don't Have to Say You Love Me*. Rock-and-roll not only defeminized women. It dehumanized them. Rock music made "groupie" a new word in the English language, although the phenomenon was far from new.

American songs of the first half of the twentieth century gave us a vision of sexless love, rock-and-roll a vision of loveless sex. Meanwhile, the pornographers were destroying the mystery of woman even among children browsing at magazine racks.

It was once accurate to say that the French made comedies about sex while the Americans made tragedies about it. But boudoir farce is now common in America. This is due in part to the changed emotional climate of which the freer use of certain Anglo-Saxon words is both a consequence and a cause.

As for English, that hybrid tongue once confined to a small island country, it has become the first true world language. In the number of people who speak it, it is second only to Mandarin Chinese and to none at all in the area of diffusion. About 300,000,000 people speak English as their first language and another 120,000,000 as their second. Meanwhile French purists in France and Quebec try desperately in an age of international radio and television and air travel to halt the invasion of their language by that selfsame English language the Norman French created by imposing their own on a conquered people. French engineers go on talking about *les pipelines* (pronounced peep-lean) while fashionable French women praise a new fashion as *très smart*. *Cool* is the hip new adjective in Paris. One might call this Harold's revenge.

And English is growing, not only in the number of persons who speak it but in the size of its vocabulary, due partly to its capacity, far beyond French, to create words from within—*contrail,* for example, from condensation trail; *laser*; and *scuba*–and partly to its unhesitating and even eager importation from other languages, including *discothèque* from French, *marina* and *macho* from Spanish. An unabridged general dictionary of English contains more than 500,000 entries. Language experts say that English dictionaries of 750,000 entries will soon be in use.

And all this, the songs and the profanity and the neuroses and this expanding powerful language, because of Charles the Simple. And his treaty of St. Clair-sur-Epte.

Pavilion in the Rain

On warm summer nights, in that epoch between the wars and before air conditioning, the doors and wide wooden shutters would be open, and the music would drift out of the pavilion over the converging crowds of excited young people, through the parking lot glistening with cars, through the trees, and over the lake—or the river, or the sea. Sometimes Japanese lanterns hung in the trees, like moons caught in the branches, and sometimes little boys too hung there, observing the general excitement and sharing the sense of an event. And the visit of one of the big bands was indeed an event.

The sound of the saxophones, a sweet and often insipid yellow when only four of them were used, turned to a woody umber when, later, the baritone was added. The sound of three trombones in harmony had a regal grandeur. Four trumpets could sound like flame, yet in ballads could be damped by harmon mutes to a citric distant loneliness. Collectively, these elements made up the sound of a big band.

It is one that will not go away. The recordings made then are constantly reissued and purchased in great quantities. Time-Life re-creates in stereo the arrangements of that vanished era, while the *Reader's Digest* and the Book of the Month Club continue to reissue many of the originals. Throughout the United States and Canada, college and high school students gather themselves into that basic formation—now expanded to five trumpets, four trombones, five saxes doubling woodwinds, piano, bass, drums, and maybe guitar and French horns too—to make their own music in that style. By some estimates there are as many as 30,000 of these bands. The sound has gone around the world, and you will hear it on variety shows of Moscow television—a little clumsy, to be sure, but informed with earnest intention.

Why? Why does this sound haunt our culture?

For one thing, it was deeply romantic. In 1983 the Bureau of the Census reported that people over sixty-five for the first time in American history outnumbered adolescents. More than a quarter of the population was over fifty. These people remembered that era. They once courted to it. With the mean age of the population about thirty, it could be said that half the population of the North American continent was sired out of the moods and marriages and affairs inspired by that music.

It was also a dramatic sound, which is why it has remained in uninterrupted use in film and television underscoring since Henry Mancini, Johnny Mandel, and a few other composers, who had themselves been nurtured and trained in big bands, began toward the end of the 1950s to convince producers of its effectiveness.

The era that gave birth to that sound, and which that sound dramatized, defies—like all historical periods—tidy definition. It begins more or less in the early 1930s, but its elements were in place by the 1920s. It ends in the late 1940s, although five of its principal leaders, Count Basie, Duke Ellington, Woody Herman, Harry James, and Stan Kenton, were out there traveling, leading their bands, in the 1970s, and Basie and Herman went on into the 1980s. For the most part, however, the tradition had to be carried on by what came to be known as rehearsal bands and a few that came together more or less regularly to record and make brief tours, such as the Rob McConnell band in Canada and, in Europe, the Clarke–Boland big band led by the late American drummer Kenny Clarke and the Belgian composer Francy Boland.

In broad essentials, however, it was an era of about fifteen years, compared with the rock era that has now persisted for forty. It was an era when a lot of popular music was good and a lot of good music was popular. This fact has led many of those who grew up in that time to sentimentalize it, which requires forgetting that the music was not all unalloyed gold. If it was the age of Ellington, Basie, Herman, Kenton, the Dorseys, Chick Webb, Glen Gray, Jimmie Lunceford, Lionel Hampton, Earl Hines, Erskine Hawkins, Lucky Millinder, Will Bradley, Freddie Slack, Bobby Sherwood, Boyd Raeburn, Charlie Barnet, Claude Thornhill, Elliot Lawrence, Glenn Miller, Alvino Rey, Artie Shaw, Teddy Powell, and Sonny Dunham, it was also the era of Kay Kyser, Shep Fields, Sammy Kaye, Blue Barron, Art Kassel, Tommy Tucker (for whom Gerry Mulligan briefly wrote), Orrin Tucker, Wayne King, Freddy Martin, Clyde McCoy, Richard Himber, and others in that vastly successful group known to the fans of more fastidious preferences as the Mickey Mouse or ricky-tick bands. To these hipper fans, the giant in this latter category was Guy Lombardo, who was regularly voted King of Corn in the annual *Down Beat* poll of its readers. They harbored a peculiar hatred of Lombardo, as if his existence somehow posed a threat to the music they admired. The threat was elsewhere.

There are those who think Glenn Miller belonged in this category, thanks in part to the band's use of clarinet lead on the saxophone section, a much-vaunted sound that was cloying in persistent use. Jo Stafford, who in the early 1940s sang with the Tommy Dorsey band, a collection of rugged individualists with a fierce collective pride, said years later, a little hesitantly, as if confessing to an American heresy, "You know, in the Dorsey band, we thought Glenn Miller was ... kind of corny." But Miller, like John Lennon, has been canonized, and one does not question the status of icons.

The Miller band could play ensemble jazz of a kind, recorded some good instrumentals, and claimed Bobby Hackett, who played guitar in the rhythm section and soloed on cornet, in its personnel. Hackett lent a certain Bixian beauty to the interlude of *A String of Pearls*, written by Jerry Gray.

The classification of these bands was neither easy nor clear, since some of the dance bands, such as that of Charlie Spivak, embodied a decent level of taste. All the jazz bands played for dancers; and some of the most commercial dance bands occasionally put out something that resembled jazz. Kay Kyser, whose arrangements were a cut above those of most Mickey bands (no doubt because George Duning, later a film composer, wrote some of them), now and then startled audiences with some ensemble swing. It was even rumored that the Sammy Kaye band, in many ways the corniest of them all ("And now this lovely refrain sung by ..."), could do it. The best of the bands, however, the elite of them, leaned strongly into jazz. Their captious members wanted to lean even further into it and played dance music only as a concession to the exigencies of continued employment. The best of these best—a group that included Basie, Ellington, Shaw, Herman, Tommy Dorsey, and the brilliant Jimmie Lunceford orchestra—played excellent jazz, framing the work of some highly individual soloists in ensemble structures of remarkable discipline and power. To hear one of these bands straining the walls of some arena or theater or pavilion, without all the paraphernalia of modern amplification, was one of the great thrills in music.

The tributaries of this vast river of superior popular music arose in the 1920s, although its instrumentation grew out of the marching bands of New Orleans. The instruments were those that could be played while walking and were loud enough to be heard in the open air.

By the 1920s, bands were sitting down, playing for dancers. Benny Carter recalls that when he was in the Charlie Johnson band in that period, its instrumentation was three trumpets, two trombones, three saxophones—two altos and a tenor—and four rhythm, including tuba bass. Not until the bands forgot their ambulatory origins entirely did the string bass, a more flexible instrument than the tuba and certainly a more pulsating one, become the rhythmic and harmonic footing on which all bands to this day have built their walls of sound.

Leading figures in this evolution were Duke Ellington, Bill Challis, Ferde Grofé, Gene Gifford, and Don Redman. Redman worked out the organization of trumpets, trombones, and saxophones into choirs working over the rhythm section. Ellington, who even then was using baritone saxophone to add color and fortify the bottom of the orchestra, was moving in a somewhat different direction. Whereas Redman, whose thinking affected Fletcher Henderson and, through Henderson, other writers, maintained the identity of the sections, Ellington was using his instruments in unusual combinations, mixing them up through the sections, as it were. Ellington was becoming more and more adventurous in explorations of harmony, influenced in part by the French impressionists. Eventually he voiced the band to produce strange, almost disembodied, and highly idiosyncratic sounds.

The practices of these two men, modified and transmuted to be sure, have dominated serious non-classical orchestral writing in America and much of the world ever since. It is startling to consider that Don Redman is one of the most influential composers of the twentieth century, when most people have never heard of him, including some of the arrangers and composers who daily use the orchestral tools he explored so effectively.

Benny Carter, who joined the band of Henderson's brother Horace in 1926, said that Fletcher Henderson's arrangements, written for his own band but copied and given to his brother's band, were his first real encounter with the Redman–Henderson mode of writing. Benny Goodman too acquired some of the existing Henderson arrangements and hired Henderson to write more. When Goodman became a success, other musicians formed bands on his model or steered existing bands in the direction pointed by Henderson. A few looked to Ellington for inspiration, particularly Charlie Barnet and, less obviously, Claude Thornhill, who altered the color of big band sound, partly by adding French horn, partly by hiring Gil Evans, whom he had known in the Skinnay Ennis band.

The repertoire of the bands was hybrid, drawn from the movies, the blues, Broadway, and even grand opera. The instrumentals were usually original compositions by members of the band or staff arrangers, such as Goodman's *Six Flats Unfurnished* by Richard Maltby.

Most of the bands carried singers, the "boy singer" and "girl singer," as they were coyly called, such as Frank Sinatra and Jo Stafford with the Tommy Dorsey band and Sarah Vaughan and Billy Eckstine with Earl Hines. And many of them had vocal groups, such as the Modernaires with Miller and the Pied Pipers with Tommy Dorsey. Artie Shaw carried only a girl singer, resented even having to do that, and made no secret of his contempt for dancers. The music comprised fast or medium-fast instrumentals and slow vocal performances of songs written mostly by Jewish composers and lyricists. In the big band era, the two most important streams of American non-classical music fused—the black and the Jewish.

The Big Band Era was also the Age of the Movies. Movies came into their own with the addition of sound in 1927. The bands were already taking the form they would have through the 1930s and 1940s. The band era and the movie era coincided, and they died together in the late 1940s, for related reasons. But while they lasted, they profoundly affected America's way of thinking and living.

Because of what were deemed sexual excesses in the movies in the 1920s and then scandals in the film industry, the motion picture studios set up a system of self-censorship. The movies made under that restraint presented a false picture of life.

The songs of the time reinforced the view of life presented by the movies. Jo Stafford sang, "A heart that's true, there are such things." Helen Forrest sang, "I never thought it could be but there you were, in love with me." Sarah Vaughan sang, "Then you and I came wandering by, and lost in a sigh were we." Love was a fragile thing, attainable, if at all, only by the pure of heart, yet without which life wasn't worth living, and the loss of which was the ultimate personal disaster.

"I'll never smile again . . ." Only occasionally, as in Bob Russell's lyric to *Do Nothing till You Hear from Me*, which deplores the pain caused by gossip, did popular music deal with something like reality. In his excellent—and overlooked—lyric to Carl Fisher's tune *We'll Be Together Again*, Frankie Laine touched the ground with "Don't let the blues make you bad."

The big band leaders were big stars, and the movies were quick to conscript them into service—white ones, anyway. Artie Shaw appeared with his band in *Second Chorus*. Tommy Dorsey's band was in *Ship Ahoy*, the Glenn Miller band performed in *Orchestra Wives* and *Sun Valley Serenade*, while Harry James turned up in *Swingtime in the Rockies*. In such films, the band would break out its instruments and start blowing with little or no provocation, even on buses and trains. If there were some Negro porters standing by, they would turn out to be as talented as the Ink Spots or the Mills Brothers, and they would join in, in perfect impromptu harmony. In real life, the musicians on band buses were more likely to be found sleeping, drinking, smoking joints, or groping the girl singer as meager consolations for the monotony of the road.

In *Sun Valley Serenade*, such was the supposed *joie de* musical *vivre* of the Miller band that they played in open sleighs passing though the snowy countryside. How the brass and saxes could hear the rhythm section, how the musicians kept their hands warm enough to play, and how the instruments remained in tune in the cold were questions left to the nigglers in the audience.

Growing up in this false picture of life and love generated by popular music and the movies, the young people of the era were naively unprepared for life. It was accepted that only virgins were nice girls, even by the boys striving assiduously to reduce their numbers. When the libido did its programmed thing, girls (and some boys) persuaded themselves the feeling had to be love, and not infrequently rushed into inappropriate marriages that ended in divorce. Even then they rarely awoke to the possibility that their ideal of life might not be in harmony with reality. Instead they concluded that *this* marriage just wasn't "it," the great love that solves everything, as in the songs and movies, and went on to the next.

The few realistic songs that were written were not widely heard. For radio, which was exercising an increasing hegemony over music, was deeply if unofficially censored.

The era of the big bands and grand movies was also the era of the Broadway musical, and since its audience was limited to a well-to-do stratum of society, freed by its money from such inconveniences as the consequences of inadvertent maternity, stage composers and lyricists had considerably more latitude than those working in movies or Tin Pan Alley.

The musical was passing through its own golden age. Evolving from the plotless meringue of the 1920s into integrated well-structured near-operas, musicals were often urbane and wry and occasionally realistic works of art, such as *Pal Joey, Carousel,* and *The Most Happy Fella.* But Broadway produced a special and better brand of popular music. For the most part the songs heard on the radio were in keeping with the everything's-lovely-and-Andy-Hardy-Goes-to-College image of life presented by the movies. There were no whores in western movies, only dance-hall girls. In *By the Mississinewa*, Cole Porter managed to touch on miscegenation, lesbianism, fellatio, cunnilingus, and the daisy chain, but the song, needless to say, was never heard outside the Broadway musical for which it was written. Lorenz Hart wrote *Bewitched, Bothered and Bewildered* for *Pal Joey.* The line "until I could sleep where I shouldn't sleep" was altered in the out-of-show version to "till love came and told me I shouldn't sleep," which doesn't even make sense.

Occasionally somebody wrote a "naughty" song such as the sophomorically smirking *She Had to Go and Lose It at the Astor,* at the end of which it turns out that all she'd lost was her sable cape. But then for a movie called *The Shocking Miss Pilgrim,* Ira Gershwin put words to one of his late brother George's unpublished melodies and called the song *Aren't You Kind of Glad We Did?*

In the film *Broken Arrow,* James Stewart marries the Indian girl. To be sure, the girl dies in the end—but at the hands of white racists. The viewpoint of the film is firmly on the side of the Indians and the marriage, and the picture was an important departure. Then Aldo Ray married a Japanese girl in *Three Stripes in the Sun,* which wasn't a tragedy but a comedy of manners, and Otto Preminger released *The Moon Is Blue,* a comedy so ordinary that the public might not have noticed it had the Motion Picture Code seal of approval not been withheld because its dialogue contained the words "virgin" and "seduce."

Songwriters pressed against the censorship of the radio stations and networks—who were themselves under constraints from the Federal Communications Commission—and occasionally slipped something suggestive past the watchdogs, such as Alec Wilder's *If You See Kay.* It was broadcast a number of times before some network executive got the point and bounced it off the air.

By the 1980s, when the American population had progressed far toward the universal drug use and casual coupling foreseen by Aldous Huxley in *Brave New World,* and porn video and "marital aids" approximated the feelies he described, it was difficult to remember how constricting the moral tone of that time really was, and how much people suffered because of their hormones. Certainly it was not the Big Band Era of later false memory. The serious musical experiments of the bands usually turned up in instrumentals on the B sides of more commercial songs. If it was the era of Herman's *Your Father's Moustache,* it was also that of *Cruising Down the River, The Hut-Sut Song,* and *Mairzy Doats.* (*Papa Loves Mambo* and *How Much Is that Doggie in the Window?* came a little later.) If it was—and it was—the golden age of American song, awash in melodies of Kern, Gershwin, Porter, Arlen, it was at the same time an era of trivial, preposterous, and idiotic songs.

And in the end, the adventurous and exuberant experimentalism of the bands would lose its constituency as radio and the record industry proved that Gresham's law operates in aesthetics as well as economics.

Seeking a wider pallette of colors, at least five of the bands—those of Artie Shaw, Tommy Dorsey, Gene Krupa, Harry James, and Stan Kenton—tried using string sections. The effect left much to be desired. A full symphony orchestra requires up to sixty strings to balance its comparatively sedate brass and woodwind sections. Jazz brass is much louder. Yet for reasons of economics, the bands could not employ large string sections. Dorsey carried thirteen players. At its worst, the effect was ludicrous—watching Gene Krupa's fiddles saw away inaudibly, for example.

The main direction of this music's evolution was harmonic. For years the thinking of the arrangers had been well in advance of that of the players. In the 1940s, big band harmony became much more complex and "dissonant." Experiments with polytonality were under way. Stan Kenton pushed his band toward the symphonic, sometimes to laudable effect, sometimes not. Other bands, including those of Woody Herman, and Claude Thornhill and the postwar Artie Shaw band, partook of the bebop revolution. The famous soaring trumpet passage in *Caldonia* is a transcribed solo by Neal Hefti, which, Neal said, was very much in the manner of Dizzy Gillespie, while the sax passage in *I've Got News for You* is a transcription of a Charlie Parker solo on *Dark Shadows*. Herman was one of Gillespie's early admirers, and Dizzy did some writing for that band.

But that era, when hundreds of bands criss-crossed America and hundreds more played in their immediate regions, was over. Like so many epochs in art, it attained some of its finest moments just before it ended. While the prewar records in this idiom today seem thin and archaic, partly, to be sure, because of primitive recording, the best of the band records made after 1945 retain their freshness and vitality. They do not sound callow; the music has attained its maturity. The rhythm sections have adapted to the newer music, and their motion is strong, fluid, and natural. The arrangers, from Redman through Henderson, Sy Oliver, Pete Rugolo, Ralph Burns, Ernie Wilkins, Eddie Sauter, and more—with Duke Ellington, Billy Strayhorn, Gil Evans, and Gerry Mulligan off in a slightly different direction—explored the first important new orchestral formation since the symphony orchestra took shape in the time of C.P.E. Bach and caused the spore-burst of brilliant music that we think of as the Big Band Era.

What happened to them? Why did the big bands fade away?

Aside from the yearning for lost youth that doubtless comes to everyone but the most convinced reincarnationist, the lament for that era carries an assumption that there was something inevitable about it, ordained by deity or at least guaranteed as part of the American birthright. But the bands were born and flourished in a confluence of social conditions and dwindled out when those conditions changed.

One author of the era was Irving Berlin, whose name we seldom encounter in jazz histories, except perhaps in a cavil that *Alexander's Ragtime Band* was not a rag. So it wasn't. But it was important to the development of what we came to call jazz in that, first, the song, published in 1911, initiated the fascination with the duple meter that became known as the fox trot, and, second, it freed American music from thralldom to Viennese operetta (imported or domestic) on the one hand and ersatz Irish balladry (such as *Ireland Is Ireland to Me*, all by Ernest R. Ball, who was born in Cleveland) on the other. After Berlin's rise to success, American popular music took on its own character and color, which he in part determined, as Don Redman would a few years later.

Two more names one will not encounter in conventional jazz histories are Vernon and Irene Castle, the popular dance team whose example set off a craze for ballroom dancing in the United States. Between 1912 and 1914, the Castles campaigned to refine the barn dance, cakewalk, two-step, Boston, and turkey trot. One consequence was the Castle Walk, a new style that utilized a naturalistic walking motion as its foundation and made it possible for every left-footed clunk in the country to make at least a pass at dancing. The early fox trot also evolved from these experiments, and its popularity influenced the character of the emerging American music. By 1927 the Lindy Hop, named for the new hero Charles Lindbergh, had arrived. And the Lindy led to the phenomenon called jitterbugging, whose better practitioners took dancing to virtuosic levels of acrobatic ingenuity. And this opened the way for bands to play fast instrumentals. Dancers provided the foundation of employment for the bands. This fact is central to any understanding of the era.

Finally, there were the Toonerville Trolleys.

The Toonerville Trolley was the name of a syndicated newspaper cartoon that expressed a sort of nostalgia even then for a more bucolic America. All over the United States and Canada, electric railways linked cities to smaller surrounding communities that often were the loci of amusement parks in which there usually were dance pavilions. E. L. Doctorow, in his novel *Ragtime*, has one of his characters travel from New York to Boston by going from one electric railway to another. It was possible.

The late Robert Offergeld, the classical music critic and historian, who grew up in eastern Michigan, recalls the line that linked Saginaw, Bay City, and Traverse City. "They were wonderful," he said of the big old trolley cars. "You could hear the whine of them coming well in advance. They used to do about 60 miles an hour, rocking along the tracks, and they'd scare you half to death. And they took you to those little places by the shore, and girls wore boaters. I learned to dance after a ride on one of those trolleys. There was always a candy vendor, and a pavilion, and it was all rather free and innocent."

"The biggest system of them all," said David Raksin, who has taught both composition and urban affairs at the University of Southern California, "was in Los Angeles–the Big Red Cars. They linked Hollywood to Santa Monica and Chatsworth. In fact, they ran all the way out to Mount Lowe." It was indeed the biggest. The Big Red Cars, the popular name for a system owned by the Southern Pacific Railroad, along with a smaller system known as the Yellow Cars (the Los Angeles Railway Company), covered a thousand miles of track. Together they constituted possibly the finest public transit system in the United States.

The amusement parks with their dance pavilions would not have come into being without the urban and interurban railways. And those pavilions formed a series of links in the chain of locations along which the bands traveled. They also provided employment for countless musicians in the local or regional groups known as territory bands.

These factors–a taste for a more American music initiated by Berlin, a penchant for dancing inspired by the Castles, a style of dancing that was appropriate to fast instrumentals and therefore encouraged their composition, and a chain of dance pavilions and ballrooms that had grown up along the urban and interurban railways–were all there when in the early 1920s a final, critical, catalytic ingredient was added to the mix: radio and, most important, network radio.

The record companies, which were thriving when the new medium came into being, were fearful that "free" music would cut into their sales. Therefore they would not allow their product to be played "on the air." Record labels bore the motto *Not licensed for radio broadcast.* The broadcasters ignored it. A number of artists, including Fred Waring, Walter O'Keefe, Donald Voorhees, Lawrence Tibbett, and Paul Whiteman, sued various broadcasting corporations to halt the playing of their records on radio. Finally, in 1940, the U.S. Supreme Court ended these actions by refusing to review a decision against Whiteman and his record label, RCA Victor, by the Second Circuit Court of Appeals in a suit Whiteman had brought against WBO Broadcasting Company, owners of WNEW in New York City. Judge Learned Hand had written the decision, in spite of the fact that he was an opponent of "judge-made law." Revealing ignorance of the essential nature of artistic copyright, Hand wrote, "Copyright in any form, whether statutory or in common law, is a monopoly. It consists only in the power to prevent others from reproducing the copyright work. WBO Broadcasting has never invaded any such right." The premise is false, the deduction wrong. To play a record on the radio is in and of itself to reproduce the music. One way or another, it is done for profit. And the so-called automatic license provision of American law makes it all but impossible to "prevent others from reproducing" one's compositions. Hand's ruling has had lasting and terribly damaging social and aesthetic consequences.

American copyright law has always been weak. Until the twentieth century, the United States was a net importer of music. And business interests wanted then, as they do now, to get everything they could for as little as possible, the ultimate of which of course being nothing. This resulted in the theft—in effect—of Gilbert and Sullivan operettas by American producers, who presented them without paying the authors. Gilbert, himself a lawyer and former magistrate, and Sullivan had no recourse to American courts, which did not recognize foreign copyright claims. This is why in 1885 they premiered *The Mikado* simultaneously in London and New York. It was a way to establish American protection for the work.

Hand's ruling was in keeping with that American tradition of weak copyright. Subsequently, unable to bar records from the air, the record industry reversed itself and strove to get them exposed on radio, soliciting that exposure to the extent of the institutionalized corruption of disk jockeys, program directors, and music librarians with payola ranging in form from cash to drugs to airline tickets to romantic places.

Nearly all of the program content of American radio is recorded music. But in the early days, and before Judge Hand established the curious legal principle that one industry had the right to live off another, radio had to generate a good deal of its own material, partly due to pressures from the American Federation of Musicians. Even small stations in small towns employed musicians and singers. Radio drew into service artists from other fields, from Grand Ol Opry and grand opera (making household names of such singers as John Charles Thomas, Vivian della Chiessa, Helen Jepson, Lawrence Tibbett, and James Melton), as well as from the nation's symphony orchestras (making Arturo Toscanini, Howard Barlow, and Leopold Stokowski known to laymen everywhere). That public taste is not inherently as bad as the apologists for the record and broadcasting industry would have you believe is illuminated by who and what did become popular when a wide range of music was given exposure.

It was not coincidence that between 1928 and 1948 a "golden age" occurred not only in big band popular music but in movie-making and theater, and for that matter in the novel as well. These years were the youth of the new communications, communications beyond print. The conglomerates had not yet taken over and debased them. The broadcasting industry's pioneers, particularly William S. Paley of CBS and David Sarnoff of NBC, presented material of a high order along with more obviously popular entertainment. It would be naive to ascribe noble motive to them. They programmed music and people who were esteemed and famous, which happened to include Toscanini. Whatever their motives, broadcasting in its early days substantially fulfilled its potential as the most powerful educational facility ever invented, and it offered a cultural education that all the schools and universities of America combined could not equal. It not only made "culture" available, it made it attractive. The result was a ferment, a leavening of the general public mind that no system of imposed formal education could achieve. Radio caused an epidemic of excellence in America. Later, in symbiosis with the record industry, it would debase American taste to an extent inconceivable in the early 1940s.

Live music of high quality, performed by superior bands and singers, was ubiquitous in radio. Every comedy show had its own orchestra. Bob Hope's program featured the Skinnay Ennis orchestra, whose members included Claude Thornhill and Gil Evans, making the band significant in the evolution of jazz to an extent impossible to estimate. Ennis was later replaced by Les Brown. Phil Harris's band was heard on Jack Benny's show, the Billy Mills orchestra on *Fibber McGee and Molly*, and that of Ozzie Nelson on the Red Skelton show. Fred Allen's *Town Hall Tonight* featured one of the best vocal groups of the time, the five DeMarco Sisters. Bing Crosby was the star of *The Kraft Music Hall*, which for two years presented the Jimmy Dorsey band, later replaced by one led by John Scott Trotter, and a vocal group called The Music Maids. Guest performers included Jack Teagarden, Joe Sullivan, Joe Venuti, and Louis Armstrong. Dinah Shore was heard with Paul Lavalle and the Chamber Music Society of Lower Basin Street. Raymond Scott performed regularly on radio.

Johnny Mercer, Jo Stafford, Benny Goodman, Paul Weston, Woody Herman, Glenn Miller, and Harry James were heard on regular broadcasts. So were John Kirby and Maxine Sullivan, whose show had a long run. Mildred Bailey had a show. Both shows regularly presented black artists such as Coleman Hawkins and Teddy Wilson. Those local shows that did play records might follow Woody Herman's *Wildroot* or Ellington's *Take the "A" Train* with Freddy Martin or Henry Busse.

It was a glorious and indiscriminate melange in which jazz and classical and country music were heard on the same station or network, so that it was impossible not to know what the full range of America's music was, no matter what one's personal and primary preference might be. A Count Basie fan was also aware of Spade Cooley and his Western Swing. Those who have grown up on format radio—all rock, all jazz, all Beautiful Music (which it rarely is)—cannot imagine what network radio was like. In the compartmentalization of broadcasting that has since occurred, it is difficult for a rock fan to discover Mahler or Thelonious Monk. In those days one's awareness was expanded without one's knowing it. Expansion of one's cultural knowledge and taste today takes determination and effort.

Historical speculations over the rise of the big bands tend to slight the influence of radio broadcasting—and the fact that this was also a golden age in popular music, theater, and movies. Although broadcasting's purpose was to make money for its proprietors, the unprincipled avarice that became the industry's distinguishing characteristic after the 1940s was not yet obvious. Radio created the public taste that embraced Cole Porter, George Gershwin, Duke Ellington, and Harold Arlen, instead of the musical primitives who came to dominate American popular music from the 1950s onward.

The Swing Era is by custom dated from the sudden fame of the Benny Goodman band. Goodman did nothing first. The style and instrumentation derived from the work of Bill Challis, Don Redman, and Fletcher Henderson. Henderson had failed as a bandleader, and had Goodman not hired him as arranger and taken up some of his previous writing, some of the masterpieces from the Henderson pencil might be lost to us. Some jazzmen were working in the dance bands. Whiteman had popularized the *idea* of the big jazz band, whether or not his band achieved anything approaching swing. Everything was in place when Goodman's band, on the verge of failure, arrived at the Palomar Ballroom in Los Angeles in August 1935.

One of the reasons for the band's explosive success at the Palomar was the three-hour time difference between the East and West Coasts. The Goodman band's broadcasts in the East were heard late at night, when most Easterners, and certainly those who had to get up for school or college in the morning, were asleep. But they were broadcast on network at a much earlier hour in the West, and by the time they reached the Palomar, young Californians had become excited about their "swing" music.

Word of the band's West Coast success made show business headlines, the band then made a series of coast-to-coast (as they were called in that age before Comsat) broadcasts from the Palomar Ballroom, and the "swing era" began. Goodman went on to play for eight straight months at the Congress Hotel in Chicago, his home town, broadcasting the while for Elgin watches. And soon the booking agencies were signing up every leader in sight who could front a band that purported to swing.

It was not lost on the advertising agencies and their clients that the young people had a new fad. A great deal can be learned from considering who sponsored what in the next few years. In the 1980s and '90s, the tobacco companies denied that they were trying to addict the young through their advertising. The denials rang rather hollow when that is precisely what they did in the 1930s and 1940s.

Kool cigarettes presented Tommy Dorsey on radio. Artie Shaw was presented by Old Golds. Chesterfield sponsored Glenn Miller, *Your Hit*

Parade, as well as *Kay Kyser's Kollege of Musical Knowledge*. In fact, the campaign to turn young people into cigarette smokers dates from 1928, when George Washington Hill, the legendarily tyrannical president of the American Tobacco Company, decided to sponsor the Lucky Strike Dance Orchestra under the leadership of B. A. Rolfe.

Further support for a thesis that the tobacco companies and their advertising agencies consciously sought out the impressionable young is found in the character of the few other products that sponsored the bands. They were all "youth" products. Wildroot Cream Oil presented Woody Herman, Fitch's Dandruff Remover Shampoo *The Fitch Bandwagon*, and Coca-Cola *Spotlight Bands*. Products consumed primarily by adults presented more sedate music, mostly what is called light classical, Strauss and Waldteufel waltzes, the *Oberon* overture, Massenet's *Elegy*, Smetana's *The Moldau*, some Grieg, Tchaikovsky's *None but the Lonely Heart*, that sort of thing.

This flood of live, free, non-recorded music was augmented by the "remote" broadcasts from hotels, ballrooms, and pavilions, which were critical to building the reputations of bands. The four networks—NBC's Red and Blue Networks, CBS, and Mutual—all did them, and did them every night.

It would be remiss to omit mention that the networks did not pay for these remote broadcasts. The musicians were paid by the ballroom or hotel or pavilion where a band was appearing. Furthermore, the ballroom operator sometimes paid for the network's engineer and sometimes even for the installation of the line. The networks' attitude was that the operator would make back his money through the increased attendance this "free" publicity would generate. Radio, then, was already manifesting the extortionist philosophy that remains one of the distinguishing characteristics of American commercial broadcasting. It continued into the age of television. Guests on "talk shows" are minimally paid on the grounds that the publicity of an appearance will bring about bigger nightclub salaries, larger sales of one's book, bigger receipts in concerts. This outlook caused a famous confrontation between Frank Sinatra and the late Ed Sullivan. When the film *Can Can* was about to be released, Sullivan wanted to present clips from the picture framed by a walk-on appearance by its stars, including Sinatra. Sinatra refused to appear on Sullivan's show on grounds that Sullivan and his network would be getting expensive entertainment for almost nothing. Sullivan denounced Sinatra, and Sinatra took out a trade-paper ad saying, "Dear Ed: You're sick. Frank Sinatra. P.S. Sick, sick, sick." Sinatra was in the right. The attitude that the publicity of broadcast exposure is far more valuable than the entertainment the artist provides—and that someone else unspecified has the onus of paying the artist—is the key to American broadcasting.

There was, then, in the late 1930s and early 1940s, an extraordinary amount of broadcasting devoted to the big bands. And these were live, not recorded, performances. The bands were not dependent on records for exposure; they achieved it directly through radio. Record sales were only a secondary source of revenue for them. So much a part of American life did the bands become that probably no one noticed that their very existence hung on the whims of the broadcasters.

During this period the Broadway musical was evolving and expanding in terms of both dramatic content and musical worth. Broadway had attracted such composers as Irving Berlin, George Gershwin, Cole Porter, Frank Loesser, Vincent Youmans, Richard Rodgers, Jerome Kern, Harold Arlen, and Arthur Schwartz, and such lyricists as Dorothy Fields, P. G. Wodehouse, Johnny Mercer, E. Y. Harburg, Howard Dietz, Lorenz Hart, Ira Gershwin, and Oscar Hammerstein II, as well as Porter, Loesser, and Berlin, who wrote both words and music. These were the people who produced the Broadway scores that became the mother lode for the Hit Parade of the day. The bandleaders in large measure determined what songs would be exposed on the radio, and they had a taste for the better material. With that era's young people absorbing and memorizing well-made songs, it is little wonder that they are today so often much more literate and better-spoken than their children and grandchildren.

With a superb musical theater as a source of popular music, with other excellent songs, such as those of Harry Warren, coming out of the movies, with other writers like Richard Whiting, Duke Ellington, Hoagy Carmichael, and Matt Dennis adding to the flow of material, American popular music attained a stature it had not had before and almost certainly never will again.

And then the music business suffered a series of blows.

One of these was the World War II 20 percent entertainment tax. And of course a large part of the audience for the music, the young men who used Wildroot and Fitch's and smoked Luckys, was overseas in military service, along with some of the best musicians and bandleaders.

Another blow, in the view of many people, was the activation in 1941 of Broadcast Music Incorporated (BMI), a new licensing organization owned by the broadcasters. The American Society of Composers, Authors and Publishers had demanded a substantial increase in the fees radio paid for the use of songs by ASCAP composers. The stations refused to pay it. ASCAP forbade the radio performance of its music—the entire modern American repertoire. The stations had to play music that was in the public domain. Under the copyright law of the time, this meant music more than fifty-six years old. For a brief time, as a result, Stephen Foster's *Jeanie with the Light Brown Hair* made the Hit Parade. The broadcasting industry had in 1939 set up their its own performing rights society, financed by the sale of stock to broadcasters. This corporation sought out songwriters not affiliated with ASCAP. They were not hard to find, since ASCAP showed a distinct bias toward the Broadway composer, who had since its founding dominated it. It was necessary to have five songs published before you could get into ASCAP, and movie composers were not admitted at all. When ASCAP pulled its music off the air, BMI became an active entity. ASCAP lost $300,000 a month and finally surrendered to the broadcasters. It not only did not get a fee increase, it meekly accepted a reduction in fees from 5 to 2.5 percent.

BMI's critics have argued that the corporation materially contributed to the decline of American popular music, but that theory is no more credible than the contention that bebop killed the big bands. BMI did indeed build a large pool of musical flotsam, but no radio station had to play it. More complex and compelling forces caused the end of the Big Band Era. If a demon be needed, James Caesar Petrillo was type-cast for the part. It is not that his cause was unjust but that his strategy was suicidal.

A self-important, obstreperous, tyrannical little man, James Caesar Petrillo was president of the American Federation of Musicians and perhaps the best-known labor leader in America after John L. Lewis of the United Mine Workers. Petrillo commissioned Ben Selvin to determine whether the play of records on radio and jukeboxes was costing musicians jobs. Selvin, a bandleader who had conducted recording orchestras under innumerable pseudonyms, had worked for the radio networks, and had been a recording executive, read his report to the AFM convention of 1941. He said that the record industry made work for musicians and was paying them millions of dollars. He said it would be "unwise, if at all possible, to curtail the industry when such large amounts are spent on musicians. There are remedies for the unemployment caused by the mechanization of music, but a knockout blow, which could not be delivered, is not the answer." The delegates give him a standing ovation. The membership, including all the major bandleaders, agreed with him.

But Petrillo ignored him and the obvious wishes of his own membership, not to mention Learned Hand's ominous ruling. He demanded that the record companies refuse to allow records to be played on radio stations and jukeboxes unless they paid a fee. In an astounding act of intransigence, he ordered musicians to stop recording. They did so on August 1, 1942. But the singers did not.

Singers were not required to be members of the AFM and indeed were not accepted as members, no doubt in reflection of the instrumentalist's condescension toward them. And so young vocalists who for the most part had been trained in bands began recording with choral groups. These soupy loo-loo-looing accompaniments were triumphs of banality, but the records helped thrust into fame such singers as Dick Haymes, Perry Como, Nat Cole, and, most significant, Frank Sinatra.

Twenty years earlier, audiences had been wary of singers with bands. One of the first band singers was Morton Downey. Paul Whiteman signed him to a contract in 1921 but was so doubtful about featuring him with his band that he put him with farm-team orchestras for two years, finally presenting him with his main band in 1923, and then only infrequently. And Whiteman thought it necessary to put an instrument in Downey's hands to justify his presence on the bandstand, at first a saxophone and later, for whatever strange reason, a French horn, neither of which Downey could play. But Downey made several successful records with Whiteman and then, portentously enough, left to become successful on his own. Later, Bing Crosby too left Whiteman and repeated the pattern.

The singers held secondary positions in the bands, sometimes barely suffered by the musicians and leaders. The pattern of recording usually entailed an instrumental chorus followed by a vocal chorus and perhaps a half chorus of instrumental going out. But then some of the leaders, including Tommy Dorsey and Harry James, began to build up the role of the singers. "With myself and Frank and the Pied Pipers and Connie Haines," Jo Stafford said, "Tommy really created what amounted to production numbers." Asked what had killed the big bands, her husband, Paul Weston, who had been one of Dorsey's arrangers, unhesitatingly replied, "The singers." Alvino Rey gave the same answer to the question.

The seeds of the bands' destruction, then, had been within them since Whiteman hired Downey. Vocal records—by Crosby, Downey, Buddy Clark, Lanny Ross, Gene Austin, Kate Smith, Russ Colombo, and others—had existed side by side with band records, a popular music for listening as opposed to the music for dancing of the bands. Petrillo's recording ban did the same thing to the singers that atomic radiation does to the creatures in cheap sci-fi movies. It made them grow big.

Petrillo's ban continued through 1943, despite efforts of the War Labor Board and finally a direct appeal from President Franklin D. Roosevelt to end it. Petrillo scorned the president as he had scorned his membership. The first company to come to terms was Decca, which signed a contract with the AFM in September 1943. Johnny Mercer's fledgling Capitol followed a month later. Columbia and RCA Victor held out until November 1944.

What Petrillo got out of the strike was a form of tax on record dates, paid by the record companies, which went into a trust fund to pay for

free concerts throughout America. In effect, the work of the best professional musicians was taxed to subsidize the mediocre. This was resented
by many professionals, among them the late Stan Kenton, who tried in
vain a few years later to establish an exclusively professional musicians'
union. Ultimately Petrillo helped destroy thousands of jobs for musicians. Having engineered a disaster, he behaved like the true politician
in proclaiming the settlement "the greatest victory for labor in the history
of the labor movement."

By the early 1940s the audience was becoming divided into two fac-
tions, those who came to dance and those who came to listen. Wherever
one of the jazz-inflected bands appeared, a mass of young people would
be seen dancing at the rear of the floor while a smaller group pressed
close to the bandstand and stood in rapt attention, preoccupied with the
skills of the players. To the latter, every side man—Ray Nance, Tricky
Sam Nanton, Johnny Hodges, Joe Thomas, Arnett Cobb, Cat Anderson,
Mel Powell, Charlie Kennedy, Charlie Christian, Buck Clayton, Don
Byas, Lester Young, Ziggy Elman, Corky Corcoran, Willie Smith, Bill
Harris, Zoot Sims, Pete Candoli—was a star. That crowd at the front was
the constituency for jazz as a concert music, and some bands came more
and more to cater to it. The instrumentalists wanted the music to go in
that direction and so did some of the bandleaders, particularly Stan
Kenton. Musicians repeated with glee a story about a trombonist who,
asked by someone from the audience, "Why don't you play something
we can dance to?" replied, "Why don't you dance something we can
play to?"

If you want to name a point when the era ended, that may be it.

Paul Weston said the beginning of the end came with a shift in tempos.
Earlier arrangements had been designed for dancing, with even the ballads moving along on a comparatively brisk one-and-three beat. "Then
the ballads became slower to accommodate the singers," he said. "And
the instrumentals became faster to show off the soloists."

"The bands became mere accompaniment to the singers," Alvino Rey
said. "And then there was the Kenton phenomenon. Stan Kenton's was
not a dance band, except in the early days. When we tried to be more
like it, people said, 'Why aren't you like your old self?' The bands
became too symphonic. Too many chords. I was one of the worst offend-
ers, because I loved all that stuff. And then, once the remotes went off the
air, we had a real problem. Records couldn't build a band the way all
those live broadcasts did."

A few people have tried to argue that bebop killed the big bands. But
this hypothesis is patently absurd. "It's ridiculous," Gerry Mulligan said.
"If anything, bebop came along and revived the musicality of the bands."

Nobody forced people to listen to the few bands who embraced bebop. The alternatives were always there, and it certainly didn't kill Guy Lombardo's band. Benny Goodman never liked and didn't play bebop, and his band went out of business. Woody Herman did like and did play it, and his band was one of the few to survive the era, continuing right into the 1980s. Indeed, the bands that outlived the era–including James, Kenton, Basie, Ellington, and Herman–all embraced or at least accepted the practices of bebop. If bebop was all that inaccessible, the boppers should have slipped away into a seemly unemployment while the more conventional groups continued on, awash in public adoration. It didn't happen that way, and, although he led small groups, Dizzy Gillespie, one of the fountainheads of bebop, turned out to be the most enduring and revered jazz star after Louis Armstrong.

A change was occurring in the audience. Returning from military service, the young men who with their girls had been the natural constituents for the bands were preoccupied with something else, namely, breeding and feeding fans for the Beatles, Bob Dylan, and Mick Jagger. TV would prove appealing to people with problems in finding baby-sitters. And since the birthrate fell during the Depression, the next generation of young people was a smaller one. Meanwhile, the public transportation system, so important to the outlying amusement parks and dance pavilions, was falling apart–or, rather, was being systematically dismembered.

Harry Chandler, owner of the *Los Angeles Times* and of vast real estate holdings in and around the city, was on the board of the Goodyear Tire and Rubber Company. He had interests in road construction companies and substantial investments in the Southern California Rock and Gravel Company and Consolidated Rock Products, as well as several oil companies. Chandler and his family stood to make money on everything related to automobiles and highways. The *Los Angeles Times* became for all practical purposes a publicity organ of the automobile interests, including the California Automobile Club–itself a lobby for those interests–of which he was a charter member and director for more than thirty years.

"At a tremendous rate," a *Times* article happily stated at one point, "the wild virgin areas of Southern California are being broken down to the uses of progress and yielding up their beauties to the motoring public."

In the 1920s, socialists and "progressives" tried to stop the deterioration of L.A.'s rail system by having it taken over by the city. The *Times* opposed this movement, using the usual tactic of painting its proponents Red. In 1936 a group of corporations that included General Motors, Standard (Oil) of California, Firestone Tire and Rubber Company, B. F. Phillips Petroleum, and Mack Manufacturing, maker of Mack trucks, organized a company called National City Lines. Its purpose was to buy up street railways throughout America and convert them to bus lines. National City Lines would then buy buses and oil and gasoline and tires from the parent companies. In 1937 the Southern California Auto Club called for the elimination of the interurban railway lines and their replacement by buses and automobiles. National City Lines, through an affiliate, began buying up the Los Angeles railway system. It removed cars from operation, forcing people to longer and longer waits for them. Then the company obtained permission to tear up the track, with the help of some of its own agents in the Public Utilities Commission.

The railway unions fought to impede this wrecking process, backed, interestingly enough, by the Hearst-owned *Herald-Express*, which had a large working-class readership. Finally, in 1947, after ten years and not until the damage was irreversible, the United States Justice Department brought an antitrust suit against National City Lines and its owners, whose executives in due course were convicted. They were fined one dollar.

The L.A. *Times* continued its assaults on rapid transit systems, and in 1963 the last of the Big Red Cars was taken out of service. By then the *Times* had taken up the cause of smog abatement.

In the 1940s few young people had automobiles or the immediate hope of owning them, which is why Ford, Cities Service petroleum products, Texaco, and General Motors slanted their radio programs toward those older people who did. The young were largely dependent, except for occasions when it was possible to borrow the family car, on tramways to get them to the pavilions and ballrooms. It is impossible, then, to estimate the effect on the band business of the dismantling of the urban and interurban railways, and in any case it cannot be extricated from the other major changes that were occurring.

In consequence of the rise of television, the great radio networks were also being dismantled. (In theory they still exist, but they are little more than a string of news outlets.) Within five years of the incipient proliferation of television, both baseball and movie attendance had declined drastically, the latter to the point where the National Association of Theater Owners was concerned whether "hardtop" theaters, as they were known in the trade—those with roofs on them—could survive. The drive-ins were doing well as the campaign to force people into cars succeeded and young people acquired jalopies and hot rods. The drive-ins were, besides, great places to grope a girl, eliminating the preliminary folderol of dancing that went with big bands. Ministers of the gospel railed against "passion pits" and were mocked for doing so, but in fact the drive-ins did contribute to the loosening of restrictions and inhibitions and led us toward our present age of casual and perfunctory encounter. Many hard-top theaters went out of business, and their premises were converted to other uses. Suddenly one viewed the curious spectacle of supermarkets with marquees, on which were emblazoned not the names of movie stars but the price of lamb chops.

The peak business year for the motion picture industry in the U.S. was 1946, when box office grosses reached $1,692,000,000. That was the year the soldiers came home and took their girls to the movies. The large-scale production of TV receivers got under way in 1947—and motion picture grosses dropped immediately by a hundred million dollars. From there on, attendance at the movies and other out-of-home entertainments declined steadily. Not until 1974 did the movie industry exceed its 1946 box-office take, and when it did so it was in watered dollars. In 1946, ninety million movie tickets were sold per week in the United States; in the early 1980s, the figure was twenty million a week and dropping, although the population of the country had nearly doubled.

The tendency of the public to stay home and watch the glass box was not the end of television's mischief. Caught up in the profitability of TV, which revealed an astonishing capacity to move merchandise, the networks let national radio fall into desuetude. Gone were *The Fitch Bandwagon* and all the rest. Gone were the remotes from the Palomar, the Trianon, and Frank Dailey's Meadowbrook. And local stations, no longer able to depend on high-quality programs piped from New York, Chicago, and Los Angeles, perforce relied more and more on records. In turn the music industry, unable to look to network radio for exposure, and largely ignored by television on the grounds that music wasn't "visual" enough, became dependent on the airplay of records by local stations. The disk jockey became a crucial link in the sales chain of the music business.

Some of the disc jockeys—including Dave Garroway in Chicago, Fred Robbins, Symphony Sid Torin and Martin Block in New York, Ed (Jack the Bellboy) Mackenzie in Detroit, Jimmy Lyons and Al (Jazzbo) Collins in San Francisco, Al Jarvis and Gene Norman in Los Angeles, Sid Mark in Philadelphia, Felix Grant in Washington, Dick Martin in New Orleans, and Phil McKellar in Windsor, Ontario (whose clear-channel station reached much of North America)—fought a rearguard action for good music, jazz in particular. But station management wasn't interested in music. It was interested in cost per thousand—the advertiser's cost of reaching a thousand persons.

To a commercial radio station, it is of priority importance to reach the widest possible audience, for the sake of higher advertising rates. To do that, American stations in the early 1950s began emphasizing music that was the equivalent of dime-store prints of mountain stags in polychrome sunsets. This was the early phase of the musical decline, characterized by *Music Music Music, You You You, Wanted, Wheel of Fortune, The Tennessee Waltz*, and the like, which led down to Bill Haley and the Comets, Elvis Presley, and the dark at the bottom of the stairs. The decline began in the late 1940s, accelerated in the 1950s, and took the great plunge when Todd Storz dreamed up his "jukebox of the air."

Storz, of the New Orleans–based Storz broadcasting stations, observed that the same songs were played over and over on jukeboxes. He reasoned that the radio public would similarly take to a restricted list of hit songs constantly repeated. Their selection would not be according to such vague standards as esthetic worth but to a strict commercial criterion—popularity, as determined by such supposedly objective indicators as the charts published by *Billboard*. The Storz format proved successful and soon was emulated by stations throughout the United States. They played music from lists limited to forty songs, around the clock, seven days a week. Thus Top Forty radio was born. In later years, some stations tightened the playlist to fifteen.

By 1970, computerized "jukeboxes of the air" had come into existence—stations programmed by companies such as Drake-Chenault. A visit to such a station could be unsettling. Banks of large machines sat there, still. Suddenly one machine would start up, following the command of a computer, and play a song over the air, although in the station itself there might be only an antiseptic silence. Then it would stop and another machine would start. One spool would contain current "hot" tunes, another a collection of "golden oldies." Some songs were described as they begin to play, others were "back-announced," all according to commands from the computer, which also ordered the play of commercials and even the recorded on-the-hour news required by the Federal Communications Commission.

Who killed the big bands? A good case can be made against a group of people that includes James Caesar Petrillo, Todd Storz, Learned Hand, Harry Chandler and all his heirs and minions, and the heads of General Motors, Firestone, B. F. Phillips, Standard of California (which means the Rockefellers), and the Mack Truck company, as well as a forgotten functionary who thought up the wartime entertainment tax, which lingered on into the 1950s, still harming American music.

Los Angeles has the worst public transport of any major city on the North American continent, along with the coagulated freeways and all too visible air that GM and Standard and the Chandlers forced on it. A stretch of rail runs beside Santa Monica Boulevard from the Hollywood line on through Beverly Hills almost to the San Diego Freeway, where it trails out. It is a vestige of the Red Cars. Elsewhere in America, you will find odd lyrical memories of the Toonerville trolley: level straight strips of land sentried by maples or cottonwoods or sycamores, grown deep in grass and milkweed and Queen Anne's lace. The steel rails are for the most part vanished, long since torn up and melted for scrap, remembered by creosoted wooden ties. Sometimes, though, you will find the rails themselves, rusting among the wildflowers.

Whether consciously or not, Johnny Mercer caught the end of an era in his lyric for *Early Autumn*:

> There's a dance pavilion in the rain,
> all shuttered down . . .

The Squirrel
Yip Harburg

Back in the 1960s, when I was living in New York, I was asked by the Canadian Broadcasting Corporation to do a series of radio documentaries on various songwriters I admired. Some of them, of course, were already gone, but I did do interviews with a number of those who were still available. One of these was Mitchell Parish, whose body of work, while small, contains one of the most breathtaking lyrics in the English language, *Stardust*. What a piece of writing that is! The aesthetic application of Gresham's law was already at work, and rock-and-roll was taking over, turning its listeners into an ahistorical generation. Parish was outraged by it. I wanted to talk about his youth in New York City, about his associations with such composers as Hoagy Carmichael. I wanted to hear his reminiscences about walking around Tin Pan Alley on a summer day when the music then being born was coming out the open windows. He kept returning to his anger.

I interviewed Arthur Schwartz, an elegant man and one of the most elegant composers of that whole glorious era, and Harry Warren.

I interviewed Johnny Mercer, of course. If Yip Harburg was, as he said, his mentor, Johnny certainly was one of mine, and a few years before had become a good friend. We always talked about lyrics. Johnny urged me to do a broadcast on Harold Arlen. I told him I didn't know Arlen, and had heard that he lived in melancholy and seclusion after the death of his wife, Anya. Johnny said that was just the reason he wanted me to interview him: he thought it would be good for Arlen to come out of his isolation to talk to me. He called Harold and I spent several hours with him in his apartment on Central Park West. Arlen or Mercer suggested that I interview Yip Harburg, who lived a few blocks up Central Park West from Harold. One or the other called him, and I spent time with him, too.

In a 1970 history called *Broadway*, the critic Brooks Atkinson wrote, "Harold Arlen's *Bloomer Girl*, full of comedy and nostalgia, and Burton

Lane's *Finian's Rainbow*, full of political satire and comic caprice, helped to redeem Broadway from drudgery."

Both shows were essentially Harburg's, as his son Ernie, a social psychologist and epidemiologist at the University of Michigan, points out in a book called *Who Put the Rainbow in the Wizard of Oz: Yip Harburg, Lyricist*. The book is cowritten with Harold Meyerson, who is executive editor and political columnist for the *L.A. Weekly*. "With," they write, "all due respect for the prodigious musical achievements of Arlen and Lane, Atkinson's assessment refers largely to Yip, who not only coauthored *Finian*'s book (with Fred Saidy) but directed *Bloomer Girl,* and for both shows conceived the theme, wrote the lyrics, provided the politics, the satire, the caprice, the comedy, and was their guiding spirit. Indeed ... Yip was, after Oscar Hammerstein II, one of the key figures in the transformation of the Broadway musical revues into the musical plays of the '40s and '50s and thereafter."

Harburg helped initiate the Lyrics and Lyricists series, in which lyricists talk about their craft, at the 92nd Street YMHA in New York City, and in 1980 was its first featured speaker. He asked: "Why the anonymity of the lyricist as against the recognition of the composer?" and then examined what he called "the genesis of this small injustice."

Harburg clearly believed, as I do, that music preceded speech. I have noticed, both in languages I understand and languages I don't, that certain intervals are common to them, falling thirds and fourths, the first inversion of the major triad (a rising sixth falling a major third to the tonic has a peculiarly playful quality and turns up in children's songs), all of them conveying emotion: resignation, anger, amusement, caution. The melodies of laughter and anger are international, which is one reason I have never been able to accept serialism. I think music has inherent, not conditioned, emotional content.

Harburg continued, "It was eons before man ... began to invent language. Man could growl and grunt and groan, yodel and sing. When he dragged his Neanderthal bride over the threshold of his cave his larynx was able to warble a cadenza of joy long before he could say, 'Baby, it's cold outside.' This perhaps explains why people today can hum a tune, but can't remember the words.

"Music, which is an extension of our emotions, comes naturally. It is the vested interest of the heart, a very ancient organ. The word must be worked at and memorized, for it is the vested interest of the frontal lobe, a rather recent development. . . .

"[The] magic in song happens only when the words give destination and meaning to the music and the music gives wings to the words. Together as a song they go places you've never been before.

"The reason is obvious—words make you think thoughts. Music makes you feel a feeling. But a song can make you feel a thought. That's the great advantage. To feel the thought. You rarely feel a thought with just dialogue itself. And that's why song is the most powerful weapon there is. It's poignant and you can teach more through song and you can rouse more through song than all the prose in the world or all the poems.

"Songs have been the not-so-secret weapon behind every fight for freedom, every struggle against injustice and bigotry: *The Marseillaise, The Battle Hymn of the Republic, We Shall Overcome*, and many more. Give me the makers of the songs of a nation and I care not who makes the laws."

Aside from the fact that it doesn't fully make sense, that last sentence is a paraphrased plagiarism. Perhaps Harburg wasn't able to trace it to the source. The exact quote, which I spent a great deal of time tracking down, is: "Let me make the songs of a nation and I care not who makes its laws." It is from an essay on government published in 1703 by the Scottish patriot Andrew Fletcher. Harburg might have commented, as I have, that rock-and-roll was the primary cause of the drug epidemic in which America is now drowning. But Harburg *did* know the darker implications of the power of song, for he said in that lecture: "A song can degrade your culture; debase your language. It can pollute your air and poison your tastes or it can clear your thoughts, refurbish your spirit. It is the pulse of a nation's heart. A fever chart of its health. . . .

"I do not wish to intimate that the lyric writer is a more evolved creator than the composer. The composer is merely luckier; he works in a medium in which the appeal is directly to the emotions. The lyric writer must hurdle the mind to reach the heart." Or as I have said, he must implant a thought that instantly arouses an emotion. He doesn't so much hurdle the mind, which implies its circumvention, as use it to cause feeling. But the thought in words must be understood if it is to move the emotions; music does it directly. What they have in common is that they are, unlike architecture and painting and sculpture, temporal and incorporeal arts. They occur in time and are instantly gone, leaving eddies of emotion and thought behind.

"The greatest romance in the life of a lyricist is when the right words meet the right notes," Harburg said.

Harburg's crowning achievement was the movie *The Wizard of Oz*, but among the hundreds of millions of people who know its songs, few realize that its lyrics are by Harburg. Ironically, several MGM executives tried to delete *Over the Rainbow*, its finest song and one of the best-loved of all songs.

The Meyerson—Harburg book makes note that Ira Gershwin, Lorenz Hart, Oscar Hammerstein II, Howard Dietz, Harry Ruby, and Irving

Caesar were all born in New York City to Jewish parents in 1895 and '96. Composer Jay Gorney, Yip's first collaborator, was also born in 1896, but in Bialystok, Russia, though his family moved to Detroit when he was ten. He graduated from the University of Michigan in 1917. George Gershwin was born in New York just a little later, in 1898. Hart, Hammerstein, and Dietz all went to Columbia College. So did Richard Rodgers, born in New York in 1902, and Arthur Schwartz, also born in New York.

Meyerson and Harburg write that what they call the class of '95–'96, in company with a few others, invented and set the standards of lyrics in what came to be considered an original American art form, the musical comedy. The hypothesis holds if the list is expanded to include a few persons born a little later and not necessarily in New York: Dorothy Fields, considered a major lyricist, was born in New Jersey in 1905. Cole Porter was born in Peru, Indiana, a little earlier than that distinguished group: 1891. Frank Loesser, eventually a composer as well as an outstanding lyricist, was born in New York in 1910. Johnny Mercer was born in Savannah, Georgia, in 1909.

The hypothesis that the musical is an original American art form is dubious: the lineage goes back to European operetta and far beyond that to Greek drama. The only truly American art form is jazz, and that too has roots elsewhere. But that a small group of Jewish males born in the same city in a twenty-four-month span, along with a few others including Mercer and Porter and one woman, Dorothy Fields, created the most brilliant body of lyrics in the history of the English language is indisputable. There is nothing in England to compare to it.

Irving Berlin, a major figure of American music, was born in Russia. Meyerson and Harburg note that his work, in the early years, "was New York to the core, but it was not yet theater song—defining, instead, the upper limit of what vaudeville and revue could do." Berlin learned to write for theater but was never adept at it. He was a creature of Tin Pan Alley more than a theater man.

The major formative figure was Larry Hart. Hammerstein and Harburg rank close to him in influence.

Harburg was a polemical lyricist, building songs and musicals around his deeply felt liberalism. He early aroused the ire of Republicans with his song *Brother, Can You Spare a Dime?*, which he said some of them tried to get barred from radio. It was too late: the song was a hit and doubtless contributed at least in a small way to the first election of FDR.

He was born Irwin Hochberg on April 8, 1896, on the Lower East Side, the youngest of his parents' four living children; six others died. His parents worked in a garment sweatshop, as did so many other immigrant Jews. I remember Yip telling me that the Gershwins were not poor: "At least they could afford a piano. "I remember the day they hauled it up the face of their building." Yip helped me realize that the rags-to-Broadway-riches myth is nonsense. Berlin too was born poor, but every other major Broadway composer and lyricist of that era was born at least to comfort and most of them to wealth. Excepting Mercer, all of them were college educated, including Harburg.

The Broadway musical theater has always been the plaything of the rich. Its songs are of the rich, by the rich, and for the rich. That Harburg alone in his crowd was not born to comfort goes far to explain his compassion for the common man and the deep difference between his work and that of every other Broadway lyricist. Alan Jay Lerner's occasional attempts to write musicals of social conscience, including the one he did with Kurt Weill, the abortive *Love Life* (1948), are awkward and embarrassing: Lerner knew nothing of poverty or poor people, being a consummate snob, for all his affectations of social conscience. I think the superficiality of Lerner's liberalism could be seen in an incident that occurred in a taxi that was reported in Leonard Lyons' column in 1959. Since Lerner himself was the only possible source of the story, he was obviously proud of it. When a cab driver disputed the route they should take, he said to Lerner, "I'm as good as you." Lerner said, "No, you're not. I'm younger, more talented, more successful, fulfilling greater responsibilities. Go up Park." That alone suggests why Lerner was unable to bring off *Love Life.*

Harburg's shows have a bite and urgency that Lerner could not attain and the others on Broadway never even aspired to. Compare Porter's *You're the Top, I Get a Kick Out of You, You're Sensational, Miss Otis Regrets, Anything Goes,* and *Why Shouldn't I?,* to Harburg's *Happiness Is a Thing Called Joe,* written for the movie *Cabin in the Sky.* "Although the cabin's gloomy and the table's bare ..." Cole Porter could never even have imagined such a line, nor any of the lines in *Brother, Can You Spare a Dime?* and *The Eagle and Me.* His *Down in the Depths (on the Ninetieth Floor)* contains the line "even the janitor's wife has a perfectly good love life." Note that "even the janitor's wife ..." tells you what his social attitudes were. Compare it to Lerner's quip to the cab driver.

A statement Yip made years later suggests that he met Ira Gershwin when they were both attending Townsend Harris Hall, which combined high school and college. But Edward Jablonski, in *Happy with the Blues,* his biography of Harold Arlen, says "Attending Townsend Harris Hall at the same time was Ira Gershwin, a neighborhood friend," which suggests they already knew each other. That is the impression I garnered from Yip in his reminiscence about watching the piano go up the face of their building. In any event, Yip and Ira remained friends for life. They wrote for their high school paper and, at City College of New York, started a column in the campus paper and studied classical verse forms. Ira dropped out of CCNY, but Yip stayed, desperately wanting the security of a degree. That parting of the ways is more than a little symbolic of what separated him from all other Broadway lyricists. Graduating from CCNY in 1917, he took a job as a manager for the Swift meat-packing people in Uruguay, staying there two years. On returning to New York, backed by money from a friend, he went into the electrical appliance business. He liked writing light verse but never gave a thought to making a living from it. He couldn't take the chance. If he failed, there was no mattress of money for him to fall on.

I heard all sorts of stories about where he got the name Yip. Since he was often called Yipper, it was suggested that the name evoked a terrier quality in his personality. I saw no such quality in him; he was a gentle sort of man, warm and accessible, with a genuine interest in the people he met. According to Edward Jablonski and others, the name was derived from the Yiddish word *yipsl*, meaning squirrel. When Yip married a Boston girl named Alice Richmond, he changed his name from Irwin Hochberg to Edgar Y. Harburg. The Y was for Yip, and from then on it was his real name, not a nickname.

By October 1929 he was worth about a quarter of a million dollars, a substantial fortune at the time. Very soon he was broke, his business destroyed by the crash. He was deeply in debt. Yip told me, and told many other people too, that he had mixed feelings about the Depression: he was horrified by it, but it gave him freedom. It got him out of business.

There are two versions of how Yip began writing songs with his first partner, Jay Gorney. Edward Jablonski wrote in *Happy with the Blues* that Gorney had read some of Yip's light verse in Franklin P. Adams' *Conning Tower* column. Yip, however, said he talked to his friend Ira Gershwin about his desire to try his hand at song lyrics, and Ira recommended that he team up with Gorney. Possibly both stories are true. Gorney had been writing songs with the brilliant Howard Dietz. But Dietz had just formed a partnership with Arthur Schwartz.

Johnny Green and Harburg got a hit song: *I'm Yours.* Then in 1932, in the depths of the Depression, Gorney and Harburg wrote a show called *Americana* whose theme was the Forgotten Man, the working man, the immigrants who had believed in the American dream only to see it betrayed by runaway capitalism. For that show, in that age when young men shuttled back and forth across the country on freight trains and once-proud men stood on street corners with outstretched hands, they wrote a song that would haunt America then and for a long time afterwards. Its lines are still chilling:

> Once I built a railroad,
> Made it run,
> Made it race against time.
> Once I built a railroad;
> Now it's done.
> Brother, can you spare a dime?

Yip's next partner was the aristocratic Vernon Duke, with whom he wrote *April in Paris, What Is There to Say?*, and *I Like the Likes of You*. In 1933, he wrote *It's Only a Paper Moon* with Harold Arlen, beginning one of the most important professional relationships of his life.

But the Depression was drying up the musicals of Broadway. Its best lyricists and composers were being lured out to Hollywood to write for the movies, among them Cole Porter, Rodgers and Hart, Harry Warren, the Gershwins, Jerome Kern, and Arlen and Harburg. Under a year's contract to Warner Brothers Harold and Yip wrote songs for three films, none of them memorable.

Then came *The Wizard of Oz* at Metro-Goldwyn-Mayer. Yip proved to have a talent for fantasy, and the project was perfect for him. He was given a great deal of latitude and authority by the film's producer, Arthur Freed, who was responsible for some of the finest musicals MGM ever made, including, later on, *An American in Paris* and *Singin' in the Rain. The Wizard of Oz* is the first great integrated film musical, and Harburg was responsible for its unity, since he wrote (without screen credit) the dialogue that fits the songs so beautifully into the picture. *Over the Rainbow* may be his greatest lyric, but the whole score, music and lyrics equally, is a stunning piece of work.

The early days of World War II saw a change in Yip's personal life. Jay Gorney and his wife Edelaine were divorced. Yip married Edelaine, known to friends as Eddy. He would spend the rest of his life with her, and raise Jay Gorney's son Rod. If there was any sort of strain between Yip and Gorney at the time, it faded, for they wrote together again later.

After *The Wizard of Oz*, Yip returned to Broadway to write a show with Burton Lane, a vehicle for Al Jolson that included *There's a Great Day Coming Mañana*, another of his satiric political commentaries. He wrote a musical film called *Cairo* with Arthur Schwartz and, with Jerome Kern, a Deanna Durbin film called *Can't Help Singing*. He and Harold Arlen worked on *Cabin in the Sky*, a film with an all-black cast that seemed to round up every black performer Hollywood could find, from Duke Ellington to Rex Ingram, Mantan Moreland, and Steppin Fetchit. The movie industry had nowhere near the pool of great black actors that it does today, and many of the performances are embarrassing. But nothing is as embarrassing as the script, with Eddie (Rochester) Anderson as a ne'er-do-well shiftless gambler, Ethel Walters as his long-suffering wife, and Lena Horne as the seductress. It is so awful, so drenched in racial stereotypes, that it exerts a certain morbid fascination. Its redeeming features are the singing of Ethel Waters and one of the three songs Arlen and Harburg contributed to it: *Happiness Is a Thing Called Joe*, in which Harburg demonstrated his ability to imagine himself in someone else's shoes, not exactly a common quality of conservatives, in or out of the arts.

Yip's next musical, *Bloomer Girl* (1944), with Harold Arlen, set in the days of the hoop skirt, treats the issues of war and peace and black and female equality, with analogies to World War II. *Evelina* and *Right as the Rain* derive from that show. But the most powerful song of the show is the one assigned to Pompey, the runaway slave of the story: *The Eagle and Me*. It was and remains a plea for freedom and the individual rights of all men. It's a marvelous song which, later, Lena Horne recorded in a passionate personal version.

In November of that year, Yip participated in a national election-eve broadcast in support of Roosevelt's third-term presidential bid. For that show he wrote *Don't Look Now, Mr. Dewey (But Your Record's Showing)*, and another intense plea for racial equality, *Free and Equal Blues*. Roosevelt made a short speech as part of the broadcast. Yip later stated that the gentle Harold Arlen said that "he thought I was too involved in politics all the time and that it was polluting the stage. The stage was not a pulpit, not a place for 'propaganda,' which he called it. I called it education; he called it propaganda." Burton Lane would make the same objection.

Yet it was with Lane that Harburg would write his best musical and most effective social commentary: *Finian's Rainbow*. It is about an Irishman named Finian who believes gold actually grows in America, steals a crock of it from a leprechaun named Og, leaves for America and in the state of Missitucky encounters a racist (modeled by Harburg on Senator Theodore Bilbo and Congressman John Rankin), whom an accidental wish turns black, causing him to discover the horrors of what he has always preached. Og has followed Finian to America, and all turns out well for everyone: there was no malice in Yip's work. Og was played by David Wayne. His understudy was Larry Orenstein, who had played trumpet and sung with Paul Whiteman, Shep Fields, and Ray Noble (under the name Larry Neill). He also was Yip's assistant on the production and, on occasion, played the role of Og himself.

Larry, who lives now in Los Angeles, says that for all its complex plot lines, "it was a beautiful show, beautifully done." And it contained some marvelous Arlen–Harburg songs: the exquisite and somewhat neglected *Look to the Rainbow, Old Devil Moon,* and *When I'm Not Near the Girl I Love,* as well as a satiric assault on materialism: *When the Idle Poor Become the Idle Rich.* The last of these is almost clairvoyant: it foresees and makes mock of the explosion of postwar American consumerism.

In a song called *The Begat* Harburg takes yet another swipe at a favorite shibboleth, the Republican party, in a line about the DAR and the Babbitt and bourgeoisie "who begat the misbegotten G.O.P." With his patriotism and faith in the United States, he had no way of foreseeing HUAC and Senator Joseph McCarthy, who would exact the GOP's revenge.

The blacklist began in 1947, when the Hollywood studios announced that ten "unfriendly witnesses" before the House Un-American Activities Committee would not work again in the movies. And Yip, who was working on an MGM musical version of *Huckleberry Finn* with Burton Lane, was dropped after three songs. Yip wrote an almost pathetic letter to MGM's lawyer, saying: "I am a Franklin Delano Roosevelt Democrat, believing firmly in everything he stood for. As a firm, almost fanatical believer in democracy, as a proud American, and as the writer of the lyric *God's Country,* I am outraged by the suggestion that somehow I am connected with, believe in, or am sympathetic with Communist or totalitarian philosophy."

Ah, but he had written those anti-Republican lyrics; forget the anti-Stalinism of *God's Country.* The elephant has a long memory.

But there was no blacklist on Broadway. Yip could write shows. His next was *Flahooley* (a collaboration with Sammy Fain), a parable set in a toy factory and satirizing capitalism, consumerism, and atomic energy, and the political witch hunts then terrorizing America. It was full of topical references, including one to Alger Hiss. One song is titled *You Too Can Be a Puppet.* The show opened early in 1951. With the Korean War under way, not everyone reacted well to a show that was critical of America's industrial power, and it was attacked by those two great thinkers Dorothy Kilgallen and Ed Sullivan. Under this kind of assault it failed.

All the while Yip was being passed over for one movie after another, including the Judy Garland version of *A Star Is Born.* MGM refused to film *Finian's Rainbow.*

Yip undertook yet another musical with Harold Arlen, one that was eventually titled *Jamaica.* It was compromised from the beginning. It was to have starred Harry Belafonte, who had proved adept at calypso and the kind of pidgin English Harburg planned for the show, a commentary on American life refracted through a view from the islands. Yip got there before Bob Marley. But Belafonte had to undergo throat surgery, and the show was tailored for Lena Horne, which altered its perspective. It still contained songs such as *Hooray for de Yankee Dollar* and *Leave de Atom Alone*, but it was not as effective as it might have been with Belafonte. *Three Monkeys in a Mango Tree* object to being considered relatives to a creature as destructive as man. The show was a success, but only as a star turn for Lena Horne.

It was Yip's last. He would never again write a major musical. Nor would he ever write another important movie, for, although the black list was gone, so were the great MGM musicals whose era he and Harold Arlen had initiated. Warner Brothers filmed a version of *Finian's Rainbow*, with Fred Astaire, but Yip had little to do with it and hated it. He wrote a musical called *Darling of the Day* with Jule Styne. It closed in three weeks.

In 1968 Yip wrote a show about the children's crusade of the thirteenth century, *What a Day for a Miracle*, with music by Larry Orenstein and Jeff Alexander. Again, he was using another time as a reflection on our own. It was ahead of its time—written by Jews, it raised the unacceptable hypothesis that Arabs could be decent people—and it never reached Broadway.

After that, Yip's professional activities were desultory. He watched the rise of the Bob Dylan generation of songwriters, so many of them pontificating on politics, their work informed by a pretentious moral superiority. None of them had Yip's leavening of wit, nor for that matter his literacy and his deep knowledge of poetry, history, and economics. He hated the illiteracy of their work.

When it came to political commentary in the form of the lyric, no one in America has ever touched Yip, and the only one in the English language who ever did was William S. Gilbert.

Style Is the Man
Arthur Schwartz

If the best American songs came out of Broadway musical theater and the movies, it was because the best young composers gravitated to these media, which promised performance of their work and, if they made it, enormous incomes. No slot machine pays off like Broadway when the lemons at last line up. But it was always a gamble in which only the rich could indulge. Countless Hollywood movies have applied the Horatio Alger rags-to-riches fantasy to musical theater—including *My Gal Sal* (1942), a putative biography of Paul Dresser starring Victor Mature that had little to do with Dresser's reality. Irving Berlin seemed to embody it, but he was an exception.

The press, I found, made a considerable to-do of Alan Jay Lerner's silver-spoon birth. This caused me to look into the lives of the major Broadway composers and lyricists of the golden age. One after another, they turned out to be from, at minimum, the upper middle class, and some of them from very heavy wealth. And by far the majority of them were university-educated.

Cole Porter was born to millions and married millions more. He went to Worcester Academy, took a B.A. from Yale, attended Harvard Law School, the Harvard School of Music, and eventually the Scola Cantorum in Paris, where he studied under Vincent d'Indy. Lorenz Hart's father was a grifter, but apparently a slick one, and the family always had servants. Arthur Schwartz was the son of a lawyer, graduated Phi Beta Kappa from NYU, and earned a master's at Columbia, after which he became a lawyer. His primary partner, lyricist Howard Dietz, graduated from the Columbia College School of Journalism.

I admired Arthur Schwartz and certainly Howard Dietz, whose command of language perhaps exceeded in precision and surprise that of any other lyricist, from my earliest days. Arthur's catalog includes *I Guess I'll Have to Change My Plan, Something to Remember You By, Dancing in the Dark,*

Alone Together, A Shine on Your Shoes, If There Is Someone Lovelier than You, You and the Night and the Music, By Myself, I See Your Face Before Me, They're Either Too Young or Too Old, A Rainy Night in Rio, Oh But I Do, A Gal in Calico, Haunted Heart, and *Make the Man Love Me,* some of the most gorgeous melodies in the whole history of song.

One day I was descending from the ASCAP New York office in an elevator. A tall, dark-haired, and strikingly handsome man in—I later realized—his seventies struck up a conversation with me. We got onto the subject of songs, and as we left the building found we were both walking north. The conversation continued. The man was elegant, poised, vigorous, articulate, and spoke with a voice of such gorgeous baritone resonance that I can still hear it in my head.

Finally, as we waited for a stoplight to change, he asked my name, and I told him. He put out his hand and said, "I'm Arthur Schwartz."

I managed not to appear foolish, and sometimes after that when he was in New York City—he lived his late years in London—I would get together with him.

Arthur combined assurance and modesty in a curious balance, and his music was exactly like the man who wrote it: elegant, intelligent, urbane, and in exquisite taste. No one in the history of American popular music, with the one exception of Jerome Kern, so embodied in his art the meaning of the word "taste." His melodies had the quality of utter naturalness, as if he had come upon them not so much by labor as by serendipity.

I asked him at some point, "How did you manage to combine careers of law and music?"

"Well, I didn't do them at the same time," he replied. "I didn't know when I was starting to write music that I'd be very good at it. I wrote very little in the early years that made me think I should do it at all as a career, and so I decided to be a lawyer and have something to fall back on in case I didn't make it in music. And so I practiced law for four years. And Larry Hart was a man I knew quite well from camp days, when we were both counselors, and I had the luck of having him advise me. I would go to him every few months, at his house on 119th Street, and spend a day or a whole weekend with him, playing tunes of mine, and having him say, 'Well that's good, that's no good, don't leave the law now, well let's think about it,' and at a certain point I played him enough stuff for him to say, 'I think if you want to take a year off and see whether you can make it, have you got any money?' I said, 'Yes, I've saved a lot of money.' He said, 'Well, if you can support yourself for a year, why don't you do it? You can't make your way on Broadway and be a lawyer at the same time.' And I did it at the time he advised me to, and it did take me a little under a year to get the first job. I was twenty-eight.

"I never had any music lessons in my life at all—of any kind. And when I told him I wanted to leave the law, my father said, 'How are you going to compete with Gershwin and Kern and all the other people when you haven't had any training?' And of course that worried me very much, because I was just an intuitive writer. I learned how to do everything—not to orchestrate, especially, but I make my own piano parts and have all my life. Just learned how to do it. But I felt that it was very risky to try to compete with people. Rodgers was a thoroughly educated man musically, so was Cole Porter. My father was right. How dare I think that I could compete with them? With luck, I was able to."

I was curious about his work habits, particularly with Howard Dietz, being adamant myself—as were Larry Hart and Johnny Mercer—that the music should come first.

Arthur said, "Dick Rodgers has an old joke about that. When asked a thousand times which came first, the words or the music, he said, 'The check.' People who write together over many years, the way most of my collaborators and I have worked, mainly Howard Dietz and myself, the songs come in many different ways, sometimes from a title, sometimes from a tune, sometimes from a whole lyric, sometimes from a portion of a lyric. I'll never forget the time when Dietz and I were working on a show called *The Band Wagon*, a revue with Fred Astaire, and I thought we had finished the score. Howard and I had a suite in a hotel where we worked while he walked down to the MGM office every day, where he was a vice president in charge of advertising, and he said, 'We have this merry-go-round, and I'm not satisfied that we have a good merry-go-round song. We ought to write another one.' I said, 'I'm through. We have enough. We have a merry-go-round song.' We had written, 'High and low, low and high, and the horses go up and down.'

"He said, 'No, no. We'll write one.' He had his coat and his hat in his hand, and he had a yellow pad. He said, 'What's the name of the girl who takes charge of this room, the maid?'

"I said, 'Louisa. Whaddya wanna know that for?'

"He said, 'Just a minute.' He wrote some words on a piece of paper, put it on the piano, and ran out to his office job. On his pad it said, *I love Louisa, Louisa loves me. When we rode on the merry-go-round, I kissed Louisa.* So I said, 'That's too good, I have to write that.' And that became the first act finale, with the merry-go-round and the horses, and it was a great performance. That's one illustration of how freakish the writing of songs can be."

"Everyone comments," I told him, "on the supreme elegance of your writing, not just the music, but the lyrics by Howard Dietz as well."

"Well," Arthur said, "he's a prime lyricist and poet and a great wit. During the many years we've lived together working, he's said some of the funniest things. I told you, we worked in hotels. We used to have to move from room to room and from hotel to hotel because people complained about the music. And after the ninth or tenth move, we finally got settled in a place we thought we would not move from. Howard Dietz said, 'You know, Arthur, nobody ever complains about the lyrics.'"

Noting that Arthur had evaded my question, I pressed him: "Asking a man to define his own being and taste is difficult. But what is the source of the elegance in *your* writing?"

"Oh, I don't know that it's all that elegant," he protested.

"You must have heard it said."

"Yes. I think that every writer of everything–prose, poetry, music, anything–has his work reflect his taste and his personality. I think that's true of any writer you can think of who wrote novels or plays in the past or today. A personality is expressed in the work that comes out. I don't feel that I'm elegant, either. I don't mean that. I feel that I have an approach toward my work, and the work of other people that I like, which is of a certain kind. I don't say it's better than other kinds. I don't think I'm that special, I don't think I'm that original."

"What are your own favorites of your songs?" I asked.

"I think I like a lot of the songs that other people like. I do like *Dancing in the Dark*, of course; I think that's probably the best-known song I've written. I also like things that are not very important and not very well-known. I do like *You and the Night and Music*, I do like *By Myself.* Very much.

"I like many styles in other people's work. I like very much the kind of music I can't write and don't write. For example, one of my favorite songs is *I'm Just Wild about Harry*, by Noble Sissle and Eubie Blake, written about 1921, I think." (He was right; it was written for the show *Shuffle Along*.) "I would have given anything to have written that. It's just a very original tune. It goes on to phrases without repeat and has an ending that is unlike the beginning, and it has surprises. I also like *The Floradora Sextet* by Owen Hall and Leslie Stewart, and I've often said that that would be a great sort of thing to try to duplicate, that is, a piece of music and lyric which constantly goes from one melody to another without stop and yet is at the same time a unit." He sang the opening lines of the song, which was published in 1901, *Tell me, pretty maiden, are there any more at home like you. There are a few, kind sir.* "And it goes on and on. It takes about six minutes to get through it, and there are probably nine or ten tunes."

"The AABA song is comparatively modern," I said.

"Oh it is!" Arthur said. "But there are people who avoid it. And there are people who wrote AABA who wrote many other types of structure, including myself. Do you know a song of ours called *New Sun in the Sky*? 'I see a new sun up in a new sky, and my whole horizon has reached a new high, da-da-dum, so forth.' So you have sixteen measures before you repeat. So it's half a chorus and half a chorus with a different ending. I don't try to write in any particular form. I once wrote a song with Frank Loesser for a movie, and after it was quite successful, I realized that the main strain was seven measures: *I'm Riding for a Fall.* It sounds like eight, but it's seven. And who cares?

"Ira Gershwin, with whom I wrote a show once, told me that when he and George Gershwin were writing *Girl Crazy*, they came across a song called *I'm Bidin' My Time* and they were going to have the next eight bars repeat. And it was Ira who thought that if it didn't and just went on, it would sound more like the folk song they were trying to write. The next year I was writing for a show with Dietz a song called *Louisiana Hayride*, and I thought, subconsciously, 'If you don't repeat, and go on to the next phrase, it will seem more like a folk song.' So we left out the repeat. I'm fascinated with novel structures."

I asked Arthur about the difference between theater songs and those written directly for the marketplace, for what used to be called Tin Pan Alley.

"You take songs that were very good popular songs, a song such as *Smiles.* That's a very fine popular tune. [*Smiles* was published in 1917.] But if you heard that as a theater tune, you'd say, 'Well, that's a little below the level of theater music.' There is a difference in style. I would feel that, too, about *Hello, Dolly.* I think that's one of the greatest popular songs ever written; it happened to be in a show. There is a difference between theater music and outside-of-theater music, and outside-of-theater music on the individual basis, although that is changing. It is different from popular-song writing, and it expresses the difference between the people who are writing theater music–their personalities, their backgrounds, their tastes–and the same elements in people who are not writing theater music.

"Style is the man; the man is the style."

Jeepers Creepers
Harry Warren

The name of Harry Warren is sometimes invoked in support of the Horatio Alger myth: son of immigrants, born poor (in Brooklyn, like Arthur Schwartz) growing up without education, somehow fighting his way to the top with only his raw and untrained talent. Harry Warren was one of the most successful of all American song composers in that golden period. In the fifteen years from 1935 to 1950, he had forty-two songs on the top-ten list of *Your Hit Parade*, a network radio program that monitored the success of songs through a complex process of surveys. Next in success was Irving Berlin, who had thirty-three songs on that list in the same period.

"In 1938," Harry told me, not without pride, "I had two songs with Johnny Mercer, *Jeepers Creepers* and *You Must Have Been a Beautiful Baby*, that were both on the *Hit Parade*, one and two." Harry neglected to mention that in 1941 he and lyricist Mack Gordon had four on *Your Hit Parade*: *There Will Never Be Another You, I've Got a Gal in Kalamazoo, Serenade in Blue*, and *At Last*, the latter three hits with the Glenn Miller orchestra, all written for the film *Orchestra Wives*.

Warren wrote the music for two Broadway shows before going to Hollywood where, in the twenty-five years from 1932 to 1957, he turned out songs for movies at four major studios: Warner Brothers, Twentieth Century-Fox, Metro-Goldwyn-Mayer, and Paramount. He wrote something like 250 songs in that period, fifty of which became standards. He was the songwriter on a number of the extravagant Busby Berkeley musicals. Berkeley, who had been a Broadway choreographer, first worked with Warren on the film *42nd Street* which, as it happened, was the film that also took Harry permanently to Hollywood. Berkeley's exaggerated choreography, with complex geometric patterns of dancers, was featured in two more pictures with Warren–Dubin scores and starring Dick Powell–*Gold Diggers of 1933* and *Footlight Parade*.

Warren worked with some of the finest lyricists of his era, among them Al Dubin (probably his primary collaborator), Johnny Mercer, Arthur Freed, Ralph Blane, Ira Gershwin, Mack Gordon, Leo Robin, and Sammy Cahn. His various publishers printed about fifty million sheet-music copies of Warren songs, yet his name remained largely unknown to the American public, unlike that of Gershwin or Porter or even Arlen.

"This is a cross I've had to bear," Harry said, kidding on the square, to the late actor and author Tony Thomas, a prominent film historian and biographer. "Even my best friends don't know who I am. I've never been able to figure it out. I guess I don't look like a songwriter, whatever a songwriter is supposed to look like. At the Academy Award show in 1936, when they gave me an Oscar for *The Lullaby of Broadway*, I had trouble getting past the guard.

"I hardly ever hear a disc jockey mention my name when they play my songs, but they often mention the lyricist. The very first record I ever had was *Rose of the Rio Grande* in the '20s by Vincent Lopez and his band, and they left my name off the label. I've had whole albums devoted to my songs, and you usually have to read the liner notes to find out it's my material."

Harry's feelings about fame were ambiguous. If he complained about being ignored, he didn't like public visibility either. He once was induced by friends to hire a press agent, and when the publicist actually got Harry's name into a newspaper, he fired him. He said it was embarrassing.

A famous illustration of Harry's spleen involved Johnny Mercer. Johnny wrote *On the Atchison, Topeka and the Santa Fe* with Harry and recorded it in 1945. A record store in downtown Hollywood did a window display on the song, proclaiming on a poster, "Johnny Mercer's *On the Atchison, Topeka and the Santa Fe.*" Harry was incensed, claiming Mercer was trying to take full credit for the song, and even sent his long-suffering wife Jo down to the store with a camera to get a picture of the window, which he planned to use in evidence in a lawsuit against Mercer. Nothing ever came of the lawsuit, of course, but Harry retained a certain prickly rancor toward Mercer ever afterward. Various people, including Paul Weston, told the story, but oddly enough it is with amusement and with affection for Harry.

"Harry took offense easily," Tony Thomas remarked with a slight chuckle. "And once he did, he carried it for life. Don't forget, his people were from Calabria." Calabria is in the south of Italy. Among Italians, the Calabrese are known for intractable stubbornness.

Harry was a great opera lover, with a particular penchant for Puccini, whose music strongly influenced his own. As pianist and composer Gene DiNovi, like Harry a Brooklyn Italian, notes, "Just look at his bass lines.

Puccini." When I asked Harry if it was true that he was one of the more serious Puccini freaks, he said, "I hope I am. That's my idea of music." Harry was born December 24, 1893, when Puccini was twenty-five and still struggling to establish himself. Puccini's first successful opera, *Manon Lescaut,* was produced that very year. Puccini died in 1924, when Harry was thirty-one and an established songwriter. It is curious that with so strong a Puccini influence in his work, Harry should seem—and was—so American a songwriter.

I no longer remember how I came to know Harry. It was probably through Johnny Mercer and, if not Johnny, Tony Thomas. In any case, when I used to come out from New York to Los Angeles on some job or other, I would sometimes call Harry, and of course always called Johnny. Harry, a really dedicated connoisseur of Italian food, gave me a guided tour of some of the better Italian restaurants in town.

He lived on Sunset Boulevard in Beverly Hills, in a house at the end of a long lane walled by high shrubs. He had been there since Beverly Hills was a sleepy place, thinly populated. I always enjoyed talking to Harry because he was living history, and indeed a chat with him was a journey to and through an America that no longer was. I had a long conversation with him one day in 1975. Harry was then eighty-two, feisty and energetic and still writing melodies, though none of them turned up in pictures; his era was gone. His voice was rather high, with a touch of Brooklyn accent. He didn't quite say *woikin* for *working* but he came close. And there was an under-color of laughter in his voice.

"My father, Antonio Guaragna," Harry said, "originally went to South America. He was in Argentina when he was twenty-one years old. He was a bootmaker, made riding boots. And they wanted people in South America with different crafts. This was about 1871. He didn't like it. He went back to Italy and got my mother and my three sisters and my oldest brother, got on one of these boats that took like two months to come over here, and they cooked their own food in steerage. A lot of people died in those boats in those days, coming over. They landed in New York, didn't know anybody. It takes a lot of nerve to do that. And they weren't even chased out of any place, either. They wanted to come to America. He made boots here, because of course in those days a lot of people rode horses. He used to make all my shoes. My other two sisters and my brother and I were born here.

"My brother Frank used to deliver the boots and the shoes. We lived down at Columbia Heights. That's right under the Brooklyn Bridge, near the St. George Hotel. That's where I was born, Christmas Eve, 1893.

"The family name was Guaragna. My father changed it. I never changed it. I went through school with the name of Warren. We never lived in an

Italian neighborhood. We were a very Americanized family. We didn't like being Italian in the old days, because they were picked on a lot, like they pick on the Mexicans now. They thought we just smelled of garlic, and that's all. Don't forget, the people who came over here came from little towns in Italy. They weren't educated, most of them couldn't read and write. I don't understand how my father did it, I really don't."

Harry emphasized that the family was never poor. The house in Brooklyn Heights—still a fashionable neighborhood, with a spectacular view across the East River to lower Manhattan—was large. Their father's custom boot shop was on the ground floor. Harry was drawn to opera, Italian folk songs, and Catholic liturgical music. His hunger for music, he said, was insatiable. He sang in his church choir because, he said, he read well.

"We used to sing quartet, four-part harmony in our house when we were kids," he said. "I always wanted to write songs, I guess, as far back as I can remember. I learned to play piano by myself, I had no formal education. At first I was a drummer. My godfather had a band, and I used to go on tours with him in the summer. We worked with a carnival show up and down the Hudson River, into Connecticut and Massachusetts. I picked up the piano, and got to like to play the piano much more than drums. And I finally got a job playing piano in Sheepshead Bay. I was also an assistant director for Vitagraph. I had so many jobs. I found out they needed a baritone singer for the Vitagraph Quartet. I went down and applied for the job and I got it.

"Then I got a job as a property man, and then as an assistant director. I used to play the piano for scenes there. I also played for ballroom dancing, because they had to have a tempo to dance to. But then they got a phonograph, and beat me out of a job. That's how I started. I started to play piano a lot, improvising, singing.

"The war came along, and I went in the navy. When I came out, I tried to get into the music business. I met two fellows in Sheepshead Bay who were music publishers. So I said to them, 'I have a song I'd like to have you hear.' It was called *I Learned to Love You When I Learned My ABC's*. They said, 'Gee, that's a cute song.' Don't forget, in those days Woolworth's sold sheet music. The title page of the sheet music determined how it would sell. If it was a pretty title page, people bought it. They never looked inside.

"They were about to print it when they took the music counters out of the stores. The fellow said, 'Do you want a job here?' I said, 'Yeah.' He said, 'Twenty dollars a week.' That's how I got in the music business.'

"I did the first show of Billy Rose, *Sweet and Low*, which had *Cheerful Little Earful* and *Would You Like to Take a Walk*. That was a revue. And I did a show for Ed Wynn called *The Laugh Parade*, which had *You're My*

Everything. And I did another show for Billy Rose called *Crazy Quilt.* That had *I Found a Million Dollar Baby in a Five and Ten Cent Store.*

"My film career really starts with *42nd Street.* I did one before, in 1929, called *Spring Is Here,* an old Rodgers and Hart show. I don't know why they asked us to write extra songs for that. That always puzzled me. The people in the picture business didn't know anything about songs or show business. Most of them were dress-makers. Coat cutters.

"I remember Johnny Mercer and I did a picture for one producer who was a horse player. He had a list on his desk of all the tracks in the United States, and he'd call up his book-maker. He'd tell you to stop playing or singing until he called up his book-maker. In New York, it was later than here. He'd get the New York results first. In between these calls he said to me, 'You're the lousiest piano player I ever heard.' I said, 'If I played good piano, do you think I'd be writing songs? I'd play with an orchestra.' And he said to Mercer, 'You really stink as a singer!'"

"Since you're not enamored of these people," I said, "tell me, Harry, how a good New York boy got sandbagged into Hollywood and the movie industry?"

"It was easy. I was a staff writer at Remick Music Company. Remick guaranteed me, which I had never heard of before, $200 a week drawing account. I had been making $45 a week. I couldn't turn that down. It was good money, I bought a house. That was about 1924, or '25. It was all against royalties, which I never earned, by the way.

"Warner Brothers bought Remick, as well as Harms and Witmark, and paid in those days something like $4 million, which was a lot of money. My contract expired. Max Dreyfus, who had been the owner of Remick, sent for me. He always liked me, I don't know why. I liked him too. He was responsible for developing Kern, Gershwin, everybody. He had a great sense of humor, you know. Drank nothing but imported beer, had it imported from Germany. He had great taste. He had a big farm up in Brewster, New York; his wife raised Percherons, beautiful big horses."

Max Dreyfus is a comparatively unsung hero in the development of the American song. One of the major figures in the history of American music publishing, he encouraged and nurtured almost all the major show composers of the 1920s, '30s, and '40s, including Cole Porter. He would sign them to contracts and let them do pretty much as they pleased. In his ability to sense talent even in the formative stage, he was to songwriting what Maxwell Perkins was to novelists, and we shall not see the likes of either man again.

Harry said, "Max said to me, 'Your contract's up. What do you want to do about it?' Uncle Max, I used to call him. I said, 'What do I want to do about it, what do you want to do about it?' He said, 'We'll re-sign you.' I said, 'At the same money?' He said, 'Do you know you're overdrawn $40,000 already?' He whispered to me, 'I don't care about the Warner Brothers. I'm going to re-sign you for $500 a week drawing account.'

"I said, 'How about going out to California?' He said, 'I'll put that in the contract, that you'll have to be in California for six months a year, and while you're out there you'll have to get a thousand dollars a week.'

"I said, 'Fine.' And I signed the contract. Poor Max. He hated his job. He was now working for the Warner Brothers. He'd sold his company. He was in there as an adviser. He was waiting for the time when he could go back into business. According to his contract, he couldn't for ten years. He owned a piece of Remick, and also owned Harms, and T. B. Harms, which became Chappell.

"Well, I was sitting around doing nothing. Warner Brothers got the galley proofs of *42nd Street* and somebody thought it would make a good musical. They called up Buddy Morris, who was now in charge of Witmark, and said, 'Who have you got there who could write music for a picture like that?' Buddy gave my name.

"And that's how I came to California. I *hated* it. I couldn't stand this place. It was corny then. It was nothing like New York. At least now it's a cosmopolitan city. You know, you couldn't get a good meal out here! The coffee was like black soup. Bernstein's Grotto and Victor Hugo's in downtown Los Angeles were the two best restaurants. But there wasn't any place to eat. I remember Gus Kahn, the lyric writer, and I went to a restaurant one night and ordered a steak, and we couldn't cut it. I asked the guy for a sharp knife, he brought another, we still couldn't cut it. We went hysterical, we went berserk. Even the hamburgers were lousy. There were no delis out here. When we worked at the Warner studio in Burbank that summer, 1932, when I came out, there wasn't a soul on the lot, except the two guys writing the script for *42nd Street.* We looked out our window, you couldn't see a thing for miles—there wasn't a building."

"Why did they build Warner Brothers way out there in the sticks?"

"It was cheaper, probably. They probably bought the land for two dollars an acre. When I first came out in '29, the First National studio on Sunset Boulevard was the one where they did everything. They recorded everything on huge discs. I often wondered how they kept track of all that stuff. They didn't have tape, they didn't have sound on film even.

"I went to Fox in 1940. I did the last picture Shirley Temple made, called *Young People.* If you drove out the Santa Monica or the Pico Boulevard gate, you wouldn't even see a car—nothing. Now it's a teeming city. You go to downtown Beverly Hills, you'd think you're in New York.

"But I wouldn't go back to New York now. I kept going back, and as I kept going back, the more I disliked it. We always went back first class, because I was making good money, and we stayed in the best hotels. I still didn't like it. I wouldn't go back now because my friends are dead. There's nobody there I could even visit. All the publishers I knew are gone.

"I loved the train trips."

"Is that why you wrote two train songs, *On the Atchison, Topeka, and the Santa Fe* and *Chattanooga Choo-Choo?*"

"Also *Shuffle Off to Buffalo* and *Rose of the Rio Grande*. I didn't even know where that was. I had an old jazz tune that Bix Beiderbecke played called *Clementine from New Orleans.*

"I used to love that train whistle. There was nothing like the wailing of the whistle at night, and the clanging of the bell as you went through a little town and you're lying in your bunk. In the early days when I went back east, I couldn't wait until we got to the Hudson River to lift up the curtain and see the river."

"Johnny Mercer wrote a lot of train songs," I reminded Harry.

"Yeah. He was great. He'd come up with great lyrics."

"Was he hard to work with?"

"No. He just didn't talk, that's all. He wasn't friendly. He'd sit there and stare at you. That's why I called him Cloud Boy. Cloud Number Five. He'd just sit there and stare at you, see? When we were working at the Metro lot, I asked about his wife. I said, 'How's Ginger?' I went to lunch, came back two hours later, and when I walked in he said, 'She's fine.' I said, 'Who's fine?' He said, 'Ginger.'"

I said, "Harold Arlen told me a story about Johnny. He said they were working on a picture at, I think, Paramount, and Johnny walked out right in the middle of a meeting and came back two days later and went on with the conversation as if nothing had happened."

"Harold had a great disposition," Harry said. "I don't have that kind of disposition. I get offended very easily. I don't know why, I shouldn't be that way. I guess the fact that I was the baby of the family, nobody could pick on me. But Harold laughed at everything. I used to say to him, 'Walk two Oscars behind me,' and he thought that was hilarious. We used to go to Palm Springs a lot in those days. If somebody said that to me, I wouldn't like it. But he laughed. I couldn't take John when I worked with him. Too bad we didn't have tape in those days. I could have given him a tape and he could have taken it to his house. Mort Dixon was like Johnny. A great lyric writer, but a big drinker. He killed himself. He'd sit there and look at you. He was another guy like Mercer, he'd come out with the whole lyric, you know, not just two lines, like Mack Gordon, who'd give you a line at a time. Al Dubin too. They always dug for a title. Once they got the title, the lyric was easy."

"If you haven't got a title, you haven't got a song," I said.

"I refused to work with Dixon. He didn't talk. We used to work in the office at Remick at night in New York, and he'd just sit there."

Mort Dixon is one of the forgotten lyricists. With Harry he wrote *You're My Everything, Nagasaki, Would You Like to Take a Walk?, I Found a Million Dollar Baby in a Five and Ten Cent Store*, and *Flirtation Walk*, and, with others, *That Old Gang of Mine, Bye Bye Blackbird, River Stay Away from My Door, I'm Looking Over a Four Leaf Clover*, and *The Lady in Red.* Harry, in common with Richard Rodgers and quite a number of composers, had little understanding of the vague associative process through which lyrics are written, often in great agony.

Harry said, "I'd play the tune three or four times. I said to Mack Gordon, 'I can't keep playing this tune. I'm beginning to dislike it.' I made him get a piano player, I wouldn't do it. I only play a tune once. I don't want to play it after that. That's it.

I asked, "Did you find singers hard to work with?"

Harry said, "I was in the picture business from '32 to '69, I would say, and never had a singer say, 'I didn't like that song.' I never had that happen to me. I'm a lucky guy. Even when I did a picture with Bing, *Just for You*. We had nine songs in that picture. We wrote a song called *Zing a Little Zong*. He looked at the song and said, 'Fine,' and walked out.

"Al Jolson was another story. Jolson would never give the songwriter credit. He was a guy who liked to cut in on songs. He'd say, 'How about it, fellas, am I in on it?' I said, 'No, sir. No chance.' We were up in Big Bear, working on the songs for a picture for him. Al Dubin and I had written *About a Quarter to Nine*. We were on the way back. Jolson had a Mercedes. He always had some la-de-da stooge with him. He said, 'Gee, Al, I loved those songs. Who wrote 'em?' I said, 'Go ahead, tell 'im, *we* wrote 'em.' His days as a big shot were over. When I was struggling, I wrote a song with Irving Caesar. Jolson put his name on those lyrics. I got my half, but Irving Caesar didn't."

Jolson was notorious for this kind of extortion. His name is listed as cowriter on an enormous number of songs he didn't write, including *Avalon, California Here I Come, Sonny Boy, There's a Rainbow Round My Shoulder*, and *Me and My Shadow*. He was intensely disliked by songwriters.

I said, "You wrote songs for a lot of those band pictures, I remember. *I Had the Craziest Dream* came from a Harry James picture, *Springtime in the Rockies. Serenade in Blue* came from *Orchestra Wives. Kalamazoo* is one. Where did that come from?"

Harry said, "When I played in the band with my godfather, we stopped in Kalamazoo. I must have been fifteen years old. And there was an old wooden station there. I remember carving my initials on the wood. We were on our way up to Allegan, Michigan, a county fair we were going to play. They didn't even know what Italians were up there, never heard of them. All dirt roads. The farmers came up with their carriages and horses, with all this produce and chickens and cows. You'd think they were just coming across the United States in their Conestoga wagons. I remember a real old-time guy pulling a string out of his inside pocket, he had his money tied up there. Because the pick-pockets used to play all the carnivals, y'know. And also the fortune tellers."

"Also," I said, "you and Al Dubin wrote the first dope song–*You're Getting to Be a Habit with Me.*" The song, which was in the score of *42nd Street* in 1932, uses symbols of addiction throughout, including the line "as regularly as coffee or tea." Tea was a common term for marijuana at the time.

"Yeah," Harry said, completely unabashed. "We did." And then he flabbergasted me. He said, "Would you be interested in writing with me?"

"Yeah!" I said without a moment's hesitation.

He said, "I've got a tune I'd like you to look at." He got out a cassette recorder, sat down at his piano in his studio at the back of the property on Sunset Boulevard, and taped a tune for me. "Take it home and see if you can come up with something," he said.

Harry then suggested that we go for lunch at the Bel Air Country Club, one of his hangouts. After lunch we were heading down a sidewalk toward the parking lot when we encountered a certain famous singer who was coming in with his little daughter, a pretty girl no more than seven years old. The singer made a fuss over both of us, telling his daughter–who I'm sure was less than enthralled by this information–that Harry and I were songwriters, and telling her the names of the songs we had respectively written. Harry and I were embarrassed. Then the singer, said, "I'm getting ready to do a new album. I wish you'd both send me some songs."

We nodded noncommittally and took our leave. As we crossed the parking lot, Harry said, "You know, that guy only ever recorded one of my songs. Did he ever do any of yours?"

"Yep," I said. "Two of them. So I'm one up on you."

I opened the front passenger door for Harry. He paused as he was about to get in and shot at me, "Are you going to send him any songs?"

"Nope," I said.

"Right," Harry said. "Fuck 'im."

I still have the tape Harry gave me that day. I never found a lyric for the melody. Harry died December 2, 1981. Sometimes I look at that tape, even listen to it, the piano playing awkward and rocky but the melody beautifully contoured, as one would expect of a Harry Warren tune, and feel guilty. I would love to find a lyric for it, just so I could say I once wrote a song with Harry Warren.

Roses in the Morning
Johnny Mercer

It is often difficult to recall where and when you met someone, but in Johnny Mercer's case I remember exactly. He was in my opinion the finest lyricist in the English language, an exquisite craftsman and the one with the most personal voice. I had arrived in Los Angeles from New York and called a friend to ask if we might have dinner that evening. She said she had to attend a birthday party for John Williams, then asked, "Would you like to go?"

"Since it's my birthday too," I said, "I'd love to."

It was John's thirty-sixth birthday. I remember that because everybody brought him three dozen of something. Someone brought him thirty-six baby turtles, on whose fate we can only surmise, and someone else gave him thirty-six Black Wing pencils. Black Wings were the pencil of choice of composers in those days. Because of those three dozen Black Wings, I can set the year as 1968, when John Williams turned thirty-six, the date as February 8, and the time at shortly after 8:00 P.M. That is when I met Johnny Mercer.

He was standing with Henry Mancini and a portly man who turned out to be Dave Cavanaugh of Capitol Records. I did not have to ask who he was: I knew that pixie smile from a thousand photographs. When I was in high school, he was a very big singing star, though to the day he died he was never sure of that. He founded Capitol Records during World War II and turned out record after record that a wartime generation of young people found compellingly interesting. You could not get them in Canada and so I would slip across the border to Niagara Falls, New York, to buy them—Mercer's own and those of the stable of fresh talents he assembled for the company—and take them back under the seat of a bus. I was always in fear of being arrested for smuggling and sent to

prison forever. I was about fifteen. I dreamed of playing piano like Nat
Cole and writing songs like Johnny Mercer.

Hank Mancini introduced us. He said, "Gene's a writer from the East."
The East being New York. And Dave Cavanaugh said something kind
about my lyrics. I said, "Well, Mr. Mercer, if I know anything about writing lyrics, I learned it from Cole Porter and you and Charles Trenet."

"How'd I get in there between two queens?" he said with a quick smile.

One learns not to embarrass one's heroes with overpraise or dumbstruck attention. After some restrained statement of my admiration for
his work, I excused myself and went on about the party, a Hollywood
affair of demonstrative embracing, kissed cheeks, gushing compliments,
and maneuvering for professional and social advantage.

Two or three days later I got a note from Mercer at my hotel. I couldn't
imagine how he'd known where to find me, although the answer turned
out to be a simple one: he'd asked Henry Mancini. He said that by coincidence he had, the day after the party, heard a lyric of mine, *Someone to
Light Up My Life*, sung by Vic Damone, on his car radio. "That is some
elegant lyric," he wrote. "It made me cry. I wish I had written it." Long
afterward, I learned that he treasured a telegram from Cole Porter saying
something similar about one of his own lyrics.

Thus began a friendship. Whenever John came to New York or I to Los
Angeles, we'd booze and talk shop, sometimes about lyrics, sometimes
about the corruption of the music business. "Whatever we do," he said,
"the publishers will always be two jumps ahead of us." I was warned
against drinking with Mercer, told by various persons that he could
become suddenly and sullenly—and articulately—nasty. It was notorious
that he would get drunk at parties, turn vicious toward friends and
strangers alike, and then, shaken with guilt and hangover the following
day, send them roses. He was always cautious with Jo Stafford. She has
bearing and presence. Nonetheless, once, at a Capitol Christmas party,
John, already well into the wassail, started in on her.

Jo said, "Please, John, I don't want any of your roses in the morning."
That stopped him.

Some of the stories were funny but many were not, and some people
came away from parties bearing an abiding dislike for Mercer. An executive at RCA Victor in New York, who had idolized him for years, wanted
to meet him. A mutual friend introduced them in the Rainbow Room at
the top of Rockefeller Center. Alas, he caught Mercer on one of his bad
nights, and afterward said he wished they'd never met because now his
illusion was shattered. Carlos Gastel, for many years Nat Cole's manager, once told Mercer off in a bar, saying, "Talent gives you no excuse

to insult people." I know two or three people who despised Johnny Mercer. For others, it wasn't that simple. The songwriters Jay Livingston and Ray Evans, while nursing no illusions about him, never let anyone forget that Mercer's recommendation of them for a motion picture assignment he was too busy to take himself launched their professional careers. John was as generous in his praise of good songwriters as he was quietly critical of the shallow practitioners of the craft. As for me, I liked John. A lot. And we got along, perhaps because we shared the lyricist's paranoia, which John once perfectly expressed in a single line: "You get tired of being everybody's lyric boy." He was referring to all the lead sheets and demo tapes sent to you by musicians who think lyrics are dashed off in a moment from ideas picked casually out of the air. Music, as they see it, is the important art. Everybody uses words, don't they? And music may be the more important art–even the most important of them all for, as Walter Pater observed, all the arts crave after the conditions of music. But it isn't the easier art. "I think it takes more talent to write music," John said to me once, "but it takes more courage to write lyrics."

Although John sometimes wrote quickly–*Days of Wine and Roses* was written in five minutes, *Autumn Leaves* in a taxi on the way to Los Angeles airport–he often suffered for a lyric, as every conscientious lyricist does, and the exquisite *Skylark* took him a year. "Sometimes you get lucky," he said. "But not often." Asked what was the hardest part of writing a lyric, he used to say, "Finding the title." And it is.

Once I arrived in California from New York to work on some songs for a film. I rented a furnished apartment in Westwood, installed a telephone, and called John at his home in Belair. He was away for a few days at his other home in Palm Springs. He and his wife Ginger also maintained an apartment in New York. I left a message with his answering service and went to work on my lyric assignment. John called a few days later and said in that soft Georgia accent, "Whatcha been doin'?"

"Looking for a rhyme," I said.

"Why didn't you call me?" he said. "I'da laid one on yuh."

"I did call you. You were away, remember?"

He invited me to dinner. I said that until I had this one song solved, I would be unfit company for man or beast. He knew exactly what I was talking about. He told me to call him when the song was finished and we'd go out somewhere.

Perhaps a half hour later I got a call from a Harold's Liquor Store in Westwood, saying they had some Scotch for me. "I didn't order any Scotch," I said.

"Mr. Mercer ordered it for you," the man said. "A case of Glenfiddich."
On an earlier trip to California I had spent an evening at John's house,
where I tasted Glenfiddich single-malt Scotch for the first time and raved
about the flavor. He had remembered.

"*How* much?" I said.

"A case."

"I'm only going to be here a month!"

"Do you come to California often?"

"Fairly."

"Well, we can send you two or three bottles now and you can get the
rest whenever you come back."

And so it happened. Every time I came to Los Angeles on a job, I'd call
Harold's Liquor Store. I drank John's Glenfiddich on and off for about
three years.

And I kept hearing how saber-tongued he could be when he'd been
drinking. Finally I asked Henry Mancini about it. "It's all true," he said.

"It's never happened to me."

"Your turn will come," Hank said with a smile.

But it never did. Once I saw John starting to get edgy with a waitress at
Charlie O's in New York. When she had gone to get us two more drinks,
I said, "John, why are you giving her a hard time? She's been perfectly
pleasant to us, and you're being a son of a bitch." I figured the friendship
might end there and then.

But John looked me evenly in the eye and said, "You're right," and
when the girl returned he was cordial to her, and as we left he gave her
an enormous tip.

His relations with his wife, Ginger, were not smooth, at least when he
had been drinking. At one period, Johnny was in love with Judy Garland.
He importuned Ginger for a divorce. She refused him. One morning she
agreed. She already knew the news. In a very short time Johnny learned
that Garland had just married composer David Rose.

Once my wife and I were visiting John and Ginger at their home in
Belair. Johnny got very drunk. He began a verbal assault on Ginger. One
chilling line sticks with me. He said to her: "You're just an ugly old
woman who keeps hanging around."

My wife, born in Los Angeles but raised and schooled in New Orleans,
said with some sort of canny instinct, "John, you're not behaving like a
Southern gentleman. What would your mother think?"

It was amazingly effective. John cooled off.

Another famous lyricist, whose career John had sponsored, told me a
story. He was with John and Ginger in a bar one night when John
decided to sit in and sing with the trio. He sat on a stool and began a

blues. The lyrics, completely improvised, were a rhymed assault on Ginger. "As a human being," the man said, "I was horrified. As a lyricist, I was astonished at his brilliance."

I was always amazed, in the years after our first meeting, how many of my lyrics he had learned. I of course had known hundreds of his all my life. I remember singing them when I was no more than ten as I rode my bicycle to the beach in the spring on graveled country roads through fields of apple and peach blossoms in the Niagara Peninsula. I was in love with songs, and undoubtedly I absorbed principles of euphony and articulation from Mercer long before I ever knew him or even imagined that I could know him. One pub-crawling evening we wandered around New York singing fragments of each other's lyrics back and forth, like musicians trading fours.

I loved John's work more than anyone's, more even than Howard Dietz's, Yip Harburg's, or Cole Porter's. I loved it–even before I knew enough about the subject to understand that these were my reasons for loving it–for its perfect literate craftsmanship and for the powerful vivid use of Anglo-Saxon imagery. And of course for his range.

Every singer knows that the most singable vowels are *oo* and *oh*. In *I Remember You*, John used both sounds, and particularly the *oo*, throughout the song. It is an amazing lyric, so simple that its sophisticated inner craftsmanship could easily escape notice:

> I remember you.
> You're the one who
> made my dreams come true
> a few
> kisses ago.
>
> I remember you.
> You're the one who
> said, "I love you too.
> I do.
> Didn't you know?"
>
> I remember too
> a distant bell
> and stars that fell
> like rain,
> out of the blue.

> When my life is through,
> and the angels ask me to recall
> the thrill of them all,
> then I shall tell them
> I remember you.

The bridge begins and ends with the *oo* sound. And it is used as an inner rhyme in *you too.* Very few of the words end with stopped consonants, and those few fall on short passing notes. All the other words end in semivowels and fricatives—*one, dreams, remember.* The liquid semivowel *l,* occurring here as a double *ll*—in Italian, the *ll* is sustained longer than the single *l*—begins in the release and then recurs through the rest of the song: *bell, fell, recall, thrill, all, shall, tell. Shall-tell* is an inner rhyme echoing *bell-fell,* at least in American English. (In England, *shall* would not rhyme with *tell.*)

Another Mercer masterpiece, *I Thought about You,* further illustrates his grasp of the craft:

> I took a trip on a train
> and I thought about you.
> We passed a shadowy lane,
> and I thought about you.
>
> Two or three cars
> parked under the stars,
> a winding stream.
> Moon shining down
> on some little town.
> With each beam,
> same old dream.
>
> With every stop that we made,
> I thought about you.
> And then I pulled down the shade
> and I really felt blue.
>
> I peeked through the crack
> and looked at the track,
> the one going back
> to you.
>
> And what did I do?
> I thought about you.

Long notes create the rhyme points in songs. Since short syllables should be fitted to short notes and long syllables to long, the rhymes must be long sounds that can be sustained. You can sustain only the vowels, and preferably the long forms of the vowels. Consonants—*b, t, d, g,* for example—cannot be sustained, with the exception of the fricatives *f, s, sh,* and *th.* They can be sustained, but the sounds they make are silly and unattractive. Short vowels as in *bit* and *up* can be sustained but they have a somewhat abrupt sound. One would normally avoid using as a rhyme a word with the kind of abrupt termination you find in *back* or *crack.* There are four consonants that can be sustained to euphonious effect. Known as semivowels, they are *l, m, n,* and *r.* Mercer used open vowels and words ending with the semivowel *l* in *I Remember You.* Words like *train* and *lane, stars* and *cars, stream* and *dream, down* and *town,* containing semivowel endings, are also good rhyme words. Now, notice how Mercer uses the open vowel *oo* and semivowels at rhyme points through most of *I Thought about You* and then, toward the end, deliberately brings in the abrupt consonant *k* to evoke the click of a train's wheels. The word *clack* is never even used; yet you hear the clacking in your mind. It is implied by the sound and the rhyme.

"Do you think Johnny was conscious of these things?" his wife, Ginger, asked me, after he was gone. I am sure he never gave them a thought when he was writing. But he assuredly was aware of them. I know because we occasionally touched on them in conversations. He had an enormous sensitivity to language and the way it works. "We all come from Gilbert," he said to me once, referring to William S. Gilbert. The tradition is rooted in Gilbert. It came to America through the Gilbert and Sullivan operettas and, later, through Wodehouse, who was known in his time not only for his satiric fiction but also for some very good lyrics for music by Friml, Romberg, and Kern.

Aside from its craftsmanship, I love John's writing for its emotional warmth, a warmth always controlled by a fastidious restraint. He never overstated. Everything was subtle: "as if the mayor had offered me the key ... to Paris."

The vast body of our best song literature came from the Broadway stage roughly between 1920 and 1955, at which time it began the long decline to its present squalor. But Mercer's work, a catalogue of about 1500 songs, was written mostly for movies. He wrote seven Broadway shows: *Walk with Music*; *St. Louis Woman,* which later toured Europe with an all-black cast under the title *Free and Easy*; *Texas Li'l Darling*; *Top Banana*; *Li'L Abner*; *Saratoga*; and *Foxy.* But he wrote lyrics, and occasionally music as well, for nearly thirty movies, and maybe more, including *Hollywood Hotel, Cowboy from Brooklyn* (for which he wrote *I'm an Old*

Cowhand), *Going Places, Naughty but Nice, Blues in the Night* (which originally had a quite different title; the producers changed it when they
heard Mercer's lyric), *The Fleet's In, You Were Never Lovelier* (which score,
written in collaboration with Jerome Kern, produced *Dearly Beloved* and
the splendid *I'm Old Fashioned*), *Star Spangled Rhythm* (which gave us the
haunting *That Old Black Magic*), *The Harvey Girls, Out of This World, The
Belle of New York, Seven Brides for Seven Brothers, Daddy Long Legs, Merry
Andrew, Breakfast at Tiffany's* (which produced *Moon River*) and *Days of
Wine and Roses.*

Johnny Mercer was born in Savannah, Georgia, November 18, 1909, and
never severed his ties to that city. He was a Scot by ancestry and had
cousins in Scotland. He was the son of a successful real estate man and
the grandson of a colonel who served under Robert E. Lee. Harold
Arlen's nickname for John was "the colonel." John's adopted daughter,
Amanda, told me there was some Polish on his mother's side.

The South virtually exudes poetry, or at least it used to. Heavily populated by the Irish, who have been called a word-drunk people, and by
Scots, who rival them in a passion for imagery, the South has a language
to which the black population has also made a substantial contribution.
Mercer grew up surrounded by black people, at ease in the rhythms of
their speech. Of all the awards he got in his life, he was proudest of one
he received in 1944: a black boys' club in Chicago voted him the outstanding young Negro singer of the year.

Whatever the historical reasons for it, Southern literature—as repre-
sented by Thomas Wolfe, William Faulkner, Carson McCullers, and
many with Celtic names—is memorable for rich poetry, and Southerners,
black and white alike, have a taste for arresting imagery to express their
visions of ideas and events. They seem unself-conscious about it, not
afraid of appearing "literary" or "poetic," as one would be in the stiff-
jawed industrial North or the taciturn farm valleys of Vermont. And all
Mercer's lyrics, at least in the use of language, were deeply Southern,
though not in ways that limited them. Rather, they were Southern in
ways that made Mercer's diction free and flashing and open: "The clouds
were like an alabaster palace."

The Mercer family had a summer home at Vernon View, twelve miles
out of Savannah. The attic of John's mind was crowded with images of
unpaved roads covered in crushed oyster shells and winding through
trees hung with Spanish moss, of azaleas and marsh grasses and inlets of
the sea, of kerosene lamps seen through the mosquito netting that hung
around beds. The family was well-to-do, and surrounded by colored, to
use the term of that time, servants with whose children he played mar-

bles or one-o-cat–softball. They spoke Gullah, a dialect so dense that it almost isn't English, and John understood it. He was steeped in their music–lullabies and work songs and that of their Sunday church services. He sang in the Christ Church from the age of six until he was seventeen, amused relatives by singing such party songs as *The Goat that Flagged the Train*, sang in quartets songs like *You Tell Me Your Dream*, collected records, knew all the Harry Lauder numbers by heart, and about the age of fifteen wrote a song called *Sister Susie, Strut Your Stuff* in the style of many songs then in fashion. He listened to Louis Armstrong, Bessie Smith, Red Nichols, Bix Beiderbecke, and Frank Trumbauer.

Mercer's songs tend to fall into four primary groups: his train songs, like *I Thought About You,* and *Laura; Autumn Leaves, Once Upon a Summertime,* and *When the World Was Young,* which capture to a striking degree a French viewpoint, although John spoke hardly a word of French; his bird songs, such as *Bob White, Mister Meadowlark,* and *Skylark,* one of his most exquisite lyrics; and his Southern songs, such as *Lazybones, Blues in the Night, Ac-Cent-Tchu-Ate the Positive,* and *Any Place I Hang My Hat Is Home.* There is a recurring theme of aging and time past, which begins cheerfully in *You Must Have Been a Beautiful Baby* and evolves sadly into *The Summer Wind, Days of Wine and Roses,* and the aforementioned *When the World Was Young,* which people often call *Ah, the Apple Trees,* one of the most poignant brief phrases in all his songs.

Mercer's politics seemed vague but they were of conservative bent. He believed in the American system but he wasn't happy about the suburban sprawl that was occurring, and as time went on he struck me as troubled by the social inequalities of the country. Certainly he was saddened about the deterioration of the environment.

Johnny seemed to feel that he had never really made it on Broadway. He may have been right. Some of his shows were successes but none was a really substantial hit. The reason perhaps was in John. In writing lyrics for the stage, one must become the characters whose words you are creating; like an actor, you must take on other identities, think and thus write in the tone and style of those characters. And John was always John, at once country boy and cosmopolite, Southerner and American, American and internationalist. Therefore he was truly in his element in films, where a personal style has often been valued more than a general flexibility, whether in songwriters, directors, or actors. He remained a Georgian, remembering the littoral wetlands and the clouds of pink flamingos and terns and gulls that used to be there, and the quick slithering alligators. "Now it's all freeways," he said with simple sadness one night.

John was an odd sort of duck, cantankerous and kind, humorous and morose, a compound of compassionate poeticism and personal bitterness. Very Celtic. The bitterness never colored his work; you will find no trace of it in his lyrics, although there is often a sardonic self-mockery, as in the lines "When an irresistible force, such as you, meets an old immovable object, like me . . ." The music to that song was Mercer's. So was that of *Dream.*

"He never had any musical training," his wife said to me once, "and he was hesitant." That is unfortunate. Frank Loesser, another brilliant lyricist spawned by Hollywood, never had any training either, but he wrote wonderful melodies. So, occasionally, did John.

John said once, "I tried to be a singer and failed. I tried to be an actor and failed. So I just naturally fell into lyric writing." But he hadn't failed as a singer. Perhaps because he founded Capitol Records—with Glenn Wallichs and fellow songwriter Buddy De Sylva—and thus recorded for his own company, he may have felt he had not made it fair and square. But I loved his singing, which had great humor, and a lot of people did.

Hilaire Belloc wrote, "It is the best of all trades, to make songs, and the second best to sing them." A small framed copy of that quotation hung on the wall of John's studio, fifty yards or so behind his house, snuggled in a canyon's foliage in Belair, next to a golf course on which deer sometimes wander. But he never really saw it that way. In his heart he felt it was best to sing songs.

Once, when we were hanging out in New York, I said to him: "Have you ever figured out what makes us write songs?"

"I don't know," he said. "I think it comes from a creative urge when you're little. Of course I was always stuck on music. I gravitated to songs because I loved music so much. I would like to have been an advertising man, I think I wanted to be a cartoonist, I was an actor. But all the time I was listening to songs, buying songs, writing songs. And I think that's what I was really cut out to do."

John believed that in most instances, the melody of a song should be written before the lyric. My own experience confirms him in this. Only a very few composers in history, Richard Rodgers among them, have been able to lift words off a page and make them sing. Given finished lyrics, composers often come up with melodies that are a little wooden, a little academic, tending to *recitativo.* They do not seem to be as sensitive to the music in speech as lyricists are to the speech in music. "I've lost a lot of good lyrics by turning them over to composers," John said.

That afternoon in New York he said, "A tune writer has to know how to build up a lyric so that the laughs come through, and the lyric writer has to know how to baby that tune, when he gets a good one, to search and search till he gets the right lyric to it. You can ruin great ideas if they're written improperly. I find that there's a very strange alchemy about working too little or too much on a tune. Sometimes if you work too much and you're *too* careful, you lose the whole thing. But if you get a fine fire going at the beginning, and you control it, you can rewrite enough without rewriting too much. That's the best way to write, I find."

"What do you think of contemporary lyrics, as a whole?" The year, I think, was 1970.

"I think in the main what we're going through right now is a lot of drivel. A lot of people who can't write are trying to write. And I think those who do write well are basing most of their stuff on a modern-day kind of hobo philosophy. It's a futility because of the war in Vietnam and because of crime and violence and everything. And it's built on an Elizabethan structure, and hill music, which is also based on Elizabethan structure. And so a lot of these kids who are writing, like Simon and Garfunkel and Jimmy Webb and Johnny Hartford and the kids down in Nashville, take the guitar and try to philosophize to a hillbilly tune with chords that come from 'way 'way ago. That's the general picture. Of course, there are many exceptions, including a guy like Alan Jay Lerner. I think Webb is a superior writer—I didn't mean to classify him with the others. And Burt Bacharach is trying very hard to be different, too hard as far as I'm concerned, although I think he's gifted. I don't know. What do you think?"

"I pretty much agree. I like Webb's things too. *By the Time I Get to Phoenix* is a very good song. Why don't you record again?"

"I'd like to. I'm singing really not too badly, so they say. I think my voice is deeper. I think I know better how to sing in tune than I used to. I don't think anybody cares, that's the main thing."

"I think there would be considerable interest. You always did your humorous things. You never recorded your ballads. Why?"

"I can't sing well enough."

"I don't agree."

"I could try it now. I think I'm a little better than I used to be."

Some time after that, John recorded two excellent albums for the Pye label in London. Whether my urging had anything to do with it or not, I do not know, but he recorded some of his ballads, such as *The Summer Wind*, to poignant effect.

"I don't think," I said, "that I've ever heard a song of yours that didn't have a payoff in the last line."

"Well, I think that's kind of the way you approach writing; if you're brought up in that school, you don't even *begin* a song if you haven't got an ending of some kind."

"Have you ever started out when you didn't know what the ending was going to be?" I said, and we both laughed.

"Yeah, I *have*. Sometimes I *wound up* without having an ending!"

"That's a desperate feeling!"

"It is!"

"And particularly when you've got some good lines in there and you don't want to lose 'em, but you have to top 'em."

"That's right," John said, and we laughed some more.

"Let me ask you about a couple of people you've worked with. One is Jerome Kern."

"Well, Mr. Kern was kind of the dean. He was the professor emeritus. He was the head man. And everybody respected him and admired him because his tunes were so really far above the others. He was new and yet he was classical in feeling. He had great melodic invention, he had great harmonic things. So he was at home with the professional composer. They respected him above all, he taught all of them something. The lyric writers liked him—if they could ever write with him. Strangely enough, he wrote with about ten or fifteen lyric writers, more than people think he did, although of course his biggest collaborator was Hammerstein."

"Well, there was Harbach, and Ira Gershwin, and Wodehouse, and yourself . . ."

"Well I wrote one picture with him, and Dorothy Fields may have written two or three. He was a fascinating guy. He was small. He wore glasses. He had a prominent nose and a very quick, alert mind. He was terribly curious. Berlin has the same kind of mind. Porter too, although Porter's mind was a little more sophisticated, more effete. Kern was terribly interested in anything that went on around him. He loved to play Indications, he loved to play Scrabble. If you brought him a brand new game, he'd be like a child about it. He'd want to play that for a week. He'd give parties and they'd play these games. He collected first editions and had a fabulous library which he sold for I think about a million dollars. He also had a coin collection which he sold for a lot of money. He was interested in everything all the time. He interested himself in the book and in your lyrics and the costumes and the choreography just as much as he did in any other part of the show. And because he was good, he had a kind of conceit about him. But he also, like most men of that much stature, had a kind of modesty about him too. I liked him very much."

"Was he easy to work with or hard?"

"He was hard to work with because his standards were high. With me, it was nothing at all, it was really fun, it was an enjoyable job. Of course, I didn't work that long with him. I didn't have a fight with him. If I'd had to write six or seven shows with him and he'd thrown his weight around, I guess he could have been a son of a bitch. But he wasn't."

"How about Harold Arlen?"

"Harold Arlen is a *genius.* I don't know what to say about him, except he doesn't write enough. He's been bothered by illnesses and the various mundane things of this world. But if he were writing like he wrote twenty years ago, I don't think you could catch up to his catalogue. I think he's been inactive so long that people have sort of forgotten about him. He's wonderful. I think he'd *like* to write. I think he probably *needs* to write, for his spirit, for his heart. He's a very tender, very sensitive man, and he writes so beautifully. It's easy for him. It sounds terribly inventive to us, terribly difficult, what he does, but not to him. It's like turning on a tap. It just flows out of him. We did two shows together, *St. Louis Woman* and *Saratoga*, which is kind of a quiet score. Not many people know it and not many people have heard it. Maybe that's because it isn't too good. It wasn't a hit. We did about ten movies at Paramount. The songs that came out of them were songs like *Out Of This World, That Old Black Magic, Acc-Cent-Tchu-Ate the Positive, Come Rain or Come Shine.* We had a lot of songs that are people's favorites that you don't hear much, like *Hit the Road to Dreamland, This Time the Dream's on Me. Blues in the Night* is probably our best-known song."

We talked about *Days of Wine and Roses*, written with Henry Mancini for the film of that name. The title comes from Dowson: "The days of wine and roses, they are not long . . ." Mercer's remarkable lyric consists of only two sentences. In them he expresses the startled sadness of everyone's eventual dawning perception that time has slipped irretrievably away and some things have been lost forever, including the joy of naive discovery, and that one has begun to grow old. It is a brilliant lyric, a jewel of the form. In a way it is typically Mercer. Paul Weston told me, "John was worried about time and his age when he was twenty-eight." Once John and I were walking down a street when two truly beautiful girls passed us, going in the opposite direction. John and I both looked over our shoulders to watch them walking into their future and our past, chatting happily and oblivious of the darkness ahead. John said, "I'm still looking but they're no longer looking back." *Days of Wine and Roses* expresses John's haunted preoccupation with time. It could be argued that the modern era of lyric writing dates from that song–in English, at least; the French, Charles Trenet being one of their best, have been writing songs in this manner for eighty years or more.

"You think so?" John said. "You see a thing in that song that I don't know if I see."

"A quality of abstraction."

"Yeah," he said. "Well, I'm not so sure it's purposeful on my part. I don't know whether when Dali painted his pictures, he did it purposefully or he just said, 'I've just got to say something I feel here, and this is the best way to say it.' I'm not sure it was all that intended."

"Oh, I'm not saying that it is or has to be intended. I'm just saying that things you wrote there and ways you wrote there would not have been acceptable or understandable to the public of the 1930s."

"Well, I'll tell you, maybe I give them more credit. Irving Berlin said a long time ago, 'Johnny gives everybody credit for knowing what he's talking about.' You don't write down to the ten-cent-store girl or anybody else. I don't. You certainly don't. And when I try to be literate, I just assume they know what I'm talking about. When I try to do what we're talking about right now, to get images—we did it in *Charade*. In the middle part, where it goes, 'in the darkened wings, the music box played on,' I assumed they know what I'm talking about. I can't stop to say, 'You know, there's really not a music box, it's really the orchestra.' You take that to Andy Williams, who's really a fine, intelligent cat, and he says, 'There's always something in these songs I don't understand. But I'm gonna sing it anyway.'"

I took a photo of John that day. After he was dead, Ginger told me it was one of the few pictures of himself he ever liked. Maybe I caught him the way he saw himself. Or maybe, and this is more important, I saw him the way he saw himself; or better yet, that he let me see himself as he was. The relationship was that of two professional lyricists who enjoyed talking about the work to someone else who understood the mechanics of the craft. Somehow the ease of the relationship is in that photo, it is in the eyes, and in the slight gentle smile. There is kindness in those eyes, and laughter, and sadness. It's John, at least the John Mercer I knew.

As the day faded into what the Brazilians call—magnificent term!— *tardinha*, the little afternoon, John and I went somewhere and had a few Glenfiddiches and then dinner, and when we emerged into the streets it was late sunset. White windows shone on the faces of buildings that stood like black cardboard against a rose-colored sky, and high above those deep streets the purple clouds looked solid, carved, sculpted. We took a cab and suffered minor spinal traumae as we bumped over the potholes to some club in lower Manhattan where Jimmy Rowles, with whom John had written several songs, was working. I think Jimmy Rowles was Johnny's favorite pianist.

It is more than difficult to evaluate Johnny Mercer's effect and influence on the American culture. It is impossible. John infiltrated our minds, a benign alien who captured our very processes of thought. Those who grew up when Mercer was at his most active had an advantage over the young of today. We absorbed into memory lyrics by Lorenz Hart and Howard Dietz and Tom Adair and Mercer, those magnificently literate men who gave us, in collaboration with some very gifted composers, the common, everyday, garden-variety popular songs of the period. One assimilated from them one's sense of the English language. They were glorifying and elevating it, not in inaccessible works of High Culture but in popular music that you heard every day on the radio. And Mercer was the best of them all. Today we hear illiteracy rampant in popular music and in television commercials, since those who now write advertising copy grew up on the Beatles and Elvis Presley and thus have been conditioned to the defective and inarticulate use of the English language.

John heard and used the American vernacular with great sensitivity and skill. He was remarkably in tune with it, using it as it evolved in such songs as *Jeepers Creepers* and *Acc-Cent-Tchu-Ate the Positive*, and he sometimes hastened that evolution by popularizing words and phrases. *Acc-Cent-Tchu-Ate the Positive* became a phrase of American English, complete with black Baptist rhythmic emphasis. And *latch onto*, which was jazz slang when Mercer used it in that song, turned up by the late 1950s in a *New York Times* editorial.

Mercer chronicled his time in songs. He noted the urbanization of America in *I'm an Old Cowhand*, with lines such as "I ride the range in a Ford V-8." He made fun of the affectations of his adopted home in *Hooray for Hollywood* "where you're terrific if you're even good." When the war came, he made humor of the training of the soldiers in *G.I. Jive*. And more seriously, as they began to move out to the blood baths of Normandy and Iwo Jima, he caught the anguish of those last moments of young couples in:

> This will be my shining hour,
> calm and happy and bright.
> In my dreams, your face will flower
> through the darkness of the night.

And when that night was over, and the survivors came home, Mercer threw them a party in the song *In the Cool Cool Cool of the Evening*. ("If I ain't in the clink, and there's something to drink, you can tell 'em I'll be there.") Later, in a song written with pianist and singer Blossom Dearie, he made witty fun of the coldwar paranoia inspired by the FBI and CIA:

Everywhere you go,
I think you oughta know,
I'm shadowing you.
Turn around and find
I'm half a step behind.
I'm shadowing you.

In Venice,
I'll be a menace
in your Italian hotel.
In Paris,
I shall embarrass
you on the rue d'la Chappelle.

His lyrics were only part of his influence on America and on twentieth-century music. Mercer was one of the three founders and the first president of Capitol Records, a company which had overwhelming influence for the good in the 1940s and, later, a comparable influence for the degradation of music.

The label was founded in 1942, during the darkest days of the war, when the Germans were winning everywhere and the U.S. Navy's Pacific fleet had been almost completely destroyed at Pearl Harbor. The sources of shellac in the South Pacific had been cut off by the Japanese conquests. Where Capitol got its shellac was for a long time a mystery. The answer is this: Mercer signed to the label a young man who led a dreadful band–and whose father owned a warehouse full of shellac in San Diego.

Capitol was off and running, an innovative and tremendously creative company that gave a great lift to American music. If it had a weakness, it was that its president, Johnny Mercer, had no interest whatever in the business end of the company. He was interested only in the music. Once, during the company's early days, when its headquarters consisted of one small room over a store on Vine Street in Hollywood, Mercer and Paul Weston were listening to some of their newly recorded material. Cofounder Glenn Wallichs was on the telephone. Mercer liked to listen to music loud. Finally Wallichs said, "Johnny, would you turn that down? I'm on long distance, trying to line up a distributor in Pittsburgh."

"Ah, to hell with that," Mercer said. "Let's listen to the music."

Variety predicted that Capitol would fail in the face of competition from the big three, Columbia, RCA Victor, and Decca. But it did not fail, and demonstrated that good popular music could succeed with the people if only they could be exposed to it. Capitol was to prove to be, in its early years, the most creative and innovative of all the large record companies, one of which it rapidly became, spreading its influence in American music to an extent that is beyond estimate. Without it, we might never have had the Stan Kenton band, the bulk of the recordings of Nat Cole, the consequent dissemination of Cole's influence as a pianist on Oscar Peterson and Bill Evans and all those whose work flows from them, the brilliant recordings of Peggy Lee, those of Andy Russell and Jo Stafford and Margaret Whiting, the second career of Frank Sinatra, and so much more.

Mercer operated from a philosophy that is strange by today's standards. He believed that you should not release a record unless you liked it. The idea of making a record for purely commercial reasons was beyond his comprehension, and the concept of regularly scheduled releases was alien to him. And the label–silver lettering and a picture of the Capitol dome in Washington, D.C., against a simple black background–was generating excitement throughout America. There was something new going on, and the young people knew it.

Although it has become fashionable to denigrate Stan Kenton in recent years–and his excesses justify it–it should not be forgotten that the band in its early days was really startling. The good instrumentals from big bands usually came out on the B sides of more commercial pop records. The Kenton band was noted from the beginning for its instrumentals. Such records as *Artistry in Rhythm, Eager Beaver, Artistry in Bolero,* and *Opus in Pastels* constituted the underscore music of a generation growing up in the middle and late 1940s. Nor is it true that Kenton made *no* contribution. He introduced an enriched harmonic palette, a powerful use of brass, an expanded application of players' technical resources, and a sort of dramatic approach to orchestral jazz that have been imitated ever since, sometimes by musicians who would deny Kenton any influence whatever.

Kenton was the most powerful force in the development of the stage-band movement in colleges and universities, which has had both good and bad effects on American music. It has undoubtedly raised the level of American and ultimately world musicianship. Kenton did that, and Mercer in collaboration with Paul Weston gave Kenton his chance.

Purely as a pianist, Nat Cole was one of the most important influences in jazz. Under Mercer's control, Capitol pushed a jazz pianist as a pop artist. But Nat was also a superb singer, with impeccable time and bounce. That whispered throaty sound, coupled with his cultivated enunciation, influenced other singers, and some of them quite far away. Nat was visiting Germany when he went one evening to a restaurant where a blond singer and pianist was doing Nat's material and imitating him perfectly. Amused and pleased, Nat attempted to pay his compliments. The

German did not recognize him. And he spoke not a word of English. Nat realized that the slavish imitation was entirely phonetic.

Nat's influence extended far beyond voice, since he was the first to recognize and hire Nelson Riddle as a vocal arranger. Would Sinatra's second career have taken off without Nelson Riddle—and if Capitol had not signed him after his original label, Columbia, dropped him?

Would Jo Stafford have become a star if Mercer had not founded Capitol?

It has been said that an institution is the lengthened shadow of one man. It is impossible to measure the length of Mercer's shadow, given the influence of his lyrics and the way Capitol Records shifted the course of American music.

Mercer's lack of interest in business was the company's fatal flaw.

Mickey Goldsen, who was head of publishing at Capitol for some years, recalls a disagreement he once had with a songwriter wanting yet another advance on his songs. When Goldsen refused him, the man went to Glenn Wallichs and intimated that Goldsen was cheating him. Wallichs was disturbed. He and his associates prided themselves on Capitol's honesty, which alone made it a novelty in the record business, and he summoned Goldsen to his office to say that he was hurting the company's reputation. Goldsen flared. He shouted, "It's in the newspapers that Buddy De Sylva's got his secretary knocked up, and Johnny Mercer's in the nearest bar insulting everybody, and *I'm* hurting the company's reputation?"

Others were brought in to fill the deficiency caused by Mercer's indifference to business, including Jim Conkling, who had been a college classmate of Paul Weston's. But Mercer was never comfortable with the company's size and success.

In time De Sylva took sick and wanted to sell Capitol. Mercer was a holdout. But finally, he and Wallichs and De Sylva sold the company to Electrical and Musical Industries (EMI) of England. And the standards of Capitol Records fell when it was guided not by Mercer's philosophy of excellence but by corporate principles of avarice. Gone were the sense of cultural responsibility and the passion for innovation and music.

Nat Cole's sales had helped build Capitol. In the 1960s Nat made a telephone call to the company. The switchboard operator said, "Capitol Records, home of the Beatles." Nat slammed the receiver down in anger. Tony Bennett, who had a deep belief in the psychosomatic sources of illness long before the fashion of holistic medicine, has always insisted that Capitol's shabby treatment of Nat in the later years was the source of his cancer.

Mercer got a similar shock when he paid a visit to the Capitol Tower, that odd building–designed to look like a stack of records–that he and Wallichs and De Sylva had built. A receptionist asked his name. John gave it.

"Who?" she said.

He repeated it.

"And may I ask what this is concerning?" she inquired.

John was as disturbed by that incident as Nat Cole was by the phone call.

"We never should have sold the company," he said to me on several occasions. And he was right.

In the last years, he and Ginger traveled a lot. Their trips were always by train or boat. He hated flying. He worked in London with André Previn on a musical that never made it to Broadway. One day, trying to get on the back step of a bus, he lost his equilibrium and fell, giving his head a severe crack on the pavement.

He began work on his memoirs. John was the only one I ever knew who wrote lyrics on a typewriter. He had learned to type when he worked in his father's office during his adolescence, and he typed neatly and well on a machine with a cursive font that I always instantly recognized on an arriving envelope. He would sit there at his typewriter, alone in that studio, trying to preserve in words the days when he went to New York with a little theater group and then, later, obtained small roles in other plays; an early and encouraging encounter with Eddie Cantor; turning away from acting toward writing and meeting Ginger when she was a dancer with *Garrick Gaieties*; writing with Harold Arlen and Hoagy Carmichael and Kern.

After he was gone, Ginger asked me to look at the manuscript and possibly edit it, which I did. There wasn't enough there to publish, and all sorts of important things–the time he saved a drowning man in the Malibu surf, for example–weren't even mentioned. The document wasn't so much an autobiography as a melancholy musing on time gone by. He wrote of entertaining troops in California during the war. He said that they discovered California on their way to the South Pacific, and after the war came back to it with their brides and had their children and turned Los Angeles and the San Fernando Valley into the smog-choked sprawl that it is. He regretted the passing of Georgia wetlands.

"I am over sixty years old now," he wrote. "And when just the other day I heard Richard Frederick and Anna Moffo do a medley from *Show Boat*, Jerry Kern's wonderful melodies, I pulled over to the side of the road, parked, and cried like a young boy.

"I sit here in California, writing these reminiscences in a heavy rain, thinking of the fires and mud slides, and it does seem as if the magic sunny land I knew has been 'struck,' like the movie sets it built, and has disappeared overnight, all its genies gone back into bottles, leaving sky-scrapers where the orange blossoms used to scent the wind."

John had a talent for darkness, and the manuscript reminded me of one of his most vivid lyrics, written when the young men were coming back from the war to discover everything changed:

> When an early autumn walks the land
> and chills the breeze
> and touches with her hand
> the summer trees,
> perhaps you'll understand
> what memories I own.
>
> There's a dance pavilion in the rain,
> all shuttered down . . .

I learned from, of all people, Harold of Harold's Liquor Store in West-wood that John was ill. I dropped in one day to buy some Glenfiddich, the supply of which John had provided me having long since gone. I asked Harold whether he had talked to John lately and he said that John, under doctor's orders, was on the wagon. I was disturbed more than amazed by this news. John's concern for his own drinking is manifest in some of the songs, including *Drinking Again, I Wonder What Became of Me*, and *One for My Baby (and One More for the Road)*. I called him and paid a visit to him and Ginger. We talked for a while, pleasantly enough, and he confirmed that he had stopped drinking. What I did not know then was that he had a brain tumor. What I do not know to this day is whether he knew it. This was the cause of his disequilibrium.

I did not see him for several months. Then Tony Bennett and Lena Horne performed in concert at the Shubert Theater in Century City. Afterward there was a reception for friends and for people in the profession. I saw John and Ginger. There was little chance to talk, but I said, "How y' feeling, John?"

"All right," he said, "except that I keep falling down a lot." He had once joked to me that he had had a lot of practice falling off bar stools, and I thought he meant he was drinking again, as in the song. Later, as the party was ending, John and Ginger walked ahead of me toward the door. Suddenly he fell. Ginger was helping him up. I was in a dilemma. Should I help? If he had been drinking, would he and Ginger be em-barrassed by my intrusion? In the end I did nothing. He hadn't been drinking, of course. I know only that he fell that night and I didn't help him. It was the last time I ever saw him. It still bothers me a little.

The word went out that John was in the hospital. I called his house but got no answer. I called Henry Mancini, who said he had been unable to learn anything. Nor had Johnny Mandel, with whom John had written *Emily*. A strange silence surrounded him–at his own wish, as we found out later. When it became clear that John's illness was terminal, Ginger took him home. That studio in which he had written so many songs–and on whose wall hung a list of his failed projects, such was his masochism–was converted into a hospital room, with nurses attending him day and night. At the end, this master of words was unable to speak. And he died there in his studio, next to the golf course of the Belair Country Club where the deer come, in June 1976. He was sixty-seven.

In the weeks after that, I discussed Johnny with any number of his friends. No one was able to explain John, not his talent, not his anger, not his melancholy. Ginger was never able to explain him, and she was married to him since 1931 when he was trying to get established on the New York stage and she took sewing jobs to keep them going.

His flat, horizontal marble tombstone, bearing the name John Herndon Mercer, in a strangely bleak cemetery devoid of grass in Savannah, is inscribed with one of his song titles: *And the Angels Sing*.

But Mercer's best epitaph is the lyric to *One for My Baby*. The song is much like a French song in that it is a sort of short story, a slice-of-life portrait of a drinker, in which the character goes through a common progression from stoicism to self-pity to aggression to exhausted depression, and the song might justly be considered autobiographical, one of Mercer's deft sketches of himself.

> You'd never know it,
> but buddy, I'm a kind of poet,
> and I've gotta lotta things to say.
> And when I'm gloomy,
> you've simply gotta listen to me,
> until it's talked away.

> Well that's how it goes,
> and Joe, I know you're gettin' anxious to close.
> So thanks for the cheer.
> I hope you didn't mind my bending your ear . . .

No, John, we didn't mind at all.

The Paradox
Frank Sinatra

One night, when Don Rickles was master of ceremonies on a dais filled with famous faces, he introduced Frank Sinatra with these words: "Frank, make yourself at home: hit somebody."

Another comedian, Shecky Greene, has for years done the following routine: "You can say what you want about Sinatra, but the man once saved my life. That's right, he did. I was standing out in front of Caesar's Palace one night and three big tough guys began to kick the hell out of me. They were giving me a terrible beating, but finally Frank came up and said, 'Okay, that's enough.'"

Steve Allen, asked to write for *The Village Voice* a reflection on the perceived split in the Sinatra personality, said: "Are all the stories about his lifelong association with the most notorious Mafia murderers and social savages, the stories about semipsychotic rages, true? The answer, to all such painful questions is, to some degree, yes."

Everyone in show business knows this to be so, though Sinatra and his family have consistently denied it. One of his oldest friends said, "Well, let's face it. He's Jekyll and Hyde." An Italian American musician who worked with him said, "Look, I know you have a lot of Italian friends. But you don't know Italians the way Italians know Italians. Italians tend to break down into two kinds of people: Lucky Luciano or Michelangelo. Frank's an exception. He's both."

Puzzling over the phenomenon, Steve Allen wrote: "Frank Sinatra in his prime was, to put the matter quite simply, the best popular singer of them all."

A friend of mine, studying voice with an opera teacher, asked who in her opinion had the best vocal technique, thinking she would name someone in opera. She said without hesitation, "Frank Sinatra." Henry Pleasants, an authority on opera, told me once that he had rarely met an opera singer who didn't have a Sinatra collection. "They know how good he is," Henry said.

Sinatra has fascinated and puzzled people since his earliest professional days. When his career took off in the early 1940s, journalists rushed to their telephones and then to their typewriters to pose the wrong questions and come up with the wrong answers. Girls were "swooning" at his performances. What was the cause of this mysterious phenomenon?

There were two causes. The first was hunger. Some of the girls had waited so long in theater lines to see him that they fainted. The second was George Evans, Sinatra's press agent, who knew an angle when he saw one and paid a few more girls to fake it.

But what caused this flocking? The journalists went to psychologists and psychiatrists for explanations, and came away with a few, all of them silly. His thin face and slender frame, barely hanging on the microphone, touched the maternal instincts of the girls. Maternal indeed. Or it was the war: Sinatra was a surrogate for the boy-next-door who was away in service.

The journalists and psychologists alike seemed unaware of history. The Sinatra effect was by no means unprecedented, and in fact suggested a question I have not yet seen answered, or for that matter even seriously addressed.

This kind of sexual flocking had occurred around many male performers, including Franz Liszt, who plucked a large bouquet of his era's fairest flowers. So too Louis Moreau Gottschalk. It happened around Offenbach. When he arrived in Boston, aristocratic ladies unhitched his horses and pulled his carriage through the streets by hand. No doubt it happened around Spohr. Certainly in Italy, many of the great castrati were adored by quantities of women. When Henry Pleasants said so in a piece about the castrati published in *Stereo Review*, several readers wrote to argue that affairs were impossible for the castrated male. Henry replied that while castration assured sterility, it did not necessarily confer indifference, or even, for that matter, impotence.

It seems that a man, even an ugly one, need only become famous to have women fling themselves at him, particularly if he achieves his high visibility as an entertainer. Let us not even bother with the more obvious cases like Elvis Presley and the Beatles. One would be naive to think that, for example, Toscanini suffered from a dearth of opportunities. And in each instance, the phenomenon erodes the image of the male as the sexual aggressor, the female as the reluctant recipient of his brutish attentions. For there is nowhere in history a comparable example of men flocking in a sort of collective self-humiliation around a famous female entertainer—not Lily Langtry, not Sarah Bernhardt, not Marilyn Monroe, not Olivia Newton-John. But we know how women behaved toward Errol Flynn and John Barrymore, and there is no reason to assume Henry Irving or David Garrick experienced anything very different. A man, if he has the opportunity and that bent of temperament, may try to add a famous beauty to his trophy collection, but he will not stand in a screaming crowd of men clamoring for their idol, and given a choice of an anonymous but beauteous barmaid or a homely movie star, he will almost invariably choose the former. So fully if silently does society recognize this difference in behavior that a man who follows a famous woman and tries to break into her hotel room—I covered the attempted rape of Patti Page when I was a young newspaper reporter in Toronto around 1949—will end up in jail or a psychiatric ward, while a girl who similarly tracks a public idol will be dismissed more or less lightly as more or less normal.

Whatever the reasons for this mass self-debasement of women, the fact is that it happened far more to Sinatra than to Dick Haymes, Perry Como, Nat Cole, Andy Russell, or any other of the singers coming up at the time. And of course it did not happen at all to the "girl singers" such as Peggy Lee and Doris Day. Sinatra was The Man, for a whole generation of young people, for the boys as well as the girls. Indeed, the theory that he was merely a surrogate for the absent servicemen overlooked his popularity with a good many of those self-same servicemen.

He said for the boys what they wanted to say. He said to the girls what they wanted to hear. The body of excellent songs that had come into existence in the United States at last found a singer worthy of them. He was the best singer we had ever heard. He was one of the best singers in history. And we knew it. He was our poet laureate.

One of the writers at the time said, with more than a touch of condescension, that Sinatra sang those love songs as if he believed them. But of course. That was the secret. And far from manifesting a callow gullibility on Sinatra's part, this was a striking advance in the art of singing. Sinatra was to American song what Montgomery Clift was to American acting.

As for that forgotten writer's contempt for mere love songs, he apparently did not understand that there are only two things worth writing about, sex and death. The vast bulk of our literature, whether noble or trivial, is about either or both of these subjects. A suspense thriller is about the avoidance of death, the survival of the individual. A love story is about (secretly) about the survival of the species. When the hero destroys the villain and saves the heroine, he has achieved the survival, for the nonce, of the individual, and when he takes her in his arms in the fadeout, you know they are about to make their own modest contribution to the survival of the species. Essentially, then, all literature is about survival.

Almost all of our stories and songs are about love, the highest exaltation we know excepting that achieved by some people through religion, and even then the terminology of romantic love is often used in the effort to describe the experience.

Remembering her days with the Pied Pipers and Tommy Dorsey, Jo Stafford said, "Frank joined the band while we were playing a theater in Milwaukee. The Pipers were ... well, we thought we were pretty good. We were a little clique unto ourselves. Frank was very thin in those days, almost fragile looking. When he stepped up to the microphone, we all smirked and looked at each other, waiting to see what he could do. The first song he did was *Stardust.*

"I know it sounds like something out of a B movie, but it's true: before he'd sung four bars, we knew. We knew he was going to be a great star."

That was early in 1940. The style was not even fully formed. Sinatra had just come up from the Harry James band, at that time much less successful than the Dorsey band. But he had already recorded with James, and in an early Columbia side, *All or Nothing at All,* one of the characteristics of his work is already in evidence: his exquisite enunciation. His vowels are almost Oxonian. The title line comes out almost "ohllll or nothing at ohlllll. . . ."

And there is something else very interesting about the way he treats those words. When you sing a long note, it is the vowel you sustain, almost always. Certain of the consonants, voiced or voiceless, cannot be sustained: *b* and its voiceless counterpart *p, d* and *t, g* and *k.* You cannot sing thattttt. It is impossible. You must sing thaaaaat. Or cuuuuup. Or taaaaake. But certain other consonants, voiced and unvoiced–*v* and *f, z* and *s*–can be sustained, being fricatives, although I find the effect unattractive. You cannot sustain the semivowels *w* and *y.* But there are four semivowels that can be sustained: *m, n, l,* and *r.* Now, just as Spanish has long and short forms of the letter *r*–a double *rr,* as in *perro,* is rolled–correct Italian enunciation requires that you slightly sustain all double consonants. And Sinatra has always recognized this principle, whether because of his Italian background or not. You hear it when he extends the *l* in *Alllll or Nothing at Alllll.*

Sinatra posed a problem for the singers influenced by him. If you followed what he did too closely, you'd sound like an imitation of him, which of course you were. The temptation, in one's formative stages, was to affect his enunciation, with those softened *r*'s after consonants, rather broad *a*'s, slight dentalization of *t*'s and *d*'s. The sound of *t* is produced by placing the tongue on the ridge of gum just above the top front teeth and using the release of it to articulate a plosion of air. If you vibrate the vocal chords simultaneously, the *t* becomes *d.* If you place the tongue a little forward of that position, on the teeth, it alters the sounds of *t* and *d,* adding a slight sibilance. In the "normal" enunciation of the sounds *dr-* or *tr-,* the tongue's tip touches the dental ridge; but halfway back in the mouth it is touching the molars, and is already in position to make the *r* sound. If the tongue is touched to the teeth, it isn't, and must be pulled back quickly for the *r.* This peculiarly softens the *r,* as in the way Sinatra pronounces "dream" and "tree." The sound is particular to New York–area Italians. The late actor Richard Conte, born in Jersey City, had it. Tony Bennett, born in Queens, strongly dentalizes *t*'s and *d*'s.

Early recording was entirely acoustic. With the development of electrical recording, a new technique was called for, but few people grasped this. Bing Crosby understood it to an extent. He appreciated that it was unnecessary to shout into the microphone. What he did not appreciate was the dramatic possibilities opened up by the microphone and the constantly improving techniques of recording.

Of its very nature, singing through a good sound system or for recording should be as different from vaudeville belting as film acting is from stage acting. One can convey on film with a lift of an eyebrow what might require a conspicuous change of voice or tone or volume or some expansive gesture on a stage. And something similar is true of singing into a sensitive microphone.

Sinatra understood this. It seems that the comprehension came to him gradually: his evolution is clear in his recorded work.

Sinatra has on occasion said that he learned a great deal from listening to Tommy Dorsey play trombone night after night on the bandstand. Indeed, one of the myths about his work in the early days was that he learned an Indian trick of breathing in through his nose while continuing to sing. Whatever the athletic skills of the American Indians, none of them ever achieved this physiological impossibility, and neither did Sinatra. In brass and woodwind playing there is a technique in which the cheeks are filled with air to maintain pressure in the embouchure while the player inhales through the nose. Clark Terry can do this seemingly endlessly. But only a few players have mastered this technique, and Tommy Dorsey was not one of them. He did, however, have remarkable breath control, and his slow deliberate release of air to support long lyrical melodic lines was indeed instructive to Sinatra and still worth any singer's attention. Dorsey would use this control to tie the end of one phrase into the start of the next. Sinatra learned to do the same. This is evident in their 1941 recording of *Without a Song.* Since Dorsey's trombone solo precedes the vocal, the record provides an opportunity to observe how Sinatra was learning from Dorsey, and how far he had come since *All or Nothing at All.* At the end of the bridge, Sinatra goes up to a mezzo-forte high note to crest the phrase "as long as a song is strung in my SOUL!" But he does not breathe then, as most singers would. He drops easily to a soft "I'll never know . . . " This linking of phrases between the inner units, learned from Dorsey, gave Sinatra's work a kind of seamlessness.

The next time he sings "I'll never know," he hits an A on the word "know" before falling to G, the proper note for the word. This kind of glissando drove the adolescent girls wild. When George Evans had built a general national hysteria, Sinatra had only to sing one of these falls in a theater and the next four bars were drowned in a sea of shrieking. This was in fact merely another device derived from Dorsey, and natural to the trombone.

Sinatra's voice at that time was a pure sweet tenor. A year and a half later, when he recorded *In the Blue of Evening*, he was already losing some of that quality, which owed more to the Irish tradition than the Italian. His singing was acquiring strength. (The entire body of Sinatra's commercially recorded work with Dorsey has been reissued in a five-CD box by RCA, ninety-seven songs recorded in thirty-two months.)

If Sinatra had acquired a good deal of his technique from Dorsey, he seems to have drawn some of his conception from Billie Holiday. Indeed, most of the best singers of his generation, including Peggy Lee—his equivalent among women singers for dramatic intensity—seem to have paid at least some attention to Holiday.

Fats Waller is reputed to have said, "Billie sings as if her shoes pinch." Whoever said it, somebody took note of the squeezed quality of her voice. But many informed and sensitive listeners find a deep emotional experience in her work, and there is no questioning her effect on any number of women singers, including Anita O'Day and June Christy, who are her direct stylistic descendants. With a small voice and a tendency to short phrases—in contrast to Sinatra's extremely long ones—she phrases not according to the melodic structure of a song but according to the natural fall of the words. Whether she did this by design or inspired intuition, I do not know. But Sinatra does it by design.

Naturalistic phrasing, however, requires the use of the microphone. Journalists made fun in those early days of Sinatra's way of handling a microphone, his hands around the stand, just under the mike itself. They joked that he was propping himself up with it. They did not understand that he was playing it. He had completely abandoned the previous approach to the microphone, that of standing bravely facing it, using the hands for dramatic emphasis. Sinatra was moving the mike in accordance with what he was singing. And he was the man who developed this technique. In later times, when microphones had been greatly reduced in size, singers would slip them off their stands and walk freely around the stage with them. But those early mikes were bulky and screwed firmly to the top of the stands. And so Sinatra gripped the stand and drew the microphone toward him or tilted it away according to the force of the note he was putting out at any given moment. He mastered this.

The microphone made possible speech-level singing. It did not make singing unnatural; it restored naturalness to it. But, and this is insufficiently understood, the microphone is treacherous in that it magnifies not only the virtues of a performance but the flaws too. And it is a difficult instrument to use well.

For example, the plosive consonants *p* and *b*, and for that matter *t* and *d*, and sometimes even the aspirated *h*, which pose no problem to anyone singing in an opera house or a bathtub, are booby traps to a singer working close to a mike. Therefore the singer must approach them with caution. Failure to do so results in the phenomenon called popping the mike. You will hear it on many records. Some of the best singers will now and then pop one of those letters in a recording session, rattling the speakers in every living room in which the record is later played. In the entire body of his recorded work, you will almost never hear Sinatra pop a consonant.

Sinatra's stature as a performer was not fully manifest, however, until he worked outside the context of the Dorsey band. Despite Dorsey's showcasing of singers, Sinatra had been required on the whole to sing at tempos suitable for dancing. Freedom to explore a song as a dramatic miniature did not come until he made four sides for Bluebird on January 19, 1942, eight months before he left the band. These are *The Song Is You, The Lamplighter's Serenade, Night and Day*, and *The Night We Called It a Day*. The choice of composers is interesting: Jerome Kern, Hoagy Carmichael, Cole Porter, and Matt Dennis, for whose work Sinatra would always have an affinity. The Axel Stordahl arrangements were well above the norm of accompaniment in popular music. The string section comprised only four violins and a cello, but Stordahl used them skillfully. These are chamber recordings, really, designed to set off the intimacy Sinatra's work had attained. It is as if he is singing not to a great and anonymous company but to you. With these four sides, Sinatra becomes Sinatra. In later years his work would mellow, deepen, and mature, but the conception and the method were fully developed by then. Sinatra had just turned twenty-six at the time, the bird about to fly. The great shrill mobs of girls were not yet begging him to autograph their underwear, and there is captured in these four songs something "of love and youth and spring" that would never be heard in his work again. They were remarkable recordings when they came out, and they are remarkable now. It is a pity that he and Stordahl did not record two dozen or so songs in that vein at that time.

Sinatra and Stordahl would produce a superb string of recordings for Columbia Records, but the orchestras would be larger, the intimacy less, the thinking sophisticated. Sinatra was by then the biggest celebrity in America. Only a few years later, a Gallup poll would reveal that his name was better known than that of President Truman. Newspaper writers were boggled by his earnings—a million dollars a year. The record companies, further impelled by Petrillo's recording ban, rushed to get other band singers into the studios, including Billy Eckstine, inevitably promoted as the Sepia Sinatra, although his style had more in common with his friend from the Earl Hines band, the brilliant Sarah Vaughan; Jo Stafford, who thought of herself as a group singer, had no taste for stardom, and withdrew from it without fanfare in 1956; Doris Day from the Les Brown band; Perry Como from Ted Weems; Peggy Lee from Benny Goodman; Andy Russell from the Alvino Rey and early Stan Kenton bands; Kay Starr from Charlie Barnet; and of course Dick Haymes, he of the wondrous richness of sound, who had followed Sinatra through the James and Dorsey bands. David Allyn was an alumnus of the Boyd Raeburn band, a striking baritone with a dark woody timbre, a favorite with musicians, who never got the recognition he deserved. Nobody thought to do anything with Harry Babbitt of the Kay Kyser band, who I thought was one of the best band singers. There was something sunny about his work. Maybe that's what was wrong with it: it said nothing of the dark side of life. One great singer who did not come out of a band was Nat Cole. Cole was one of the most important jazz pianists, influential on Oscar Peterson and Bill Evans and through them on many others. That he sang extremely well was discovered almost by accident, and his success as a singer virtually ended his career as a pianist.

Sinatra opened the way for all of them. And for other Italians. Before Sinatra, popular singing in America was dominated for a long time by the Irish, or at least an Irish style: Morton Downey, Buddy Clarke, Arthur Tracy, and others. Then came the Italians, starting with Russ Columbo. But the full impact of Italy came with Sinatra, and after that came Tony Bennett, Perry Como, Julius La Rosa, the late and too little recognized Tommy Leonetti, the late Bobby Darin (born Robert Cassotto in the Bronx), Vic Damone (Vito Rocco Farinola, born, like La Rosa, in Brooklyn), Frankie Laine (born Paul LoVecchio in Chicago), and David Allyn (born Albert DiLello in Hartford, Connecticut) among them. Sinatra influenced at least two generations of singers, including some of those just mentioned.

But in pioneering a new approach to singing, Sinatra also created a problem. What he did seemed so indisputably right that any other approach to phrasing seemed wrong. If one phrased in the same way, one sounded obviously derivative. But what was the singer to do, not phrase for the meaning of the lyric? Actually, these singers, examined closely, do not sound all that much like Sinatra. Technically, the best male voice of all is that of Vic Damone. The instrument itself, the unbelievably open throat, is gorgeous. One of the best voices belonged to Eddie Fisher. Unfortunately, he never did find out what singing is all about, and his time, or rather lack of it, is legendary among musicians. Steve Lawrence and Jack Jones probably have the firmest musical command, although Jack Jones is inclined to waste a magnificent talent on unworthy songs. But the voices, in all these cases, bear no resemblance to Sinatra's and all of these people avoid enunciating in his manner.

There is an outstanding exception among the Sinatra derivations, one who doesn't seem to sound like him. Tony Bennett learned his phrasing from Sinatra. But Tony tapped another source of inspiration, which no one seems to have noticed: Louis Armstrong. The clue is in the vibrato. And so Tony gets away with it better than the others. It also helps that his voice is about a fourth or fifth higher than Sinatra's.

Sinatra's work, unlike that of most singers, has distinct phases to it, like the periods in a painter's life.

The first of these is the period with Harry James, which might be called embryonic. Only in retrospect do we find signs of the special. Otherwise he was indistinguishable from any number of capable but bland band singers. Then there is what could be considered the childhood, the period with Dorsey. This is followed by an all-too-brief adolescence, consisting of the four Bluebird sides with Stordahl.

Then comes the young manhood, the period with Columbia, when he turns to Broadway to find songs commensurate with his talent, essaying *Old Man River* (for which he was laughed at, although his reading of it was outstanding) and the *Soliloquy* from *Carousel*. And he is already looking to the past for material: *These Foolish Things, Try a Little Tenderness,* and *When Your Lover Has Gone* were not new even then when he recorded them. This is the first great plateau: in *Five Minutes More, I Begged Her,* and *Saturday Night Is the Loneliest Night of the Week,* the swing, if any, is rather self-conscious, advanced hardly at all since that dreadful song he recorded with Dorsey, *I'll Take Tallulah.*

And then his career slipped a cog. His record sales petered out toward the end of the 1940s. He began to have voice problems. Mitch Miller, who was then head of a&r at Columbia and already committed to the recording by various people, such as Guy Mitchell, of some appalling trash, was forcing like material on Sinatra. He even made him make a record with Dagmar, that curious lady famous for a Himalayan bust line. A side man on one of these painful sessions was a guitarist named Speedy West, who was known for being able to produce a cluck-cluck-cluckah chicken sound from his instrument. Despising the tune, his throat bothering him, Sinatra struggled through a take. A smiling Mitch Miller rushed from the booth as if to embrace him—and embraced Speedy West.

Sinatra said later, "At thirty-eight years old, I was a has-been. Sitting by a phone that wouldn't ring. Wondering what happened to all the friends who grew invisible when the music stopped. Finding out fast how tough it is to borrow money when you're all washed up."

Sinatra waited out his contract with Columbia, written off by the press, struggling with his voice, desperate. Curiously enough, one of the two times I ever saw him perform live (other than in the recording studio) was during that period. He played the Chez Paree in Montreal. He came onstage full of obvious and visible anger and anxiety, and sang with a new darkness and depth. It was shortly after this that he signed a contract with Capitol Records and made a ten-inch LP with a small orchestra. The album, called *Songs for Young Lovers*, tended to swing lightly. When your voice is not in good shape, and Sinatra's still wasn't, it is wise to avoid very slow tempos, which require the long sustaining of notes and lines. But the album was shot through with prismatic new colors. For the first time, his work takes on the hue of jazz. And the swing is insouciant, unself-conscious: he has learned to ride a rhythm section. And whatever he had lost in length of phrase (which later he regained) is more than compensated for by the emotional depth of his readings and the bounce he brings to the songs.

During the next eight years, he recorded for Capitol twenty hit albums, all ranking among the top twenty, including three at number one and five at number two, and several dozen hit singles such as *Young at Heart*, and kept up this output when he left Capitol for Reprise, a label Sinatra founded. Sinatra found some very compatible arrangers to work with, including, over the years, Nelson Riddle, the brilliant Billy May, Gordon Jenkins, Don Costa, Robert Farnon (for one album only, made in England and never released in America until the era of CD reissues), Claus Ogerman, and Johnny Mandel.

Nelson Riddle once said that the earlier Sinatra, of the Columbia days, sounded like a violin, but the later one, the one who emerged at Capitol, sounded like a viola. That is an apt analogy. The voice had acquired a slightly rougher texture. It had in fact become more Italian. There's no trace of the tenor left, not at least in the voice quality, although his range covered at least two octaves, from F to F.

There is such a thing as an Italian voice, the gravelly sound that comics affect when telling Mafia stories. You hear it not only in the voices of Italian men, such as actors Aldo Ray, Al Pacino, Robert Loggia, and Paul Sorvino, and Congressman Peter Rodino of Rhode Island, but even in Italian women, such as Brenda Vaccaro. Pianist Mike Renzi, who has such a voice, once quipped: "It comes from all the shouting and screaming at home when you're a kid."

That's funny, but in fact it is as surely a national (though not universal) physical characteristic as the commonality of blond hair in Scandinavians. There are also African voices, which have an airy sound, somewhat like the tenor of Ben Webster. Actor Danny Glover has such a voice. So does Harry Belafonte. And the late Nat Cole had the most beautiful African voice I ever heard.

The Italian voice quality is not evident in Sinatra's earliest recordings, but by the time of his work at Capitol Records it was. His sound acquired tremendous body, and although something has been lost—he never again uses head tone, and certainly not the falsetto that ends *The Song Is You*—he had arrived in the period of his finest work, the artist in perfect control of his material, recording one after another of the greatest American songs, creating albums that are like haunted rooms in a museum. Some of these performances are so definitive that a singer—male, anyway—has to think twice about taking any of them on. No doubt that is why there are not many vocal recordings of *Young at Heart, The Tender Trap, All the Way, From Here to Eternity*. There may be another reason why so few singers have done *My One and Only Love*: it climbs a twelfth in the first two bars, and there is no way of sneaking up on it.

There is no questioning Sinatra's musicianship. He has never claimed to be a "jazz singer," referring to himself instead as a saloon singer. But he is a universal favorite of jazz musicians. When Leonard Feather did a poll of musicians for his 1956 *Encyclopedia Yearbook of Jazz*, Sinatra got almost half the votes. Out of a hundred and twenty ballots, Sinatra got fifty-six, Nat Cole thirteen, Billy Eckstine eleven, and Louis Armstrong nine. Among those who named him their all-time favorite singer were Buck Clayton, Nat Cole, Miles Davis, Duke Ellington, Herb Ellis, Tal Farlow, Stan Getz, Benny Goodman, Bill Harris, Bobby Hackett, Carmen McRae, Gerry Mulligan, Sy Oliver, Oscar Peterson, Oscar Pettiford, Bud Powell, André Previn, Jimmy Raney, Howard Roberts, Horace Silver, Billy Taylor, Cal Tjader, and Lester Young.

The late Shelly Manne coached Sinatra for the drum-playing scenes in *The Man with the Golden Arm*. "He had a definite feel for it," Shelly said. "He could have played if he'd wanted to, although whether he'd have been as great a drummer as he is a singer is another question." Woody Herman toured during the 1970s with Sinatra. "How was he singing?" I asked Woody later. "Well, you know how I feel," Woody said. "He can sing the phone book and I'll like it."

In theory Sinatra can't read music. "Well he can't but he can, if you know what I mean," said one arranger who had worked with him. One of Sinatra's early friends was the late Alec Wilder, who wrote the *a capella* arrangements for the first Sinatra Columbia sides, including *The Music Stopped* and *A Lovely Way to Spend an Evening*, as well as composing such songs as *I'll Be Around* and *While We're Young*. Sinatra heard acetate air checks of two pieces Wilder had written for woodwind octet and string orchestra, learned there were more of them, and determined to see them recorded, which they were, in 1945, with Sinatra conducting: *Theme and Variations, Air for Bassoon, Air for Flute, Air for English Horn, Slow Dance,* and *Air for Oboe*. (Ironically, the English horn and oboe soloist was Mitch Miller.) Years later I asked Alec whether Sinatra had in fact conducted those pieces. "Yes," Alec said, "he not only conducted, he did them better than anyone else has ever done them, before or since." The pieces, which are exquisite, must be considered experiments in a Third Stream, entailing elements of "jazz" and "classical" music. "He understood something," Alec said, "that is important in those pieces, and that the orchestra itself did not: steady dance tempos."

I watched Sinatra listening closely as Claus Ogerman ran down an arrangement at a recording session. "I think I hear a couple of little strangers in the strings," he said, and Claus corrected them—probably copyist's errors. Composer Lyn Murray recalled watching him over a period of days conduct an orchestra in rehearsal for an engagement in Las Vegas. Lyn said that he expended twenty-one hours rehearsing that orchestra, meticulously preparing every nuance of time and blend and dynamics. "When he was through," Lyn said, "every word of each lyric was laid out like a jewel on black velvet."

I was flabbergasted by the detail work in his reading of the lyric to *This Happy Madness*. The melody is one of Antonio Carlos Jobim's early ones, and the song is, again, very difficult to sing. The lyric is mine, and I think I can claim to know what its intent is—what the "undertext," as actors and directors say, is. When the record came out (the song is in an album called *Sinatra and Company*) I sat in open-mouthed amazement as he caught every nuance of the words.

The first half of the release goes:

> I feel that I've gone back to childhood,
> and I'm skipping though the wildwood,
> so excited that I don't know what to do.

I intended the first two lines as a sort of self-mockery, as if the "character" in the song finds himself resorting to an abysmal banality, a dreadful cliche (the reference is to the old song *Childhood in the Wildwood*), and a false rhyme. Sinatra caught this, and sings those first two lines with a hard and self-disgusted edge on his voice. And suddenly in the third line, the voice takes on an infinitely gentle sound, as of total wonder. I couldn't believe it when I heard it. He caught not what the lyric said but what it didn't say.

Asked once by an interviewer what he thought his most important achievement had been, Sinatra said that it was a certain approach to singing that he hoped would endure—or words to that effect. The hope was a vain one. Even as he was turning out his finest work, Elvis Presley was exploding into prominence, and the quality of commercial popular music was plummeting. Those singers who had indeed learned from him were still doing well, but by the 1960s and certainly by the 1970s they were finding it harder and harder to come by record contracts. Eventually all the major singers who grew up in his school would find themselves without major-label recording contracts, and some of the best of them simply vanished. Only Sinatra sailed on through it all, seemingly safe from the storms of fad. Rock-and-roll did not embrace his naturalism, the effect of a contained and inward drama. As amplification cranked up the volume of guitars and drums to a level dangerous to hearing, the singing became shrill, a distorted and grimaced music lacking in literacy or subtlety, a hysterical celebration of the mundane that all the press agentry in the world could not disguise. While Sinatra himself retained an audience, packing them in whenever and wherever he chose to go, gradually a great tradition was being forgotten. The fans of Billy Joel and Elvis Costello and David Bowie and Michael Jackson have never heard of Jerome Kern, chances are that few of them had heard of Sinatra, and her fans probably thought that Linda Ronstadt discovered Nelson Riddle—whose pencil was laid aside forever in 1985—when she recorded with him.

What Sinatra's legacy will be we cannot know. But for a time, for a very long time, Frank Sinatra turned the singing of the American song into an art form, and his collected output must be considered a national treasure.

GI Jo
Jo Stafford and Paul Weston

Early in Walter Murphy's novel *The Vicar of Christ*, one of the main characters, a Marine Corps sergeant major, is pictured listening on a radio to Jo Stafford's *On Top of Old Smokey* just before a battle of the Korean War.

Stafford's recording of *Blues in the Night* figures in a scene in James Michener's *The Drifters*, and a character in one of the James Hilton novels, talking about what he would select to take to a desert island, includes a Jo Stafford collection in his list.

That scene in *The Vicar of Christ* somehow sets Stafford's place in the American culture. You're getting pretty famous when your name turns up in crossword puzzles; you are woven into a nation's history when you turn up in its fiction. And Stafford's voice was part of two American wars. What Vera Lynn was to the British in World War II, Stafford was to the Americans, and the effect lingered on into the 1950s and Korea.

Possibly it was her way of *letting* a song happen rather than shoving it at you soaked in personal style. There was nothing sexually aggressive about Stafford; she did not seem to challenge anyone to conquer her. She was a very pretty girl, as seen in pictures that were hung up in the barracks of soldiers and over the swaying bunks of sailors, but she seemed more like, well, the girl next door than like the sweatered catch-me-if-you-can girls such as Rita Hayworth, kneeling on a bed, bosom bulging in a satin nightgown in that famous *Life* magazine photo. Jo seemed like the wise older sister, singing a piece of advice, "A heart that's true—there are such things." There is also a deeply maternal quality about her; sometimes when I would telephone to speak to her husband, Paul Weston, I'd halfway feel I should be saying, "Can Paul come out to play?"

She came across, in those war years, as someone who did not give a fig for stardom, did not want to stand above the crowd, did not consider herself better than anyone else. "Not caring what you own, but just what you are ..." And that impression, as it happens, was exactly correct. That is what she's like, this decent, enormously intelligent, and staunchly egalitarian lady. She was often voted "GI Jo" by companies or squadrons. The term by now perhaps requires explanation. Uniforms, rations, and other things issued to American soldiers in World War II were marked GI for "government issue," and soldiers themselves became known as GIs, or GI Joes.

At a military hospital in Europe, one of Stafford's recordings was, by vote of the patients, played every night at lights out. Once in New York, two young fliers, just back from Europe, told her that they'd almost been court-martialed because of her. Returning from a mission over Germany, they had, against regulations, been listening to Armed Forces Radio. They'd disrupted the flight pattern over their home field rather than change bands (to get their landing orders) during one of her songs.

The favorite of all her records among servicemen, she believes, was *I'll Be Seeing You.*

Jo Stafford slipped almost unnoticed into the American consciousness as the lead singer with a Tommy Dorsey vocal group called The Pied Pipers. That's what she liked doing, group singing, and she became a star half by accident because of a song called *Little Man with a Candy Cigar.* She went to Dorsey and said, "Tommy, this is the first time I've ever done this, and it'll probably be the last, but I want a favor of you. I want to do the record of *Little Man with the Candy Cigar* solo." He said, "You got it." From then on he assigned her a lot of solos. For the rest of the 1940s and well into the 1950s she was part of the fabric of American life, as she is now part of its memories. A retired Army general, well advanced in years, wrote her that he was so disgusted with the state of the world that he wanted to retreat to a farm with his Jo Stafford records and just forget it.

Like all of us, Jo has aged, but she hasn't really changed that much, and time after time people recognize her in supermarkets or gas stations and tell her how much this record of hers or that one meant to them during the war years. She still receives mail from old soldiers and fliers and sailors who were consoled by her voice during that ordeal now more than fifty years in the past, and remains touched by them, and answers them.

"Yes, it means something to me, those letters," she said. "I'm a very patriotic lady, and in those years I felt very deeply about those kids. I used to see a lot of them at the Paramount Theater, because New York City was their embarkation point, and they'd be on their way, and my dressing room used to be full of them all the time. I couldn't turn them away."

"Your patriotism, however," I said, "is anything but the uncritical kind—the love-it-or-leave-it stuff."

"Oh absolutely not, that's like saying if you love somebody very deeply, you never criticize them." She looked at Paul, with a strange mixture of affectionate smile and gritted teeth and said, "That isn't true, is it?" And Paul laughed, probably at something that had happened that day.

She never did want stardom and eventually gave it up, not with a conspicuous public announcement of retirement but gradually and quietly, first by withdrawing from public performing and later by ceasing to record. She concentrated on raising her two children.

Stafford's marriage to Paul Weston was settled, steady, and warm. Product of a profession whose practitioners are noted for psychological instability, she is sane, steadfast, and as far as I can see, very calm.

One day in 1947, when she was at the height of her stardom, Jo passed Country Washburn, chit-chatting with some of his cronies, in a corridor at Capitol Records. "There's the girl who can do it," she heard him say. That's a line to catch your attention, and she asked what it was that she could do. Washburn explained that he was planning a satiric recording of *Temptation*, as it might be done by a hillbilly singer–the term in use in those days. The girl he had scheduled for the session had, for one reason or another, fallen out, and he thought Jo could do it. So Jo made the record under the pseudonym Cinderella G. Stump. The song in its hilarious new incarnation was called *Timtayshun*. It was an immediate and enormous hit. The entire record industry, and its press, was speculating over who Cinderella really was. Not even Jo's manager knew. When at last he found out, he was furious. He asked her what kind of deal she had made for herself. She told him there was no deal; she had made the record for fun, and for scale, and was receiving no royalty at all.

What made the record only the funnier, and this is true of her second and later alter ego, the astonishingly incompetent society singer Darlene Edwards, was the sheer accuracy of it, the authenticity of the style. You cannot satirize what you do not know, and Jo knew whereof she was singing.

Her mother was Anna York Stafford, a distant cousin of Sergeant Alvin York, the farm-boy sharpshooter decorated in World War I. Anna York was born in Gainesboro, Tennessee, where she was noted as a virtuosic player of the five-string banjo. She married Grover Cleveland Stafford, who moved west in the hope of making a fortune in the California oil fields. He never did, but he always worked, first as a roughneck, then as a driller, finally as a foreman. Life for the Staffords was sometimes hard during the years of the Great Depression, and they lived from paycheck to paycheck. Jo was born the third of four girls on a tract of land known as Lease 35 at Coalinga, California, a small town that lies between Highway 101 and Interstate 5 in a limbo about halfway between Los Angeles and San Francisco. The land thereabouts is dry.

Hard at times or not, the Staffords' life was full of music. "When I was in high school," she said, "I had five years of classical voice training—all the breathing exercises, lying on my back, bouncing books on my diaphragm, doing scales. I had eyes to be an opera singer. I was always in the glee club in high school, and I thought to be an opera singer would be a good thing. But it takes more than five years to become an opera singer, and when I got out of high school, I had to go to work." The training helped make her a sight-reading shark and contributed to her accurate intonation. Her ear is so precise that she makes her fictional Darlene Edwards sing sharp or flat to ear-grating effect. It is hard to sing out of tune on purpose, only too easy to do it inadvertently, but Jo could do it effortlessly at will.

Years ago she told me that the trick to that kind of accurate vocal intonation is to think the tone just before you make it.

"I can't tell you physically how you do it," she says. "It's a mental thing. You know the song, you know the note you're going for. And a split second before you sing it, you hear it in your mind. And it gives you a real edge on hitting that note right."

Yes, but that doesn't fully explain it. The phenomenon of pitch in the voice is a mysterious one anyway, since the vocal cords contain no sensory nerves, which is why laryngitis is painless.

"Do you think that discipline grew out of your group-singing experience?" I asked her. "When you have to sing lead, you're responsible for the pitch of everybody."

"Yeah," she said, "you're responsible for the shape of the whole chord, as a matter of fact. You change everything . . . How can I explain this? I did a multiple recording of Christmas songs. I had done multiple recording years back on *The Hawaiian War Chant*. I did the lead first and then filled in the three parts underneath. When I heard the results, I said, 'I will never do that again.' So when I made this Christmas album, I put all the parts, starting with the bottom one, in first, and sometimes there were as many as eight tracks. I put the lead on last. Then I could control the way that sound was.

"In different chords, Paul made me realize, although I'd always done it, you do not sing A-flat the same as G-sharp. When you're sitting on top of the chords, you sing the lead differently on each one. I think it has a lot to do with overtones.

"I have a theory that when you sing absolutely straight tone, without vibrato, you lose overtones. So if you aren't dead center of the pitch when you take the vibrato out, it's going to sound awful."

But it takes great security and control to do what she did, since it involves, at least in legato passages, thinking one tone while you are still producing the one that precedes it. Paul said to her, "I still don't know how you do that." Jo said she doesn't have absolute pitch. "But I have pretty good relative pitch," she said.

Jo joined her older sisters, Pauline and Christine, who were already in the music business, to form a vocal trio. It was an age of sister groups, producing the Boswell, Andrews, DeMarco, Clark, Dinning, and Clooney Sisters, and more; Jo considers the best of them the King Sisters. Girl vocal groups, she said, normally have a high light texture because of the range of the female voice, but Alyce King was able to sing quite low, which gave body to their sound. "Alice had a B-flat down on the bottom," Paul said.

The Stafford Sisters had their own radio show on Los Angeles radio station KHJ. They performed as well on *David Brockman's California Melodies* and, for five nights a week, on *The Crockett Family of Kentucky* shows. "The Crocketts," she said, "were a real, authentic, country group— not Nashville country, but country country. Folk. They were awfully good, good musicians. We had a couple of arrangements, my sisters and I did, that were satires on country folk singing." All three Stafford girls did studio work as well, running from one movie studio to another on their appointed rounds.

Jo remembers that when she was singing back-up for Alice Faye in films, the latter would, at the end of a day, deliberately fluff a take, to force the job into overtime so that the girls could earn a little extra money. Alice and Jo are still friends.

The Stafford Sisters replaced Jo with another girl when Jo joined an eight-voice group called The Pied Pipers. And it was at this point that she met Axel Stordahl and Paul Weston.

He was born Paul Wetstein in Springfield, Massachusetts, of a German Catholic father and an Irish Catholic mother. "He is Irish in everything except music," Jo remarked once. "When it comes to music, he is German." Meaning, one presumes, precise, thorough, and disciplined. His writing is characterized by spare, clean voice-leading, and it is highly individual.

Paul grew up in Pittsfield, Massachusetts. His father was a teacher in a girls' private school. The school had a phonograph, which he was allowed to take home at the Christmas break. Though it was a big and bulky machine, he brought it to the house on skis. And he brought records, the kind that were blank on one side. One of them was *Whispering Hope*, sung by Alma Gluck and Louise Homer.

After high school, Paul went on to study economics at Dartmouth. He claimed he learned just enough economics to pass the exams, but this seems unlikely in view of the fact that he was graduated cum laude and

Phi Beta Kappa. That was in 1933. Like so many young intellectuals of the time, he was in love with the young music called jazz. He had led a band at Dartmouth and, in 1934, while he was doing graduate studies at Columbia University in New York, he sold some arrangements to the Joe Haymes orchestra, which the late Rudy Vallee, then the nation's heart-throb, heard on a radio broadcast. Vallee commissioned him to write some charts for him.

Paul's father was dismayed at the thought that his son might desert economics for music. But in those Depression years, nobody much was looking for young economists, and circumstance colluded with desire to make him a professional musician. His father relented when Paul sent home for deposit a check bearing Vallee's signature, which caused a considerable dither at the local bank. Paul continued to write for Vallee and Haymes and for drummer Phil Harris and his orchestra. (Harris would later marry Jo's friend Alice Faye.)

In the fall of 1935, the battling Dorsey brothers, who could never agree on anything, including tempos and the way a rhythm section was supposed to sound, broke up their band. Tommy took over the Haymes band and offered Paul a job as staff arranger. He took it and wrote for Dorsey for five years. It was a brilliant arranging staff, including as it did Sy Oliver and Axel Stordahl. The charts on *Stardust, Night and Day*, and *Who?*, among others, are Paul's.

One of his closest friends was Stordahl, whose real name was Odd Stordahl. It doesn't sound odd to a Swede, but it does to an American ear, and he changed it to something almost as odd, namely Axel. The signature on the record-date contracts for Frank Sinatra's first Bluebird sides, including *Night and Day*, reads Odd Stordahl. Paul called him Ax, and there was always affection in his voice when he said it, long after Stordahl died of a heart attack.

In 1938, Paul, Stordahl, Dorsey's featured singer Jack Leonard, and Herb Sanford, the BBD&O advertising executive who produced the Raleigh Kool network radio show on which the Tommy Dorsey band was playing, rented a house in Los Angeles. It was at this time that they first encountered The Pied Pipers. "Paul was going with Alyce King of the King Sisters, Ax was going with Yvonne King," Jo said. "The Kings knew about the Pipers. They'd heard us. They told Paul and Ax, 'You really ought to hear this group.' So one afternoon we went over to Paul and Ax's house and had a sort of singers' jam session."

"Half the group singers in town were invited," Paul said. "Like the Music Maids from the Bing Crosby show, and the Kings. The Pied Pipers came in the front door, and they went right to the refrigerator and ate up everything in the house."

"We were very poor," Jo said almost plaintively.

"Even the ketchup. Ax and I never got over that. The ketchup was all gone, everything that was in the refrigerator."

"I don't remember that ketchup," Jo said, laughing.

"Then they started singing. They had Jo and three guys and four other guys, and they worked in sections. Like, they'd have a sax section versus the brass section, then the two sections would be together, and four of them would sing unison here against four parts. We'd never heard anything like it.

"At this point Herb Sanford came home and heard them and went crazy. He went to Tommy and said, 'We've got to have them on the Raleigh Kool program.' And Tommy saw a chance to get the Pipers on the program without his having to pay anything, since Herb was pushing them. The band went back to New York, and the Pipers got in their cars and drove to New York. On the basis of doing one radio show!"

"You have to be awfully young to do that," Jo said.

"The sponsor," Paul said, "was in England. Each week the agency mailed a recording of the program to the sponsor. One of those great big glass discs. But as they took it to the post office, they broke it, so that it got to England in pieces, so this old Sir Hubert or whatever his name was didn't know what the hell was going on. He knew he had Tommy Dorsey and he knew he had big ratings. Unfortunately for the Pipers, he came to America. He was sitting up in the booth, at NBC. Now their arrangements were pretty crazy anyway, but they were singing '*Hold Tight*, hold tight, foodly racky-sacky, want some sea food, Mama.' And this Englishman jumped and clawed at the glass and said, 'Get them off my show, get them off!' So they were fired. They stayed in New York for a few months."

"We stayed until we had just enough money left for our train tickets home to Los Angeles," Jo said. "I had gone down and picked up my last unemployment check. It was pretty panic city. And I got home and there was a message to call an operator in Chicago. I didn't know anybody in Chicago, but it was a collect call, and I had nothing to lose. I returned the call and it was Tommy. He said, 'I can't afford a group of eight, but if you have a quartet, I'd sure like to have you join the band.' Dick Whittinghill had left the group by then, and we actually were down to four. So that was it. We went with Tommy."

Tommy Dorsey was noted for being a martinet, a volatile Irish miner's son who couldn't even get along with his own brother, the affable and widely liked Jimmy. Benny Goodman had a similar reputation for tyranny, but Dorsey, unlike Goodman, is often remembered by those who worked for him with a strange grudging affection. There is another difference. Goodman demoralized musicians. Dorsey somehow inspired them, and the Dorsey band in the years Jo was with it had an *esprit de corps* unlike any other, a collective vanity that made them think they could carve any other band. By and large they were right. It was a superb band whose recorded output doesn't seem to date. It executed excellent hot charts by Sy Oliver with burning zeal, particularly when Buddy Rich was booting it, and played ballads probably better than any other band of the period, as often as not built around its leader's mellifluous solo trombone. It was a band with an extremely broad emotional range.

And Dorsey was able to hold together some deeply disparate and brilliant temperaments, including—not long after Jo joined the band—Frank Sinatra and Buddy Rich, who were perpetually at each other's throats. How they remained friends is a mystery. What is more, they even roomed together. Sinatra has said that he himself is amazed that they both came through the experience alive. Legend has it that Sinatra once threw a cut-glass pitcher of water at Buddy backstage at the Paramount in New York. I once asked Jo if it was true. "Sure," she said. "I was writing a letter to my mother at the time, and the water splashed all over it."

Lee Castaldo, who later changed his name to Lee Castle, grew up with the Dorsey brothers, he told me, and indeed was taught to play trumpet by their father. Lee said Tommy was the kind of man who knew the diagram of every water pipe and electric line in his house, and who always knew—or wanted to know—everything that went on in his band. In another famous incident, Buddy Rich blew up in the middle of a performance at the Paramount, quit the band and walked off the stage. Buddy headed for Florida, where his mother and father were living. A day or so later, Lee got a phone call from Buddy, asking Lee to send him his drums.

Dorsey, as Lee discovered, had anticipated the call and had paid the hotel's telephone operators to tip him off when it came. A few minutes later Lee got a call from Dorsey, inviting him to come to his room for breakfast. Lee thought this distinctly strange, but he accepted the invitation, and wondered all through the pleasant matinal chit-chat what it was all about. As they finished their coffee, Dorsey suddenly snarled, "That son-of-a-bitch Buddy Rich called you to send him his drums, didn't he? Well, you're not going to do it!"

But Buddy got his drums, and in due course he and Dorsey were reconciled.

Paul and Jo both got along with Dorsey. Paul said, "I only ever had one argument with him. It was someplace like Louisville, Kentucky. He was rehearsing one of my arrangements, and he did something that he hardly ever did. He started to make some changes. Axel and I weren't used to that. And Tommy was very good about this. I haven't thought about this for thirty years. He was making the changes, and I was throwing a pencil up in the air and catching it. And the brass, the evil ones, started to laugh. So Tommy knew something was going on behind him. All of a sudden he turned around and caught me and he fired me. So I was out of the band for about three hours. A lot of people got fired from that band for a few hours."

Jo said, "One night in Texas, half of the band got fired. Tommy was in one of his drinking phases. And he was pretty well smashed. And he had almost a concert arrangement on *Sleepy Lagoon.* There's a part where he has to go up to a real high note. And this note just splashed all over the stage. So he stopped the band."

"It was such a horrendous mistake. He said, 'Stop. Take it from letter C.' So he tried. And again, splash! all over the stage. He stopped the band about three times. On the fourth time it started getting to the players. And they start giggling. The whole saxophone section started. And then it's like the measles, it spreads. Tommy turned and he said, 'You're fired, and you're fired, and you're fired.' He fired about half the band. And they all got up and picked up their horns and left. I can still see it. Freddy Stulce walked by the Pipers and said to us, 'See you later.' We played the rest of the night with about half a band."

She laughed, and Paul joined her. They reminisced about the business without regret, finding the laughter in life.

Paul said, "Did you ever hear the story about Jimmy Dorsey starting over again on a tune? It was up in Milwaukee. And there was an early morning show, and Jimmy'd had a few the night before. One of his big numbers was *Flight of the Bumble Bee,* which is not too good at 10:30 in the morning with a hangover. So he starts. And it fell apart. So he said angrily, 'Take it from the top.' And he counts it off–probably a little faster, just to show them.

"And some guy in the audience yells, 'Why don't you play it right?'"

"And Jimmy yells, 'Why don't you go and fuck yourself?'"

"The theater manager came out and took Jimmy by the elbow and led him off."

He chuckled some more at memories of the Dorseys, then said, "When Jo came with Tommy, I was just leaving the band. Dinah Shore had asked me to be her arranger and musical director, and I also had a chance to do an album with Lee Wiley. I wanted to branch out. Tommy said, 'Okay,' but then he got thinking about it, and he thought, 'I'll bet he's goin' with Glenn Miller.' And he made a speech one night at rehearsal about it. But I wasn't going with Miller. I guess," he said, turning to Jo, "I wrote one arrangement that you guys sang."

"Yeah," Jo said. "It was a Mercer song. *I Thought About You.*"

Paul settled in Los Angeles in the summer of 1940 to write for Shore, the Bob Crosby band, and for movies. He worked at Paramount Pictures with Bing Crosby, Bob Hope, and Betty Hutton. It was at Paramount that he met Johnny Mercer, who made him Capitol's musical director.

He carried on this executive position, producing such things as the early King Cole Trio albums, while turning out an incredible amount of writing for Mercer, Stafford, Betty Hutton, Margaret Whiting, and, later, Gordon MacRae and Dean Martin. In 1943 he went to work on *The Johnny Mercer Music Shop* network radio show. He also began to record a series of instrumental albums, the first of which was *Music for Dreaming.*

In the late 1950s, when stereophonic records were first released to the public, those albums were re-recorded. They are remarkably good stereo, even today, and Weston's writing remains as fresh as it was at the time. The format was that of the dance band augmented with strings, with one exception, a charming album called *Carefree* in which he used four fluegelhorns, four trombones, and four French horns, no strings and no saxes. In recording, one has two options with such an instrumentation: you can crank up the strings electronically or you can tone down the brass and saxes to achieve a natural acoustical balance. Paul did the latter, and the writing had a soft classical purity, almost a Mozart quality. Sometimes he would use four clarinets in harmony, as the Dorsey band often did in its ballads, and the Isham Jones band before it. It is a sound that is often heard in concert bands, and it is a particularly warm one, now almost vanished from popular music.

The albums had a gentle and tender quality about them, the strings forming cushions for such fine jazz soloists as the late Babe Russin, Eddie Miller, Don Fagerquist, and Barney Kessel. And they perfectly embodied Paul's temperament, sunny, sensible, warm, generous, fair, and very humorous.

Johnny Mercer had told Jo back in her Dorsey days, "Some day I'm going to have my own record company, and you're going to record for me." He was as good as his word. He signed her to the label within a year of its founding, and she began to record a string of hits, one of which came from a suggestion of Paul's: "When Jo and Gordon MacRae were going to do some duets, I remembered that record of *Whispering Hope* that my father brought home. And they recorded it. We never found a disc jockey that played it, we never found anybody that bought it. And in the Bible belt it sold well over a million copies. And it's still selling."

When in 1950 Paul went from Capitol to Columbia, Jo went with him. Paul wrote the charts on an incredible 500 or more of her recordings, not to mention sessions for Rosemary Clooney, Doris Day, and Frankie Laine. At

Columbia, her hits included *You Belong to Me, Make Love to Me, Jambalaya,* and *Shrimp Boats,* which Paul wrote. Whatever the cause of their affinity, in 1952 Jo became a Catholic convert and they were married. They had known each other twelve years, ever since she and the Pipers pillaged his refrigerator, so they hardly married in haste.

At this point we have to consider two more biographies, those of that inextinguishable duo Jonathan and Darlene Edwards.

Musical jokes are probably as old as the art itself, and fictional musicians with which to make them have been around for a long time. Peter Schickele's P.D.Q. Bach is a particular favorite of musicians. So are Jonathan Edwards, the incomparably incompetent cocktail pianist who insists that what he plays is jazz, and his off-pitch but earnest wife Darlene.

The Edwardses came into being at a Columbia Records sales convention at Key West, Florida. Paul and Jo, along with George Avakian and the late Irving Townsend of Columbia's a&r staff, were having a late dinner in a restaurant where they had to endure one of those wrong-chord pianists who somehow find work for tin-eared restaurateurs and bar owners all over the planet. The pianist left for the night, and Paul, who got more than usually funny after about two drinks, went to the piano and began to play *Stardust* in excruciating imitation of him. Avakian and Townsend fell out, as the old expression had it, and, laughing helplessly, insisted that an album should be made in that style. Avakian came up with the name Jonathan Edwards, after the famous preacher of the Colonial period, because, he said, it had a "properly ossified ring" to it.

On the way back to California, Paul had some second thoughts. He wasn't sure he could sustain the gag for an entire album. He pressed Jo into service as Darlene, Jonathan's wife. They went into the studio to make *The Original Piano Artistry of Jonathan Edwards.* The drummer on that first date was Jack Sperling. Paul had to fire him because he couldn't stop laughing. Every time they would try a take, Sperling would drop his drumsticks, collapse with face in his folded arms across his snare drum, and laugh until he cried.

The album was a best-seller shortly after its release in 1957, and the dreadful duo sustained their curious brand of artistry—bars with beats missing or added, wrong chords to befog the mind, incompleted and meandering runs and what Jo called "crumbling thirds," and Darlene's eerily inaccurate intonation—through *Jonathan and Darlene Edwards in Paris, Songs for Sheiks and Flappers, Sing Along with Jonathan and Darlene Edwards,* and *Darlene Remembers Duke, Jonathan Plays Fats.* (Ellington's *Don't Get Around Much Any More* starts on the third; Darlene starts it on the tonic and lets it fall from there.) Leaping into the contemporary market, they did a single on *Stayin' Alive* and *Copacabana.*

It is a dubious distinction to have a song in one of their albums, for Darlene has a bizarre taste in lyrics. You do not realize how dreadful the words to *You're Blasé* really are until you hear Darlene do them. ("You're deep, just like a chasm, you've no enthusiasm . . .") The same is true of *Cocktails for Two* and, alas, Ellington's gorgeous *Sophisticated Lady*, which deserved better than "smoking, drinking, never thinking of tomorrow, nonchalant . . ." and "when nobody is nigh . . ."

The recordings have had some curious effects. Paul was playing golf with the head of a large corporation, who mentioned that on a trip to New York he had picked up an album called *Jonathan and Darlene Edwards in Paris*. He asked Paul if he'd heard it, and Paul, thinking this was a joke, allowed that he had. The man said, "He's pretty good, but I don't think she's all that hot." And Paul realized the man was not joking.

In 1961—after several years of doing television in America—the Westons moved for a summer to London, where they did a series of television shows for the ATV British network. The shows were seen throughout the British commonwealth, and their faces became as familiar in England as they were in America. One night they went to a small restaurant near their home in Hampstead. The cocktail pianist smiled as they entered and immediately went into an imitation of Jonathan Edwards, which Paul and Jo thought was a charming and amusing tribute. They smiled and nodded appreciatively to the pianist. The pianist went into his next tune, in the same style. When he used a chord that possibly not even Jonathan could have come up with, Paul realized the man actually played that way. Paul had a mouthful of red wine at the time. It got sprayed all over Jo's white dress.

The fans of Jonathan and Darlene, particularly within the music business, are legion. Leonard Feather said that Darlene was the only singer to get off the A train between A and B-Flat. When the first album came out, he gave it forty-eight stars in *Down Beat.*

One of the devotées of Jonathan and Darlene is George Shearing. If he knew Jo and Paul were in an audience, he would immediately play *Autumn in New York* in Jonathan's style, to the undoubted bemusement of members of the audience not in on the joke. Still another fan is actor Art Carney, who wrote Jonathan and Darlene a fan letter—in the persona of Ed Norton.

Once you got into the lunacy of Jonathan and Darlene with the Westons, they become curiously real. Paul and Jo talked about them as if they were, and you could see that Jo had a certain strange affection for Darlene. "She's a nice lady from Trenton, New Jersey, and she does her best," Jo said. *Los Angeles* magazine sent a writer to their home to interview Jonathan and Darlene, who supposedly lived with the Westons, permanent sponges in their household. Paul and Jo slipped into the roles, and, as Jonathan and Darlene, complained about food and the fact that the Westons made them go into the bedroom when famous people came to the house.

Jo said, "It was crazy time. Because when he asked a question, the interviewer wasn't asking me, he was asking Darlene."

"Once we got into it," Paul said, "it was easy. Jonathan was saying that he played a much better stride piano than Fats, and Darlene came up with things off the top of her head. She said, 'Well, actually, a five-four bar gives you an extra stride.'"

Jonathan told the interviewer, "We do things that other people have thought of and foolishly abandoned."

"The thing about Jo," Paul said, "is her versatility. She accomplished more in more different directions than any singer I know. When you think that *Whispering Hope* was a religious seller in '46 or '47—one of the first religious songs that a pop singer had ever done.

"And then there's *Jo + Jazz*. She's not a jazz singer, but she did a good jazz album. She was the first pop singer to do American folk songs with an orchestra. And that was in 1946. She could do show songs, she could handle a rhythm song and a ballad and whatever. I sound like an agent or something. But I think people sometimes don't realize how wide her scope was, in all kinds of American music."

The one negative in her career was that some critics said her singing was cold.

"That used to be the party line," she said. "I never made it with the critics. I think what the critics didn't like was that it was simply singing."

"There was a disgusting normality about it," Paul said.

"Maybe. I don't know. I think maybe a lot of 'em resented that too. I'm basically a pretty dull person. I was never on smokin' anything or drinkin' anything."

"When you're struggling, they love you," Paul said.

"When *Little Man with a Candy Cigar* first came out," Jo said, "the critics couldn't say enough wonderful things, they were absolutely thrilled, it was marvelous. And so because of that, I thought that's the way it was going to be. But from then on, kids, forget it."

"Well, particularly when she got radio shows and hit records," Paul said. "Then it was: She's cold."

"They're suspicious of commercial success," I said. "It's an American conviction: if it's popular it can't be good; if it's good, it can't be popular. Which is odd, in view of the country's galloping commercialism. But then perhaps it's a reaction of critics against commercialism. We've all seen trash sells, but it does not follow that what sells is necessarily trash. The former is the premise of the record industry, the latter is the premise of critics."

Commercial success Jo surely had. Columbia gave her a diamond award when her sales reached 25,000,000 records—and that was *after* her period at Capitol. She was the favorite woman singer of Americans in the peak years of her career, according to the *Billboard* magazine charts.

Whether those charts are indeed an accurate reflection of popularity, there is no doubting that Jo's was enormous. In itself, it seems to have meant nothing to her. "And anyway," she said, "if I'd gone funny in any way, I had a family that would have brought me right back down to earth." Public performing simply was not attractive to her. She found far more satisfaction in the recording studio. Of all the compliments she ever received, she still remembers most vividly, and treasures, one from the late Conrad Gozzo, the great lead trumpet player whom Paul often booked for her dates. "Musicians don't usually go into the booth to listen to a take," she said. "But that day Gozzo came in, stood there listening, and at the end of the song, he pointed a finger at me, then turned and walked out. Without a word." She was always a heavy favorite of musicians. Lester Young said he wanted to have his own big band with Jo Stafford and Frank Sinatra as his singers.

Her two children were reaching the age of danger. Jo thought more and more about her responsibilities at home. In 1959, with a lucrative Las Vegas contract awaiting only her signature, she decided to give up public performing—Darlene, interestingly enough, did not—but she continued to record until the mid-1960s.

The California show business landscape is strewn with the wrecks of what have been called the Beverly Hills Brats, the sons and daughters of famous parents who have themselves attempted show business careers to embarrassing results. There are exceptions, but many of them have been burned out by drugs, drinking, or other indulgences, some of them obnoxious figures, others quite tragic. When Amy Weston was in her adolescence, she and Jo had a confrontation in which Amy defended herself on the grounds that she wasn't a doper. Later, I remember, Jo said in astonishment at the new age dawning, "I'm supposed to be *grateful* that they're not drug addicts!" Yes. Our world had come a long way from "A peaceful sky, there are such things. . . ."

But her judgment that her family mattered more than a career was obviously a right one in that Tim and Amy got through the adolescent years undamaged by the come-ons to destruction that were all around them, and Tim is now a successful musician.

Jo's passion is history, which she reads voraciously, particularly that of World War II. Her knowledge of it is almost awesome. This grew at least in part out of her symbolic association with the war and her awareness of how the young servicemen felt about her. Once I was discussing the loss in heavy seas of Allied amphibious craft during the Normandy landings at Omaha and Utah beaches. She knew exactly how many were used at each beach, how they foundered, how many were lost, and how many got ashore. During a dinner-party discussion of an action off Mindanao some years ago, a retired navy officer contradicted her on a detail. Politely but firmly, Jo held to her point. The officer said, "Madame, I was *there!*" A few days later he dropped her a note to say he had consulted his logs. She had been right and he wrong.

Jo has given a lot of her time to charity. She is a past president of SHARE, an organization devoted to work with mentally handicapped children. Well after Jo had given up performing and, finally, even record-ing, Darlene continued to work. Her last public performance was given May 19, 1978, on the occasion of SHARE's twenty-fifth anniversary. She shared the spotlight with Jo's old band-mate, Frank Sinatra.

A few years ago, Paul set up Corinthian Records to get back the mas-ters of Jo's albums and reissue them—along with those of Jonathan and Darlene. Time-Life Records issued an album of twenty of Jo's best sides, including one of Darlene's. Jo, typically, said, "I don't understand that. How can anybody listen to twenty songs by *any* singer?" Twenty-four of Paul's orchestral tracks have been reissued on compact disc.

Fortune smiled on the Westons. But she has smiled on many other peo-ple in show business who have alchemically converted her bounty into failure or disaster or tragedy, and been demolished by the hubris, indeed the madness, that intense public acclaim so often induces. The Westons handled it rationally and with grace.

Jo will never sing again. She is firm about that. She did it, she loved it, and it's over. Could she do it if she wanted to? Time takes a toll on voices, particularly those of women. The vocal cords calcify as people grow older which, in extreme age, produces a high cracked sound. But that doesn't happen to everybody, and Bing Crosby sang well in his sev-enties. Assuredly Jo could do it. One day in July 1986, when I was talking to her about some theoretical musical matter or another, she demon-strated a point. That clear voice went up and down a scale in perfect into-nation, like a flute. It was a fragment, a brief bit of music flung into time, but it was so good that it startled me.

American accents derived originally from those of England—that of Brook-lyn, for example, from that of East End London dock workers who were

brought over to do the same jobs here—and then were modified by those of
people from other places.

Scholars of dialect tell us that American accents flowed westward in
swaths, those of the American Northwest being derived from those of the
Northeast, those of the Southwest from the Southeast.

The roads around Gainesboro, Tennessee, slant south-southwest
between the ridges of the Cumberland Plateau. Gainesboro is due east of
Gallatin. It is surrounded by towns with flat-footed no-nonsense names
likes Nameless, Commerce, Gentry, Prosperity, Rough Point, Difficult,
and Defeated. Gainesboro is at 36 degrees 20 minutes north latitude.
Coalinga, California, where the roads run straight and square to each
other on the flat land of the central valley, is at 36 degrees 8 minutes.

The *g* is disappearing from the gerund in the English language. Indeed,
it *has* disappeared in many parts of England and the United States, even
though we continue to write it in a word such as *going*, as we do the vanished *l* in *palm* and *salmon*, the lost guttural in *drought* and *thought*. Jo
drops the *g* in gerunds in her speech, though not, interestingly, in her
singing. Nonetheless, she has a California-modified Tennessee accent.
She almost sings "ah" for the personal pronoun *I,* and she pronounces
"on" almost as "own." That is how strongly Tennessee persists in her
speech, not to mention her character.

One of the two main streams of American music, the one that led to
what we now call country-and-western, has roots that go back to Scottish,
Irish, and English balladry. One of the elements in its singing style is a
way of skidding up to a note from a major or minor third below.

There are two primary forms of vibrato. The first is a pitch vibrato. A
finger on a violinist's left hand slides up and down on the fingerboard, a
trombonist rapidly vibrates the slide, to produce an oscillating. If the
intonation is good, the "note" produced is the exact center of what is
actually a rising and falling sound, and the ear accepts it as that tone. The
second kind of vibrato is a volume vibrato. A note becomes louder and
softer. Flute players use this kind of vibrato. It is produced by increasing
and decreasing the force of the air pressure from the diaphragm.

In opera and most forms of American and European popular music,
singers use a pitch vibrato. But many folk and some country-and-western
singers have a volume vibrato. It is a variation of intensity.

Jo's Tennessee background shows not only in her accent but in her
vibrato. Paul was right. She's not a jazz singer. She is what one can only
describe as a highly educated folk singer working mostly in other idioms
of American music. You hear her affinity for folk music when she sings
Tennessee Waltz. She may make fun of the style in *Timtayshun*, but she sings
it with ease and respect in *Tennessee Waltz,* sliding up thirds to her notes.

But you really hear it when she does a folk song such as *He's Gone Away (Over Yandro)*, her reading of which is chillingly beautiful.

Her vibrato is puzzling. It seems to be compounded of both kinds—she says that it's quite unconscious on her part, something that just happens. You wouldn't think that such an acoustic phenomenon would be evasive of analysis, but it is. The engineer with whom she worked at Capitol used to remark on it because it never pushed the needle on the VU meter into the red. This is what probably caused some critics to call her cold, her perfect cool control, her failure to chew the scenery and make the veins stand out on her forehead.

And it is probably what caused the kids from Tennessee and Kentucky and Kansas and Missouri and Montana and Wyoming to love her, this small-town girl singing those big-city songs. And the calm of her style, that was probably just what they needed—the sound of rationality in the madness and horror of Wake Island and Guadalcanal and Iwo Jima and the Casserine Pass and Anzio and Monte Cassino and then Remagen, where the Germans forgot to blow the bridge.

No wonder they made her their GI Jo.

Jo Stafford was the voice of home.

Paul died September 26, 1996. He had been ill for some time. I waited for a time before calling Jo. She said she had no regrets. She and Paul had had a wonderful life.

And she still referred to him, as he always referred to her, as "my friend."

In from the Cold
Peggy Lee

The roads of North Dakota, like those of the other prairie states and the Canadian provinces of Saskatchewan and Manitoba that lie just across its northern border, run in straight lines, north to south, east to west. Even in the western part of the state, where the Missouri River, long ago the highway of discovery of the Lewis and Clark expedition, is in the early stage of its journey to the Mississippi, the roads just cross it in those never-ending straight lines. Their occasional jogs are arbitrary, made by man, who wrote all these straight lines on the map. There is nothing to impede the roads or the wind. It comes whistling out of the west, never slowing even at Chicago to the east. And, much of the time in winter, it comes out of the north, whipping the dead grasses that protrude from the frozen earth and its bleak skin of old snow and slashing whatever flesh is in its way like a stream of razor blades. The last winter before Norma Deloris Egstrom left North Dakota, the temperature went down to 63 below zero Fahrenheit; the following July it rose to 120. Once, when she was a little girl, she froze both her hands.

On a shelf of her home there is a book inscribed: "To a gallant and gifted survivor of the hard times. With admiration and affection, Studs Terkel." Other books and pictures bear other autographs, including that of Albert Einstein.

Her father, Marvin Olaf Egstrom, was born in New York City of mixed Norwegian and Swedish immigrant parents. He married a Minnesota girl of Scandinavian stock named Selma Andersen when she was sixteen years old. They had seven children, two boys and five girls. Norma Deloris was born in Jamestown, North Dakota, on May 26, 1920. Olaf Egstrom, called Ole, worked for the Midland Continental Railroad, which had only a hundred miles of track but linked the Great Northern and Northern Pacific railways and the Sioux Line.

"I was born in Kennedy Hospital, Fifth Floor, in Jamestown," Norma Deloris said.

"When I was between four and five, I had an imaginary playmate called Greencida. I think it was a girl. And I had some imaginary chickens. I used to feed them all the time.

"I would follow my daddy to work at the depot. I was crafty enough to follow him just far enough back so he couldn't say, 'Go home.' But one day he walked very fast, and he took big steps, because he was tall, six foot one or two.

"When he would let me walk along with him, I would run and hold onto his finger, like a handle. And then down at the depot, he was very busy. He was the station agent. He would be there with a green visor on his head. He gave me paper and those ink-pad stampers. I'd stamp everything I could lay my hands on. I actually learned a lot.

"There was a little boy in Jamestown who used to play with me at the depot. Our big pastime was to go into the warehouse and find this huge box of jelly beans. We must have eaten a lot of jelly beans. I loved the black ones.

"We'd watch the trains come in and out. Then Daddy would take me home.

"One day, when I didn't quite get a hold of his finger, I got so far behind I got lost. I was sitting on the sidewalk, crying, and a lady came out and took me in the house. She was so nice. She gave me some toys to play with. I felt a little strange, because I didn't know her and I didn't know where I was. She took care of me till Daddy came for me after work. I was mystified how he knew where to come. It took me years to figure that out. She must have had a telephone, but I didn't know what telephones were.

"When I was a little older, I was riding on the train one day. In those days the coaches were old, funny things. You pulled the windows open to get some air. There was a bottle of some kind of soda on the window. Maybe it was root beer. Root beer was very big. We used to make it. I loved it! I left my seat for a moment. When I came back, the root beer was gone. I think that was my first experience with a little bit of paranoia. Who did that? I looked from face to face. I thought about it for several years, and finally realized that it just fell out the window.

"I was a happy child in spite of everything. Basically, I think, because my mother had already established the main principles of my character. My mother was musical and she used to sing, 'You need sympathy.' She played piano, I don't know how well. But she had her own piano, which was her pride and joy. I think that's where the music came from mostly. My daddy sang. They all sang, though not professionally. They say your character is pretty firmly set by the time you're five. I still remember things of when I was two."

Her mother took seriously ill when Norma was four. She remembers her lying in a coma in a hospital bed set up in what we would now call the living room but in those days they called the parlor. Her mother fell into a coma, and died in August. The bed was replaced by a coffin. The child watched as men carried it out. Afterward she asked:

"Where did they take Mama?"

She was told: "To heaven, with God."

And she said, "Where's heaven?" and they said, "Up there."

"I can remember that," she said, "and writing my first lyric. I don't remember singing before that. I was sitting on the floor. Everything that was happening was so traumatic that I remember it vividly. I made up a lyric to that song called *Melody of Love*: "Mama's gone to dreamland on the train." That was my first lyric. Something inside made me feel not only sad but comforted, in a releasing kind of way.

"After that I began to look up at the clouds and look for Mama."

Four months or so after her mother died, her father built a roaring fire against the night's cruel cold. He and his children went to bed. She remembers sitting on her father's bed when her brother Millford came running into the room to say the house was on fire. The family fled the house in whatever clothes they were wearing into a swirling blizzard. The temperature was 35 below zero. Volunteer firemen arrived, threw furniture out the doors and windows, and poured water into the house, as well as the scattered furniture.

The family spent the next nights with friends. And soon her father was paying attention to Min Schaumberg, who had been her sister Della's nurse. She was kind and friendly to Norma. That ended the moment Min married Ole Egstrom. The child was immediately put to work. She remembers standing on a box washing dishes when she was five years old. Min began beating Norma and her sister Marianne for even minor offenses. Norma would never understand why her father married her in the first place.

Then her father was demoted by the railway, possibly because of his drinking, and posted as the station-master at Nortonville. "We moved from Jamestown to Nortonville when I was six," she said. "When we moved out of Jamestown, we got into the old world. No electricity, no gas. Just kerosene lamps and candles, then gas lamps. Nortonville was only a hundred and twenty-five people, twenty-eight miles south of Jamestown. It was an entirely different kind of life. The town, frame houses, was made up partly of farm people and partly people just living there. We had animals to raise, two cows, a Guernsey named Billy and a Jersey named Sally. A lot of chickens, and a dog named Peggy.

"I saw a tremendous amount of violence, and sadness, and later on I could always understand about singing the blues.

"I used to find Indian mounds 'way, 'way back out. I'd sit there and cry, because I knew they'd fought there. But I hadn't been to school enough to even know, so I must have known it intuitively. I found things like arrowheads and tomahawks. Just the heads, the handles were gone. Relics. I think because of Mother, and because I was looking for God, the mounds signified to me that Mama had gone to heaven with God. I was always trying to see Mama's face peeking out over the clouds. And looking off into the far, far horizon, wondering what was out there. There were very few trees or anything."

One of her closest friends was a boy named Everold Jordan, called Ebbie. One day when they were out picking beans, they saw a car half hidden in long grasses. It looked like that of a man they knew. When they approached it, they saw him dead in a cloud of flies in the front seat. Apparently he had been there for days, in severe August heat, and he was well along in decay. He had rigged a pipe from the exhaust into the car. No one ever found out why.

"We were in between eight or ten. I remember that we had a friend who was also killed. He was riding along on a bicycle with a shotgun, and it went off. I remember that we went to the funeral home to visit him, and you could see all the black marks on his face.

"Ebbie and I used to ride around on this wonderful old plow horse named Beans. I think he was a Belgian percheron. He was so big that you almost couldn't fall off. Ebbie had another horse. He was riding it one day, and the horse stepped in a gopher hole and threw Ebbie over his head and fell on him and crushed him."

Ebbie died.

"You saw a lot of death," I said.

"Yes, I did. I didn't make the connection when I was little, but now I believe we go on, I believe we live in another dimension where we're free of the physical encumbrances of this existence.

"Some of these remembrances are getting dimmer now, which is what I want them to do.

"I used to look at the horizon, and I suppose I felt a little like Columbus, wanting to find out what was beyond it. Something in me knew that I would be going out there, and I would find it, whatever it was. I knew because of the radio, that there was music, and there were other cities.

"I can't remember *not* singing. They told me that I hummed instead of cooed. Later, music always saw me through things. All kinds of things. When I'd go out after the cows, or clean the separator, or scrub the floors, do the laundry, hang it on the clothesline, I would sing all the time and keep myself happy.

"I used to wash clothes until my knuckles were red, using Fels Naptha soap. I remember the old washing machines, the wooden ones, with a handle that pumped back and forth. It didn't go around like a crank. I was alone most of the time, and singing took me through all my daydreams that would later come true. I didn't realize that this was visualizing.

"I was hearing Count Basie and Bennie Moten from Kansas City. Those were my true roots. In first grade, in Jamestown, we had a little rhythm band. It always fascinated me that I could keep time. And a lot of them couldn't. To have your hands the right distance, so that when you clap, they come together at the right time. I used to look around at everyone and think, 'I wonder why they can't do that.'

"I used to hear music in my head, in my mind. I still do."

She showed an aptitude for learning songs, memorizing lyrics on one hearing. "I must have been picking them up off the radio. We had a Victrola with a crank, and those Edison cylinders. I played it in Jamestown, before we moved to Nortonville. Music has never stopped being a consolation to me," she said.

"The first airplane I saw was when I was eight years old, I think. The trains we knew are gone now. The pot-bellied Benjamin Franklin stoves, and the coal ranges with the flat tops, the oven on the right and the water heater on the left. And the crystal sets. We didn't have electricity in Nortonville until I was ten years old. My maternal grandfather, who came to live with us when he was losing his sight, used to tell me about the Indians, and Custer, and Calamity Jane, and all those people.

"I used to be fascinated by the striped caps the railway engineers and brakemen wore. They had trains they called specials. They had a school bus, and a Model A Ford on railroad wheels, and they ran on the tracks. That was for carrying mail.

"I had a fierce, fierce allegiance to that railroad. Later on, when I was editor of the high-school paper, people would laugh at the Midland Continental Railroad. I would defend it in the paper. I would get so angry, because I thought of all those wonderful dear things that train did. Like, a mother was going to have to go to a hospital or something. She would stand by the track, and the train would stop for her and take her to the nearest hospital.

"It was a big event to see that train go by every day. It was something to break up the flatness of the prairie, that everlasting flatness.

"Along came the various cars, the Model T, the Model A, the V-8, the Essex, the Studebaker, the Hudson Terraplane, the Packard.

"Finally we got the big prop planes. The airlines wiped out all the railroads where I lived. The Superchief is gone.

"Then we went on to the jet, the 747s, global travel, the Concorde, then to the moon. This has all been in our lifetime."

Like many very bright children—she skipped third grade—she didn't think she was. "I thought I was stupid. Spelling was my favorite subject, and the roots of words. I had a photographic memory. I didn't have to study anything. That made it so pleasurable for me. I could look at something and see it. It still helps me. I loved history. I loved reading about the Indians and the Pilgrims. Geography, I loved it, but I couldn't get it in my head."

She had a deep love of animals, which she would never lose. One of them was for a stray dog she took in and named Rex. "Rex was beautiful," she said. "He had amber eyes. He was my object of love.

"There was a pack of hounds. I don't know what family owned them. They went after Rex. I remember carrying him, bloodied, up into my little room, and I tried to care for him. He thumped his tail and he died. The ground was frozen, and I couldn't dig a hole for him. So I laid him down under the railway bridge and found some old army blankets and fastened them over him with rocks, until the spring, when the ground thawed, and I buried him. I used to go down and visit him once in a while, say hello, cry. I missed him a lot. I had to be about eight years old.

"When I was a little older, I saw an advertisement in a paper or catalogue that said if you sold Cloverleaf salve, you'd get a diamond watch. So I sent away for it. They would sell you, say, twelve cans of this salve. You would sell that, and they would write to you and say, 'You have now sold so many cans, and if you sell another twelve, now you will really get the diamond watch. You almost made the mark but you didn't quite.' It was a come-on. Of course," she said, laughing, "I never got the diamond watch, but I certainly sold a lot of salve.

"I believe that, subconsciously, I always had a desire to show Min that I was going to be like my mother. And I refused to call her Mother. In fact, she beat me for not doing it. The most I would ever say was Mom, then made a bargain with myself that that didn't mean anything to me. Just so I wouldn't get beaten. But I would never call her Mother or Mama. Isn't it funny how we will make little deals with ourselves?

"That led me into an avid pursuit of studying in Bible school. That was allowed. I could take the train to Jamestown from Nortonville and go to Bible school, even though I couldn't quite believe the things they were teaching. It was a German Lutheran church, and I later heard that the pastor was a Nazi and a bund leader.

"I was sort of at the head of my class, because of two things. One, I was finding out where my Mama went. The other was that it took me away from Min for a day or two and I wouldn't get those beatings. I went maybe once a week, but not every week.

"My stepmother's home was fairly nice, and so was the rest of her family. The grandfather was all tied up with Hitler. He used to get newspapers from Germany and they would tell about this man coming up and getting the people all excited. I told him it was wrong. I knew that there was something evil about that man. I find that a little interesting for a child of ten in North Dakota to know that that was an evil man. I *knew* it."

Min's depredation continued. She would hit Norma over the head with a cast-iron skillet, beat her with a razor strap, claw her with fingernails, drag her around by her hair, and shake her confidence by telling her that her head was too small. "She was always doing a number about my hands," she said. "That they were too big. I'm still self-conscious about my hands. I force myself to forget it when I perform. And when I used to do the Revlon shows, they always took close-ups of my hands."

"A lot of things happened between the ages of eight and twelve. One of them was knowing that I would be a singer. I just knew it. There was no buildup to it. There wasn't anyone I saw and thought, 'That's what I want to be.' I just knew it. I do remember that it always felt comforting, and somehow cleansing, to sing. I'd go out to get the cows or something, especially early mornings. This is when I worked on other farms. We didn't live on a farm. In summertime until harvest, I would work with other people.

"When I had a particularly hard day's work–when I worked for other people, sometimes I cooked for thirty men–I would start a big daydream, and I'd work my way through it during the work. My biggest daydream was that one day I'd be famous, and I'd have a big car, and I would buy all these wonderful gifts, and I'd fill the car with them, and go and get my brothers and sisters. I'd see them in my daydreams and say, 'This is for you,' and they would be fabulous things, and they would be so happy, and I would be so happy.

"I didn't know how I was going to get there. I couldn't imagine. Why is it so hard to get away from nothing? I would look out at this vast expanse of flat land. There wasn't any mountain-climbing going on there!

"I used to talk to animals. I was really talking to God, wasn't I? The first conversation with God I remember was under a tree, and I remember it gave me so much comfort and courage. That always kept me sort of happy. Love is included, and wisdom, and strength, and principle. I didn't know all of that then, of course. But I realized later that that was what I was learning, and that kept me happy.

"I'd sing in the fields and I'd talk to the trees. I talked and lived with animals a great deal. I wore overalls all the time. Little girls didn't wear jeans then. I was barefoot all summer. I stepped on nails and stones. The bottoms of my feet abscessed. I lanced my own feet with my Daddy's razor. And then I tied bread and milk poultices on them. When I had appendicitis, the nearest doctor was eighteen miles away at Edgely. Later, after the operation, when I came home, Min kicked me in the stomach and opened the stitches.

"This time I thought I should tell my father. So Daddy really got into it with Min. She started beating him. She knocked him on the floor and broke a rib. She chased us both out the door with a poker. I had one overshoe. I remember Daddy saying, 'Leave it there, don't go back.' So I went with no overshoe into a blizzard. He took me to the house of some people named Bucholtz and they locked me in their house. They slipped table knives into the doorjamb to lock it. They used several, and they kept it that way for three days.

"Even the men in Nortonville were afraid of Min, and the people in the town were strong and sturdy Nordic stock.

"Daddy went back to the railroad office. Min met him down there. She missed me cleaning the house and doing all the work. So she promised faithfully she wouldn't do it any more. That's always such an empty promise with people that are cruel like that. I think somewhere in their minds they hope it might be true, but I think they also know that it's not going to be true. So Daddy came back and said she'd promised. I went back. It started again the next day."

In 1934, the railway transferred the family to a slightly larger town, Wimbledon. In the winter Norma would haul coal into the station and stoke its fires, and part of the time she ran the depot. She was now fourteen, and she was singing such songs as *Moonglow* and *Solitude*. Then a young man, a college student named Doc Haines, played Wimbledon with a band he led. Somehow she got him to hire her to sing with his band in Valley City.

"I would get a ride with a bread truck to sing with them," she said. "Then I got a radio program on KLVC." In our age of disc-jockeys and pre-recorded radio, it is hard to remember that radio stations in those days generated their own music, hiring local musicians and singers. Radio was a vast and superb training ground for talent. "I don't remember anything else I did there," she said. "Doc paid me fifty cents a night. And then the most money I'd ever made was for that sponsored radio program. It was for a restaurant. I got five dollars and all I could eat."

The moment she finished high school, she left home and, in Jamestown, got a place of her own, in the corner of a basement, with a bed and an orange crate. In those Depression days, wooden orange crates were common items of furniture, sometimes painted, sometimes skirted with cloth. Stood on end, the crates were used for storage or as bookshelves.

She sang on radio station KRMC, and then a friend arranged an audition for her on WDAY, the largest station in Fargo, a hundred miles from Jamestown. Terrified, she faced her opportunity. The station manager, a man named Ken Kennedy, summoned a pianist, presumably the station's staff pianist. With his accompaniment, she sang *These Foolish Things.* Kennedy hired her; indeed, he put her on the air that very afternoon. Such was radio in those days.

She returned to Jamestown, packed her few belongings, and left for Fargo, where she rented a room in a girls' boarding house and found several jobs. She wrapped bread in a bakery for 35 cents an hour from 4 p.m. until 4 a.m. She would go to bed about 5:30 a.m. and sleep till 9. Then she would shower and dress and hurry to WDAY and rehearse for its *Noonday Variety Show*, for each of which she was paid $1.50. Ken Kennedy, who obviously liked her, sometimes arranged for her to read commercials at 50 cents a line.

She worked briefly as a waitress in a Greek restaurant, wrote commercials for a local jeweler, played a character named Freckled Face Gertie on a show called *Hayloft Jamboree*, and did some filing work at WDAY.

She would always remember Ken Kennedy: tall, with reddish hair and a dimpled chin. He did more than give her an opportunity to sing regularly. Evidently foreseeing, if only dimly, the career ahead of her, he said, "You have to change your name. Norma Egstrom doesn't sound right. 'Ladies and gentlemen, Miss Norma Egstrom!' No, that won't do at all. Let me see. You look like a Peggy. Peggy Lynn? No—Peggy Lee!

"That's it: 'Ladies and gentlemen, Miss Peggy Lee!'"

A friend named Gladys Rasmussen who had moved to California urged her to join her there. Still dreaming of the cities and songs over the far horizon, she began telling friends she was going to go. She was certain her father would withhold his permission. To her surprise, he gave it, and even got her a pass on the railway. Now she had no choice but to go: it was a matter of her word. She sold her graduation watch for thirty dollars to her landladies in Fargo. Either it was a very good watch or her landladies were very generous. She was seventeen.

A masher tried to make time with her on the train; a Mormon woman protected her and took her sight-seeing in Salt Lake City, telling her when she left to come back, if things didn't work out in California, and stay with her family.

When Norma reached Los Angeles she had $18. She shared a room with Gladys Rasmussen, worked for a while as a waitress in Balboa, improbably became a barker at a place called FunZone, then got a job singing at a Chinese restaurant called the Jade on Hollywood Boulevard.

One night a customer offered to drive her home, but instead and over her protests took her to a sleazy club in downtown Los Angeles. Another man moved into their booth and as her abductor got drunker, said, "I'm going to get you out of here." But as they tried to leave, the drunk roused himself and started a fight with her protector who, fortunately, won it. He took her to his car and, when they had left the area, told her she had barely missed disappearing forever into the world of white slavery. He left her at her rooming house. She never learned his name.

She made only two dollars a night at the Jade and, finally, ill, decided to go home. She lived with her sister Marianne, who was supporting their siblings, in Hillsboro, North Dakota. Then she moved back to Fargo. Her mentor Ken Kennedy introduced her to the family who owned the Powers Hotel and Coffee Shop. They gave her a job singing for $15 a week, and she moved her siblings to Fargo to live with her.

With Peggy Lee, as she was now known, as their singer, the Powers Hotel was attracting audiences. The rival hotel, grandly called Le Chateau, hired a singer from Minneapolis to compete with her. Instead of competing, they became very close friends and would remain so for life. The singer's name was Jane Larrabee, but professionally she was known as Jane Leslie. Some years later, Peggy would introduce her to jazz critic and songwriter Leonard Feather, and she would marry him.

Again Ken Kennedy affected Peg's life. He told her he thought he could get her a job singing with a band led by his cousin, Sev Olson, in Minneapolis. Jane by then had returned to Minneapolis. Peg auditioned for Olson and made the move to the bigger city, living in what seemed to her wanton luxury at the Radisson Hotel. Then the Will Osborne band came to town. Osborne auditioned and hired her, and she went on the road. In St. Louis she fell ill again and underwent a tonsillectomy. While she was in the hospital, the Osborne band broke up, and she drove to California with the band's manager and pianist. She was welcomed by her old friends at the Jade, and met a lyricist named Jack Brooks (who wrote *Ole Buttermilk Sky* with Hoagy Carmichael). He recommended her for a job at a Palm Springs restaurant called the Doll House. There she was heard by a couple named Freddie and Lois Mandel, of Chicago. Freddie Mandel owned Mandel's department store in Chicago and, as well, the Detroit Tigers. Impressed by her singing, they arranged for Frank Bering to hear her. Bering and a partner owned the Ambassador East and West hotels in Chicago. Bering hired her to sing in the Buttery at the Ambassador West.

"The night before I left Los Angeles," she said, "I had my ticket but I had no money. I hadn't thought to ask for that. I remember spending the night in an all-night theater downtown, on skid row, with all the bums and smoke. I was so frightened. I had maybe a couple of dollars, but I had put it in my bra." She laughed. "That wasn't a very good place to put it. I don't even remember having a purse.

"I called Janey or I sent her a wire. I think I said something about coming to Chicago right away and bringing *Wishing. Wishing* was her big number. That was our running joke.

"She came to Chicago. I was overjoyed. I hadn't eaten. "

Bering had given her rooms at the hotel. "The hotel was beautiful," she said. "I was always impressed by carpets. Thick carpets always stood for something. I was shown to the suite. I don't know how grand it was, but to me it certainly was. Janey came in the next day, and she didn't have any money to speak of either. Her mother had sent along a box of date-filled cookies, and we lived on them for however long they lasted, maybe two or three days. And all we had to do was pick up the phone! We could have had anything under glass.

"She must have had a *little* money, because we went out once and had some kind of a dinner at a place called the Cotton Patch.

"We were living in the lap of luxury, but we weren't eating. I could have ordered room service *ad infinitum*, but I didn't. I thought I had to pay for it. I must have been really funny, with all that extreme naivete.

"Two of the maids used to bring food in from room service—hot rolls and coffee and butter. Fifteen or twenty years later, I was there to play at the Chicago Opera House in a musical review, and I saw these two maids in the hall. They were named Iris and Tillie. Now I was a guest there. And I was going to make spaghetti for my musicians. I went to get the maids to get a knife to cut the onions or something. And there they were, and I said, 'Come on in, and let's have some coffee.' They were so sweet. They came in and sat down and I said, 'There's something I've been trying to figure out all these years.' One of them had a very Irish accent. She said, 'What was it?' I said, 'How did you know we were hungry?' And she said, 'Well, we didn't see nothin' goin' in and we didn't see nothin' comin' out. So we decided we'd better feed you.'

"The Mandels introduced me to Chicago society. They had a party for me at their house in Lake Forest. It was my first champagne, and it made me sick.

"Mlle Oppenheimer lent me gowns to perform in. I think Lois Mandel was a very good customer. And I was like a model for the clothes. I felt very elegant.

"I remember that one night an artist came in to the Buttery. He was sitting in the front row, sketching me. I had no idea that he was the famous Diego Rivera. And he did a portrait of me. But he made my bust so large that I gave it away! Oh, the fortunes I have given away!

"The audience was one big ear. It was wonderful.

"Down the street from the Ambassador West, there was a little coffee shop or something. I was sitting at a table drinking a Coke and the juke-box was playing Sinatra's *This Love of Mine*. I stopped cold. You know how it is when you hear someone and know you're always going to love their work. It plasters you up against the wall. I had no idea that I would meet him, become friends, and neighbors. I had no idea I was going to meet any of those people."

During this period she would slip over to the nightclub area of Rush Street, a short distance away, where she made friends with, among others, the drummer Baby Dodds. And she was being discovered. Glenn Miller, Claude Thornhill, Charlie Barnet, and others were coming by the Buttery to hear her. One night Benny Goodman came in with Lady Alice Duckworth, who had been married to a member of the British aristocracy. Her maiden name was Hammond. She was related to the Vanderbilts, and her brother was John Hammond, the record producer and discoverer of talent. Goodman would eventually marry her, to the eternal mystification of musicians who liked her but didn't like him.

With Goodman and Lady Duckworth was pianist Mel Powell, who was playing in and writing for the Goodman band. He was a seasoned musician; and he was eighteen years old.

Goodman was about to lose his star vocalist, Helen Forrest, to the Harry James band. Peg was sure that Goodman hated her singing; he simply stared at her, his face blank, then left.

The next day, Jane told Peggy that Goodman had telephoned. Peg was incredulous.

"Well, I'm telling you," Jane said. "You should return the call. What can you lose?" Peggy called and asked for Mr. Goodman. The voice said that this was Mr. Goodman. She gave her name and asked if he had called.

He said, "Yes I did. I want to know if you'd like to join my band."

Goodman, typically, gave her no time for rehearsal: he was famous for lack of consideration and sometimes downright cruelty to musicians. He told her to wear something pretty and come to the job. The band was playing at the College Inn. Later, she often reflected on the help Mel Powell gave her. Mel, a native New Yorker, remembers his first sight of her: "this gorgeous blonde Scandinavian from the deep midwest."

"I don't know how I'd have done it without Mel," Peg said. Fortunately, she knew all the songs, but they were in Helen Forrest's keys.

"When I first started singing with Benny," she said, "I immediately caught a psychosomatic cold, because I was confused. And frightened.

"And then I realized that I was trying to fill the shoes of Helen Forrest, which were golden slippers. She was very much loved, justifiably so. And

I couldn't quite imagine that I was going to take the place of someone I'd been playing and listening to. Whenever I had an extra nickel, it went into the jukebox. And it was Benny. Or it was Tommy Dorsey. I was listening to Frank Sinatra sing *This Love of Mine*. Oh!"

"Peggy must have been a nervous wreck," Mel Powell said many years later. "Her first assignment was to make a recording. Columbia Records, to whom Benny was contracted, always came out to wherever the band was playing. So they arrived in Chicago to record. There Peg was, making a recording with Benny Goodman just a day or two after she joined the band.

"She met producer John Hammond in the control room, and he handed her the sheet music for *Elmer's Tune*. This was a pretty tough rap for a kid. There was no taping in those days. You just made records. If you blew something, you started from the beginning. You didn't say, 'Well let's take it from measure 39 and splice it.' She was so nervous. The sheet music John handed her made such a racket, and they didn't have high-tech ways of beating that, so, unfortunately, it sounded like a forest fire that was going on over the brass, over the saxophones.

"Peggy had probably been up all night learning this thing, and then she came in, and the arrangement was disorienting, because *Elmer's Tune* was very clever, very fancy, full of stuff.

"I led her into an adjacent studio and we sat down and ran through a couple of things that were in the arrangement, especially the cues for her. . . . I was cuing her about where she came in, and told her that during the recording of the arrangement, I could always improvise something.

"I also told her, 'You're going to have your first tone, Benny won't know, nobody will know. I'm just gonna pop that in there in the midst of what seems to be just a ramble over the band while the band's playing. You catch it from that; that'll be your cue, count four and go.' Well, I think she's never forgotten it."

Nor has she ever forgotten his kindness. They remain friends to this day.

Her opening with the band received scathing reviews. *Down Beat* ran her picture with the caption "Sweet sixteen and will never be missed." So hard on her were these first days with the band that she told Goodman, "I'd like to quit, please."

Goodman gave her his cool stare and said, "I won't let you."

Goodman took her to 52nd Street to hear such performers as Fats Waller. Waller was the first celebrity whose autograph she obtained. Soon she met Count Basie, whose broadcasts from Kansas City she had listened to so avidly in her strange and, to me, darkly haunted childhood. She met Duke Ellington and Louis Armstrong.

She carried a portable windup phonograph on which to play her favorite records. One of these was Lil Green's *Why Don't You Do Right?*–

words and music by Joe McCoy, publishing date 1942. "Benny heard me playing the record in my dressing room," she said. "He could hardly help it, I was always playing it. Finally he asked me, 'You really like that song, don't you? Would you like to sing that with the band?'

The song was recorded at Liederkranz Hall in New York, Columbia's favorite studio and the favorite of many performers as well. The record wasn't released for two years, however. She was earning $75 a week out of which she had to pay her living expenses. She was paid $10 for the recording session, with no provision for royalties. That was the standard contractual arrangement: the royalties went to the bandleader.

The song is a tough-minded statement by a woman to a feckless man who is unable to get his hands on money enough to support her: "Get outa here, and get me some money too." Peg could not possibly have known it at the time, but in that song she was setting the direction of her career: a remarkable gallery of portraits of women in the miniature drama form that is the popular song; or at least the best kind of popular song. In all the good ones, there is a keen sense of character, and in selecting that one, she displayed some sort of instinct about how the particular evokes the general. Why that song about the denizens of a kind of under-culture should touch people who knew nothing of it is puzzling, but it did, and that recording still sells, more than half a century after it was made.

The work with Goodman was gruelling. The Paramount theater in New York is notorious in the memory of everyone who played it. They hated it, and those who survive still do. They played seven or eight shows a day, between movies, starting at 10 a.m. And at one point, Peg remembered, the band was adding to that schedule a set at the Terrace Room of the New Yorker Hotel. There was never time for a meal: the musicians survived on sandwiches brought to them by Popsy Randolph, the band boy, later a well-known photographer. Yet the experience was invaluable. She was absorbing lessons no school can teach, things that go deep into the subconscious, into the viscera, even into muscle memory.

"Johnny said something someplace," Peg said to me in one of our conversations. There was no need to specify who Johnny was. To both of us, there was one Johnny: Mercer. "It had to do with sudden fame being so dangerous. So many people have sudden fame and they can't handle that. If you have to pay your dues, you have to do it.

"I used to call Benny Goodman's band boot camp. A finishing school.

"Time has to pass. You need a lot of experience. You learn as you go. You crawl before you walk before you run. You know how to handle a situation on the stage when some crisis comes up. If it's early in your career someplace, it doesn't matter because very few people are going to see it or hear about it, and it won't be in the trades the next day: So-and-so bombed. That's the heavy advantage of learning how to handle your stage presence by the experience you've had. If you do even a high-school play and the butler doesn't come in when he's supposed to, you learn to improvise. Or if your gown gets caught on the heel of your shoe, you learn to lean on the piano while somebody crawls under there and unfastens it.

"I had one silly thing happen like that once. I was wearing a spaghetti-strap gown with a sheath. I was singing, Max Bennett was playing the bass. He was going to dig in and really play it. And he being such a proper musician, so immaculate about everything he did, somehow managed to get his hand *under* the strings. I laughed so hard that I broke the strap of my gown. I quickly grabbed; I put my hand where most people think their heart is, and held that part of my gown up, and said to Lou Levy, who was my accompanist and music director, 'Excuse me, I'll be right back. Play something while I'm gone. Play *Bye Bye Blackbird*.' The gown was black. Lou played *Ding Dong, the Witch Is Dead.* I can still see the whole scene.

"You learn to make light of something. If you ever take it seriously on the stage, the audience becomes nervous. But if you can make a joke out of it, you're in business.

"If you have a heckler, you're fine as long as you don't do anything. The audience is with you. But just say one angry thing to the heckler.... Well, maybe you can later on, when you have some seniority. But you let the audience handle the heckler. I have seen audiences turn as one on really fine performers, because they started to dress the heckler down. It's important for young singers to learn this. And you can only get it from experience."

In 1942, about a year after Peg joined the Goodman "boot camp," Goodman hired a new guitarist, Dave Barbour. Peg seldom to this day refers to him as anything but "David." He was born David Michael Barbour on Long Island, New York, on May 28, 1912, and was thus eight years her senior. Barbour had already enjoyed a full career before joining Goodman. He worked with Wingy Manone in 1934, Red Norvo in 1934 and '35, Bunny Berigan in 1936, and Louis Armstrong in 1936 and '38. He was in considerable demand as a studio musician, primarily as a rhythm guitarist, though he was, when he chose to be, a graceful and thoughtful soloist.

Photos show that he was extremely handsome. And Peg fell in love with him almost instantly. Peg said, "David was very dapper. He wore the right kind of tweed jacket, and the birdseye shirt, and the thin knit tie, and always the right haircut." He was also a little eccentric, with a wild sense of humor. What she didn't know is that he had a drinking problem, although once she found him all but helpless in his hotel room just before a performance. A doctor sobered him up enough to play.

They were married in 1943, and left the Goodman band to settle in Los Angeles. There had always been a conflict in Peg: although she loved to sing, performing made her nervous, hardly an uncommon dichotomy.

Peg and David found a modest apartment in Los Angeles. By now *Why Don't You Do Right?* was an international hit, and she was constantly receiving offers, which she would turn down, ecstatic about her married life. Then she learned she was pregnant. She told her husband, "David, we're going to have a baby."

He paused, she recalled, then said, "Why, Peg, I hardly know you!" and smiled.

"Women do have a rough time," she said, remembering her pregnancy. "They have to take so much responsibility. After procreation is finished, he says, 'Excuse me, I'm going down to get the papers,' or something. A woman has this period of time to go through, and all of the changes in her body, and all of the emotions that they're not quite ready for, not quite ready to have the child just now. It's not convenient. But they have to go through with it. And then in about two or two-and-a-half months, they begin to love that child.

"I like it when I see men taking an interest in a child before it's born. They don't always. And the girl wanders around looking a little funnier and funnier, and the man always tells her she's beautiful. And she is. She has a certain radiance about her, because there is a life force. But then she has to look forward to who's going to take care of the child. How is she going to manage? Has she ever had a child before? Does she know how to take care of the baby? Is there someone she can go to and say, 'Will you watch my baby while I go to the store?'"

They named their daughter Nicole, but she soon was known as Nicki, a bright and beautiful little girl whom David Barbour adored. So did Peg. "I was a fearless child," Peg said. "But I became a jellyfish when Nicki was born. She was so precious to me that I didn't sleep the first year of her life."

As far as Peg was concerned, her performing days were over. And then Dave Dexter of Capitol records planned a multiple-disc album, a rarity in those days, except in the classical field with symphonies issued on several twelve-inch 78 rpm records. It was unprecedented in jazz. He asked her to be a part of it.

Peg thought, "Well I suppose I could get a baby-sitter and go down and sing a couple of songs."

The personnel of the album, to be titled *New American Jazz,* was a loose group pseudonymed the Capitol Jazzmen. It was not the same on all the records, but collectively it included Dave Barbour or Nappy Lamare, guitar; Shorty Sherock or Billy May, trumpet; Barney Bigard or Jimmy

Noone, clarinet; Dave Matthews or Eddie Miller, tenor; Les Robinson; alto; Artie Shapiro or Hank Wayland, bass; Zutty Singleton, drums; Jack Teagarden, trombone and vocal; and Joe Sullivan or Pete Johnson or Stan Wrightsman, piano.

Peg went into the studio on January 7, 1944, as the war was grinding to a close, and recorded two songs, a blues called *Ain't Goin' No Place* and the standard by Lew Brown and Sammy Fain, *That Old Feeling.* Instead of piano, Stan Wrightsman played celeste on the latter, and Eddie Miller contributed a lovely tenor saxophone solo.

Peg had no need to prove she could sing a ballad. With Goodman she had recorded, among other things, *All I Need Is You, Everything I Love,* and *How Long Has This Been Going On?* But the intimacy of the small-group setting, with Wrightsman's delicate celeste, let her go deeply into *That Old Feeling.*

Given the nature of her childhood, she had more than enough pain to draw on, and humor too—it is often overlooked that Peg is an extremely funny singer, and, in private, she is a witty and humorous woman. I once asked her if, in her moments of later triumph, dressed in gorgeous gowns and singing to vast audiences of ardent admirers, she ever thought back in mid-phrase, as it were, to that childhood.

"Oh yes," she said. "Often. My memories all served me well. I used it all later, the emotion I felt, singing. I understood the feeling, and so it was incorporated into my interpretation.

"It seems as if I really haven't understood myself. It's only in retrospect that we understand. We look back and say, 'Oh, that's what that meant!' Walter Matthau said somewhere that I was a Stanislavskian singer and that I reminded him of Marlon Brando. I didn't know how to take it at the time. I do now. I should call him and say, 'Thank you.'"

Dave Barbour felt strongly that she should not give up her career. He said that she would later regret it if she did. And the esteem in which *That Old Feeling* rapidly came to be held fortified his argument.

Peg had begun to write lyrics, encouraged by Johnny Mercer. Capitol Records at that time was housed in a little office above tailor Sy Devore's shop—a chaotic office, from all accounts, with Glenn Wallichs on the phone drumming up sales and Mercer indifferent to them, interested only in the music and always wanting to hear it loud. In that office Peg and Dave Barbour were offered contracts with the label and accepted. Dave would frequently conduct her record dates. Then there came a question of material.

During her pregnancy, she'd had an idea, while doing housework, for a lyric. She was vibrantly happy at that moment and the phrase, "Well, it's a good day!" popped into her head. She soon drafted a lyric and melody. When Dave got home, he harmonized it. She wrote another song with Barbour, *I Don't Know Enough About You*, and they recorded it December 26, 1945. *It's a Good Day* for some reason wasn't recorded until July 12, 1946.

In common with many artists, and probably all the good ones, Peg is often discontented with her work. More than forty years after she recorded it, she told me: "I don't like part of the lyric to *It's a Good Day*. The lines about 'for curing your ills. Take a deep breath and throw away your pills.' I don't like that, partly because I wish it were possible to throw away all the medicines I have to take! But mostly because it sounds a little corny to me."

Barbour had quit drinking when they were married. But now his drinking resumed. And it had grown worse. "I knew I was in big trouble," Peg said. Barbour had a taste for boilermakers, bourbon with a beer chaser. Peg claims that he even fed bourbon to the goldfish. She would try to extract him early from the parties they attended, watching as his flash point approached. She worried more when he developed ulcers.

She said, "There was a shyness about him that wouldn't let him accept compliments or anything."

Her single 78 rpm records came out in a steady stream, hit after hit: *Waiting for the Train to Come in, Golden Earrings*, and a new version of *Why Don't You Do Right?* recorded November 19, 1947. Norma Deloris Egstrom was now one of the biggest stars in the profession, and the sales of her records and those of Nat Cole were the foundation on which Capitol Records was built.

It became politically correct in jazz-criticism circles to say that her work was derived from that of Billie Holiday, but that is demonstrably not so.

She said, "Mel Powell played me the first Billie Holiday record I ever heard, which was in 1941. That was after my style was set. Then I met her and absolutely adored her. She would say, 'Hey, Peg, how's Nicki?' I can see her, just the way she was. I wrote a lyric called *She Wore a Flower in Her Hair*. She had the deepest kind of eyes. Dave and I gave a party for her. Duke Ellington was there, Tallulah Bankhead was there. It was Ralph Watkins' place, the Royal Roost, in New York. We were very big then." She laughed. "We were bigger than Sonny and Cher! We were Mr. and Mrs. Music."

"Bigger than Bonnie and Clyde," I said, and she laughed even louder. Her laughter is joyous and unrestrained.

You realize how different the two styles are when you hear Peg deliberately imitate Holiday. She has a great gift for mimicry (and various foreign dialects) and when she imitates Billie Holiday, in speech or in singing, the effect is uncanny.

Pianist Lou Levy, her accompanist and conductor over a longer period of time than any other, said, "Norman Granz, Ella Fitzgerald, Oscar Peterson, and I went to hear her at Basin Street East in New York. We were all leaving for Europe with Jazz at the Philharmonic. I had just worked with her, and we all knew her. She did her tribute to Billie Holiday. By the time she was halfway through it, Norman, Ella, and Oscar were all in tears. It was that accurate. It was eerie. I guess I was the only one who didn't cry because I was dumbstruck by what was going on. She scared Count Basie to death with it."

"I used to do it," Peg said. "But it brought so many people to tears that I stopped."

She was learning constantly, and to polish her work, she engaged choreographer Nick Castle.

"Nick would never really tell me any physical things to do," she said. "I kept saying, 'Nick, I want to move.' And he would say, 'You move enough. I just want to hear you sing.' Nick was a very wise man. He taught Mickey Rooney, Judy Garland, you name it right down the line. He used to say, when we'd rehearse, 'I shouldn't take any money for this. I just enjoy hearing you sing.' I used to love it when he'd walk into a rehearsal and throw out a big kiss to everybody with both hands and say, 'Now share that amongst you.'

"He had a great sense of humor. He was very warm, and very inspiring. Once Anna White came in to check me out. She said, 'I don't have anything to tell you. Maybe on that one little note, make a little motion with your finger.' And I thought, 'What's wrong with me?' A shyness came out, I think. I thought, 'What am I doing wrong?'

"That was in the '50s.'"

This conversation occurred as we were watching videos of two of her television shows at her home in Belair. She wore a tight, stark black gown in one, an equally tight white one in the other, and she had a gorgeous, voluptuous figure. I noticed in these shows something I had first paid attention to when she would play the Copacabana in New York: the minimal use of motion. Such, however, was the effectiveness of the focus she established that if she cocked an eyebrow, the whole audience would laugh at the minute expression.

So, watching her stand almost motionless, singing, on television, I said, "Peg, where the hell do you get the courage to do *absolutely nothing*?"

There was a long pause. Then she said, "There is power in stillness."

Then: "I do a little meditation before I go out on the stage," she said. "I didn't always do that. But the last thirty, forty years, I've done it. I stomp my foot as I'm announced, just once. It's like a demand. There's a burst of energy that almost lifts my body up. And some people tell me they think I look taller on the stage.

"I don't know what it is, but when I would walk on stage, I could feel myself get taller. It was as though there were a rubber band in my spine. Whatever that is, it's the inner me coming out. I ask for my inner self to step forward and shine. At the same time, of course, the lights come on, and they add to that. But the biggest thing that happens is an inner experience. I think there's probably a jolt of adrenalin. The whole body responds. And the body is the temple of the living God.

"I think it's because that is a moment of *very* necessary humility—when you know that you can't even take the next breath without that beautiful spirit that lives inside of you. Unless the spirit is willing, you don't have anything to do out there."

And she added: "I have outlived the intimidation."

She and David were now managed by Carlos Gastel, at that time so visible that he was a celebrity in his own right. "He was a very large man," Peg said. "His nickname, which he knew—it was no secret—was the Aga Khan. He was from Honduras. That was another nickname: the Honduran. He was well educated.

"Carlos had his own boat, a power boat. David and he were drinking buddies. I used to go along with Carlos and David on the boat to protect them from burning themselves up. They had a kind of burner stove on the boat. We had one really bad fire."

Barbour's drinking finally resulted in bleeding duodenal ulcers. He was hospitalized in grave condition. But he recovered—because of prayer, Peg believes.

When he left the hospital, they drove to Rosarita Beach in Baja California. They were impressed by the relaxed attitude of the Mexican people, in contrast to the frenetic activity of the show-business Los Angeles world that had become their natural habitat. David had a guitar with him, of course. And together they wrote *Mañana*, which they recorded soon after returning home. It was an immediate hit, with sales running into the millions. In later years, it would become controversial, with accusations that it was condescending to the Mexican people. Peg denies this, saying it was written in admiration.

Peg and David, who were living in a house they had built, now sold it and purchased a much bigger house, in French Norman style, in Westwood Hills. Her expanding circle of friends and acquaintances included many of her heroes from her childhood, among them Al Jolson, Bing Crosby, and Jimmy Durante.

Gastel's client list now included Woody Herman, who had just folded his big band and organized a small group. The group was to play an engagement at the Tropicana in Havana, Cuba. Gastel had now brought Woody to Capitol, and for the Cuban trip, Woody had hired Dave Barbour.

"I know Woody would never do anything to hurt me," Peg said. "And I was told that Woody had asked Dave to go on the Cuban trip. I'm not sure it wasn't the other way around. Or possibly Carlos Gastel arranged it. It was like Carlos to send David off someplace over Christmas and New Year's."

While David was in Cuba with Woody, Peg worked on preparing a studio for him over their garage. "I kept busy," Peg said. "I had all kinds of hobbies. I liked refinishing furniture, hand-painting it. While he was away, I worked on that studio. It was a private place where he could go and practice, with a sycamore weeping over the window, and a little balcony. I had a chair that I sandpapered and sandpapered. Then I rubbed color into it, I rubbed some gold into it. And I had 'The Happy Chair' printed on the back of it."

During this time, her father paid her a visit, told her that Min hadn't changed, and one night in tears said, "I haven't been much of a father to you." Then he went home. The next year, North Dakota gave Peg a statewide homecoming. The visit was the last time she would see her father: he died the following April.

Peg tried to get David to join Alcoholics Anonymous, but he wouldn't. Finally, afraid Nicki would see him in one of his darker tunnels of drinking, Barbour begged Peg to divorce him. "I didn't want to divorce David," she told me. "He insisted on it. He made me do it, and it was the hardest thing I ever did in my life. I never wanted anything less than that divorce." So loving were she and David at the legal hearing that the judge asked if they were there for a marriage or divorce. The night Peg gave him the divorce papers, Dave Barbour performed an odd act: he removed the strings from five guitars that he owned.

He remarried, but only for a short time. Money by then was no problem. His royalties from the hit songs they had written were considerable. He and Peg remained close. Peg said, "After he moved to Malibu, he came to the house one day looking so sad, and so pitiful. And he said, 'May I borrow that happy chair?'

"He took it out to Malibu. I don't know what happened to it. I think he thought that if he sat in that chair, some of my happiness or strength would rub off. And I always hated the idea of getting strong on someone else's weakness. It made me cry. I would run to my books and learn something and get through that period of sadness, and then I'd realize that that strength must be a trial to him. Because he wasn't getting stronger at that time. Later he did."

In the 1950s, Peg toured, playing New York's Copacabana so many times she lost count, played the Sands in Las Vegas, and continued to record one successful LP after another. She also wrote songs for films. With composer Sonny Burke, she wrote all the songs for the 1955 Disney animated cartoon feature *Lady and the Tramp*, and sang most of the voice parts, including Si and Am, the Siamese cats.

Curiously, one of her biggest hits, *Lover*, was not made for Capitol. She had an idea for an up-tempo version of the song with a complex Latin rhythm section giving the impression of a herd of galloping horses. Capitol's executives turned her down on the grounds that Les Paul and Mary Ford had just had a hit on the same tune. Her contract was expiring. She left Capitol and signed with Decca, who permitted her to make the record, which became a huge hit.

But the association with Decca was not as comfortable as that with Capitol, and after a five-year absence, she returned to the label, which had long since moved from its chaotic offices above Sy Devore's store to its round tower, designed to look like a stack of records, on Vine Street. Her producer and close friend Dave Cavanaugh took a notion from the success of *Lover* to do two albums titled *Latin à la Lee* and *Olé à la Lee*. The *Latin* album won a Grammy award in 1960.

Victor Young, the film composer, approached her about writing with him. Their collaboration produced *Where Can I Go Without You?*, which she recorded on February 7, 1963.

All the while, she was building her own classic repertoire, a gallery of women characters that really begins with her recording for Goodman of *Why Don't You Do Right?* To watch her in a concert or nightclub performance proceed through a whole gallery of characters is to take a lesson in acting. It is no accident that she was nominated for an Academy Award for her portrayal of a fading nightclub singer of the 1920s in Jack Webb's picture *Pete Kelly's Blues*. She hoped that this would open the way to a broader career in films, but it never happened, which is one of the disappointments in her otherwise starry career.

Peggy recorded (on October 17, 1958) one of Edith Piaf's songs, *My Man*. She gives us a vivid picture of a beaten creature who for whatever reason continues to endure life with an abusive man.

One of her most brilliant portrayals of a woman is the Johnny Mercer lyric (to a French tune) *When the World Was Young*, a striking picture of a world-weary demimondaine, plaything of rich men, yearning for the simple apple-blossomed sunlit days of her youth. It is one of Mercer's greatest lyrics, and one of her finest records.

Her stationery and often her advertising have long borne the inscription "Miss Peggy Lee," the very name Ken Kennedy gave her in Fargo, pointedly asserting identity as a woman.

The character in *I'm a Woman*, by her friends Jerry Leiber and Mike Stoller, recorded November 14, 1962, is not the one we encounter in *My Man*. This is no brow-beaten victim but, on the contrary, a woman boasting of her prowess at the complex of tasks that society imposes on her sex. *Big Spender*, recorded October 27, 1965, vividly conveys the mockery of a hooker putting the mark on a john, and Peg sounds truly hardbitten in her performance.

Another song in this gallery is *You Came a Long Way from St. Louis*, by John Benson Brooks and Bob Russell, which she recorded May 28, 1959. Again, it portrays a woman skeptical about a man's accomplishments. The lady in the song may be on a higher social plane than the girl in *Why Don't You Do Right?*, but the two have a lot in common in their refusal to be taken in by a man's tall tales and attempts to impress.

Happiness Is a Thing Called Joe, another portrait of a woman, this one by Harold Arlen and Yip Harburg, was recorded April 4, 1957. It is notable, among other things, for the identity of her conductor on the date: Frank Sinatra.

Yet another portrait of a woman, although this was not particularly intended to be the case, is *The Right to Love*. It is a song I wrote in collaboration with composer Lalo Schifrin, and although I did not intend the lyric to be what we might call gender specific, the fact is that it has been recorded mostly by women. Peg was the first to do so. Carmen McRae picked it up from Peg's record, and so did Nancy Wilson. The song is about social rejection because of love. Carmen used to discuss it at length before performing it in a club, pointing out that the rejection could be for any reason whatever that violated society's mores, including race. This is indeed what I intended in the lyric, back in the 1960s after Quincy Jones told me it was impossible to get away with writing a song about a mixed racial relationship.

Curiously, for all the years Peg and I have been friends, this is the only lyric of mine she has ever recorded, although she has performed others in nightclubs and elsewhere, including *Yesterday I Heard the Rain*. Her performance of it one night at the Copacabana in New York gave me chills.

Don't Smoke in Bed, which she recorded on December 2, 1947, is the work of Willard Robison, whose songs superbly evoke images of America, including *Old Folks* and *Guess I'll Go Back Home This Summer*, and of troubled family life, such as *A Cottage for Sale. Don't Smoke in Bed* is another portrait of a woman, one who is leaving a man but doing it with heartbreak. Almost certainly the song reflect's Peg's feelings over her troubled relationship with Dave Barbour. Peg wrote much of this lyric, but left the credit and the royalties with Robison.

She was still visiting Dave Barbour at Malibu, making sure that he ate properly. She remarried, three times and never for long: to actor Brad Dexter, percussionist Jack del Rio, and actor Dewey Martin. "It was always Dave," Jane Feather said.

Once their daughter Nicki gave her a jolt of reality in talking of her father, as much as she loved him. She said, "Mother, you're dealing with a child."

Peg said, "For the last thirteen years of his life, Dave didn't have a drop to drink. He asked me to marry him again. We were going to be remarried, and he had a physical. His doctor told him he was in excellent condition. Four days later, the aorta burst in his heart, and he died."

David Michael Barbour died at Malibu on December 11, 1965. He was fifty-three. His death was another in the long series of blows to her life and her emotions. And all of it finds its way into her work. In her seventies, she continued to perform, despite a series of health problems, including cardiac trouble that necessitated open heart surgery.

Because her performances are at a low level of dynamics, it is sometimes assumed that she has no power. She has power to spare. She just won't use it, for reasons of personal style and aesthetic consistency.

"Each individual voice has its own quality," she said to me once. "It's like a fingerprint. I remember when they used to say, 'Oh, using a microphone!' If I want to lay back and let one fly, I can do it, but it would offend my own ears. What you learn about the microphone is to comfortably amplify the little subtleties within the makeup of the voice."

She might have added that microphones exaggerate the flaws in singing, as well as bringing forth the virtues.

I asked her once whether stardom did not impose problems for a woman, especially a singer, in dealing with men. A singer has to be in control, and for the most part her accompanists are going to be men, who may resent her. If the musicians make a mistake, the audience tends to blame the star. A singer is out there all alone.

"Yes," Peg said. "The musicians have their sheet music, and they can look at it. *You're* looking at the air."

She chuckled: "That's why I came up with the idea that my favorite color is plaid. That's because of the diplomacy I would have to use, and the psychology necessary with men, so that I wouldn't offend them. For many, many, many years!"

"But generally the musicians are on your side."

Well, shall we say, they're on *her* side, because of her sheer professionalism and competence. Pianist Mike Renzi, who has worked with her often as accompanist and music director, said, "Aside from anything else, she has incredible time." It is a quality jazz musicians value almost above all others.

No musician has worked as pianist and conductor with Peg as much as Lou Levy, "my good gray fox," as she has always called him because of his white hair.

"Peggy Lee became half my life, and in a way still is," Lou said. "I spent fifteen years, off and on, mostly on, playing for her. I learned from her about as much about sensitivity towards music as I ever have in any situation in my life. Because it didn't involve just playing the piano. It involved lighting, staging, scripting and format.

"I learned so much through her about sensitivity in accompanying, and paying attention to lyrics, and to the whole package. Not just the chord changes. And finding what far-out chord I could play instead of this one. This was the real truth.

"When I *really* learned the value of a lyric was when I worked for her, because she is such a dramatic performer. She becomes an actress when she sings. Then I became her conductor. And you have to be really on the ball to do that. You don't just react. You listen. You pay attention. You pay attention to dynamics. Because it's different from night to night or even show to show. I learned a lot from her."

To which Peg commented, when I told her what Lou had said: "When someone says they've learned a lot from me, especially someone I respect and admire as much as I do Lou Levy, I'm always overcome–surprised and overwhelmed.

"Because when you're working together, the work takes over, and you don't notice. You put your heads and hearts together, and out of this you get a multi-dimensional view of the performance and how the audience is experiencing it.

"The other day I received a note from Lou. It was the nicest, kindest, most loving note. I got the impression that he considered those years a very special period of his life. We had a wonderful relationship. We were so sensitive to each other.

"There was a thing that happened at the Copa. I was singing *Lover* with the full orchestra. At that speed it is going by so fast and I made a mistake. I skipped a chorus. And the entire orchestra, without anyone saying anything, skipped it too! It was amazing. An entire orchestra. And there's a key change in there. They caught all of it!"

Peg's home in Belair is exquisitely decorated in the kind of faultless taste her work would lead you to expect: the carpets are deep and excellent art covers its walls. Her correspondence and telephone conversations maintain contact with friends all over the world. Her constant companion is a strikingly intuitive gray cat she calls Baby, who adores her.

One day when I was visiting her—she was sitting up in bed, clad in a pink bed jacket, recovering from a bout of illness, and had ordered tea for me—she said, "I have known so many different kinds of love. I'm very lucky."

Luck had very little to do with it.

Sweetest Voice in the World
Ella Fitzgerald

A little girl stood transfixed, eyes wide, in a California supermarket, listening as a woman wearing thick glasses leaned toward her and sang in a voice of incomparable sweetness, "Do you know the Muffin Man?"

Whether the girl's mother recognized the singer is impossible to say; the child certainly didn't. The girl was listening to the voice of Ella Fitzgerald, famous around the world. I remember getting off an airplane in the small Chilean coastal town of Arica in 1962 and hearing that voice coming from a sound system somewhere.

Ella Fitzgerald recalled: "The little girl's mother said, 'Please don't stop. Just keep on.' And then there was a little boy who followed me all around in a store, when I sang to him. And that knocks me out. I just *love* children, and I hate to see anybody do anything to hurt them. The store where I go, the kids like me to sing. They wait for me to do a song in Spanish.

"I am a sucker for children. I'll stop on the street and sing for them."

From the stage of the Apollo theater in 1934 to the late days of her life, recording a title track for a Japanese movie or simply performing for her own delight to children, Ella Fitzgerald sang in public for fifty-eight years. Hers was doubtless the longest singing career in American music, popular, jazz, concert, or any other kind of music, and it certainly is one of the most illustrious. More than a few critics have referred to her work as genius.

Occasionally through the years there has been debate over whether Ella Fitzgerald truly was a "jazz singer." If a flair for the blues is part of the definition of "jazz singer," then it didn't fit Ella Fitzgerald, whose career has been devoted almost entirely to the great American songwriters. In 1956, her manager and record producer, Norman Granz, began recording with her a series of two-LP "songbook" albums on the work of these composers and lyricists. During the next twelve years, she made so many of these albums that even she wasn't sure how many there were—albums devoted to Duke Ellington, Harold Arlen, Rodgers and Hart, Cole Porter, Jerome Kern, Johnny Mercer, George and Ira Gershwin, and more. All were successful, and some of them made the hit charts. They have been reissued in an elaborately annotated sixteen-CD package by Verve Records.

If, however, an ability to improvise vocally is part of the definition of a "jazz singer," then it assuredly fits Ella Fitzgerald, whose ability to scat sing with impeccable rhythmic imagination and accurate intonation at high speed was incomparable. Yet in the songbook albums, she sang the songs very straight, with minimal embellishment.

Ira Gershwin told writer George T. Simon, "I never knew how good our songs were until I heard Ella Fitzgerald sing them." Actually, she sings them so simply and well that one becomes aware of how cute and banal Ira Gershwin's lyrics could be, though she indeed enhances the glories of the George Gershwin music.

Musicologist and historian Henry Pleasants, in his book *The Great American Popular Singers*, wrote, "She commands . . . an extraordinary range of two octaves and a sixth, from the low D or D-flat to the high B-flat and possibly higher. This is a greater range, especially at the bottom, than is required or expected of most opera singers."

Pleasants recalled Gerald Moore, the English pianist known for his distinguished work as accompanist, telling a story about Dietrich Fischer-Dieskau. Moore and the lieder singer had finished a matinee recital in Washington, D.C. The singer was about to rush to the airport to catch a plane to New York to hear a concert of Ella Fitzgerald and the Duke Ellington band at Carnegie Hall. "Ella and the Duke together!" Fischer-Dieskau said. "One just doesn't know when there might be a chance to hear that again!"

Pleasants wrote, "Many classical singers . . . like Fischer-Dieskau are among her most appreciative admirers."

Edmund Thigpen, who was her drummer from 1968 to 1972 in a trio led by pianist Tommy Flanagan, said, "Ella's musicianship is just incredible. Playing with her is like playing with a full orchestra. She almost telegraphs it to you because of her vast knowledge of every song ever written, knowing all the verses, knowing what songs mean, and still interpreting them in her own way. Her rhythmic sense is uncanny. And she's a great listener.

"She's also one of the finest people I've ever worked with. She's a caring person, a giving person, and when she sings *People*, she means every word of it."

When I was growing up in Canada, certain things typified and embodied the faraway and fascinating places to which I yearned someday to go.

France was symbolized by the Eiffel Tower, the Champs-Elysées, the Arc de Triomphe, and the voice of Edith Piaf. England was typified by Big Ben, Trafalgar Square, the statue of Eros in Piccadilly, and the voices of Gracie Fields and George Formby. The United States was embodied in the Statue of Liberty, the Empire State Building, the Grand Canyon of the Colorado.

And the voice of Ella Fitzgerald.

That exquisite sound would come sailing across the border from radio stations in Buffalo and Rochester and Detroit, swinging and sensitive and young and absolutely pure, although she was played plenty on Canadian radio too.

It is hard to remember, in this age of talk radio, rock radio, and country-and-western radio, that what Fitzgerald did was not seen in those days as the high art it actually was. It was considered popular music, and some of her songs were very big hits.

As the years went by, her singing became more seasoned and brilliantly skilled, passing beyond anything anyone else could do. Certain of her performances linger in memory (and, fortunately, on records) as bright as jewels on velvet. But the strange thing is that the voice itself remained eternally young. In her sound, she seemed like what she was when she had her first hit: a teen-ager. And the combination, the sweet naivete of that sound coupled with the sophisticated and secure command of her art, was startling, and inimitable. To be sure, a lot of excellent singers have been influenced by her, but she remains unique, beyond imitation. An American monument.

Her long and distinguished career made Ella a wealthy woman, and she lived in a big, comfortable home in Beverly Hills, a dramatic, striking, two-story structure in Mexican hacienda style built in a U-shape around a large inner garden rich in exotic tropical and subtropical flora, receding to a swimming pool in the distance. The rooms were richly and exquisitely furnished, with a great sense of space and proportion. The walls were covered in paintings, including a striking oil portrait of her by Tony Bennett, whose abilities as a painter have grown steadily from a tentative exploratory style years ago to a daring mastery.

I had lunch there with Ella and Val Valentin, who was for many years chief recording engineer for the Verve label. Before that Val was the engineer who recorded many of the Nat Cole and Frank Sinatra albums at Capitol. He remained Ella's close friend and a sort of informal adviser.

A Swiss magazine had asked me to interview her. She was famously reluctant to do interviews, and although I had known her slightly for years, I certainly didn't know her well. Peggy Lee called her at my behest, and she agreed to see me. I think one reason she may have done so is that she had recorded quite a number of my lyrics and perceived me not as a journalist but as a songwriter. And I think Val's presence was reassuring to her.

The usual adjective for her is the exhausted "legendary." Like most legends, hers is not entirely true. According to most standard references, she was born in Newport News, Virginia, April 25, 1918, although Norman Granz says she was born two years later than that. *The New Grove Dictionary of Jazz* says, "She was orphaned in early childhood and moved to New York to attend an orphanage school in Yonkers." Variations on this keep cropping up in biographies and articles.

Ella wasn't sure what happened to her real father, whether he died or he and her mother were divorced. "I know nothing of Newport News," Ella said. "My mother left there when she married my stepfather. I don't know about my father. That part I can't tell you.

"My stepfather was Portuguese. I should have learned Portuguese. Now I'm sorry. Children don't realize the importance of learning. It was like my piano lessons. My mother couldn't afford a lot of piano lessons. I had a teacher with big hands, who could stretch. I would be so thrilled by him that by the time he got through playing, it would be time for me to go home! My mother said, 'I work too hard to let you go there and you come back and you don't know *nothin'*!'

"I'm sorry now. Had I listened to my stepfather, I would probably be real down with my Portuguese. That was the kind of neighborhood we were in–Italian, Spanish, Portuguese, and Hungarian. This was in Yonkers." Fifteen miles up the New York Central railway line from central Manhattan, Yonkers is the first city immediately north of New York City. Partly industrial and partly residential, it is a hilly community on the east bank of the Hudson River. It has deteriorated somewhat in recent years, but much of it is attractive, and it was more amenable when Ella was growing up there.

It was her mother who entered her name in the Apollo theater amateur contest in which she was "discovered." She was entered not as a singer but a dancer.

That was her burning childhood ambition, to be a dancer. "In Yonkers," she said, "I used to make my little money, standing around the corners, me and my friends, and I danced. I used to try to do Snake Hips Tucker." Snake Hips Tucker was a swivel-hipped dancer very popular in Harlem at that period. He performed at Connie's Inn and at the Lafayette and Apollo theaters, where Ella probably saw him. She said, "My friends and I would dance and people would throw us money, and that's how we'd make enough to go to the show. And my mother used to sing that song all the time, *The Object of My Affection.*" The song was new: its publishing date is 1934.

Ella says that the big influence on her mother, and on her, was the Boswell Sisters. Now largely ignored, the Boswells were three girls from New Orleans, Connie, Martha, and Helvetia, who sang complex close-harmony parts. They became internationally famous, and Connie, who was heavily featured with the group, later became a solo star, despite having to spend much of her life in a wheelchair in consequence of a childhood accident.

Ella said, "My mother liked to sing around the house, and she loved Miss Connie Boswell. Anything the Boswell Sisters sang, she liked, and she would sing it.

"There was a little Italian boy who just loved my mother so. If his mother couldn't get him to eat, she'd say to my mother, 'Please come and make him eat!' He'd come and stay with us. He wanted to go with my mother anywhere she wanted to go. And they were in the car one day. She was holding him. My cousin, who was driving the car, stopped the car fast. To save the little boy from hitting the front, my mother grabbed him, and hit her head. She got fifty-four stitches in her head.

"They didn't have all the medicines they have now, and it didn't heal. I was fifteen, going on sixteen. She had signed for me to go on the amateur hour at the Apollo." Ella was quite firm about her age at the time.

"I went on to dance. I wasn't going on as a singer! My girlfriends, Frances and Doris, were there. And of all people to go onstage, I was the first one they called out.

"They used to grab you if you didn't do right. They'd take you off, if the audience booed you. And I lost my nerve. When I walked out, I couldn't believe it. I saw all those people."

She stood frozen, frightened that she would be pulled off the stage. Someone called to her from backstage, "Don't just stand there, sing something!"

"I sang one of the Boswell songs," Ella said, and again, now, sang *That's Judy.*

She said, "I sang that and *The Object of My Affection.*"

The audience loved her, and applauded warmly, giving her the victory in the contest.

"I won the amateur contest and I got first prize and I was promised a week there," she said. "And they never gave me the week. I thought I could go to different places. I went to the Lafayette theater, and they booed me. I didn't win no first prize there. Then I lost my nerve.

"Then I went to the Harlem Opera House, down the street from the Apollo, and tried, and they gave me a week. I did a week there. My mother had signed me for one of the radio amateur hours. But then she died of the brain injury from the accident."

In the audience the night of her Apollo victory was Benny Carter, by then well established as a jazz musician, as much for his compositions and arranging as for his solo work on alto saxophone and trumpet. "I knew nothing about her fright," Benny said. "I just heard her sing and thought, 'This girl is wonderful.'

"Soon after that I took her up to Fletcher Henderson's house. He heard her and he wasn't at all interested. But Chick Webb did get interested. I took Ella to meet him." Benny was an alumnus of the Chick Webb band.

Born in Baltimore February 10, 1909, Chick Webb was a small hunchback who never let his physical handicap defeat him. He used an adapted drum set that permitted him to control a wide range of colors, and, as Val Valentin said, "If he were alive today, I think he would give a lot of drummers something to worry about." Webb had one of the best bands of the Swing Era. Much of the time it played the Savoy Ballroom.

Webb hired Ella to sing with the band for one week, and then permanently. With the death of Ella's mother, he became her guardian. Whether he actually adopted her, as is often written, is uncertain.

Ella said, "I can't say yes or no to it, but he was supposed to be my guardian, so I could travel with him. He was just a sweet person. Just a real sweet person."

It was at the Savoy that she made one of the friendships of her lifetime, a man she says was one of her important mentors: Dizzy Gillespie. Ella laughed: "Dizzy was with the Teddy Hill band and I was with Chick Webb. We used to get off the stage at the Savoy Ballroom and start dancing. We'd jump off and start Lindy hopping." The year was probably 1937. Ella was then nineteen; Dizzy was twenty.

"I learned a lot from those musicians," Ella said, "and I'm very grateful for it.

"When they used to have the after-hours jam sessions at Minton's, and another place, I used to sneak in with them. And I feel that I learned what little bop I do have by following Dizzy around these different places. I feel that that was my education. He is a wonderful teacher, and I am very grateful to him. I probably never would have tried to bop, but I wanted to do what he was doing. We used to go in there and jam all night, and sometimes we'd go down to 52nd Street to the Three Deuces and we'd sit up there and listen to Lady Day."

"And yet," I pointed out, "you developed a style that was original." There isn't a trace of Billie Holiday in her singing.

"Well I don't know how I got it," Ella said. "But I think I owe it mostly to musicians. By being around them, I learned by ear." According to some persons, she may have originated the term bebop or, as it was at first also known, rebop. They say that she used these syllables in a characteristic phrase when she was scatting with the musicians. Whether or not she really did invent the phrase, she was from the first in on the experimentation and innovation that would lead to bebop.

In 1938, when she was twenty, Ella recorded *A-Tisket, A-Tasket*—adapted from a nursery rhyme—with Chick Webb for the Decca label. It made her an immediate star, and she followed this with *Undecided*, a tune by trumpeter Charlie Shavers. The band continued to play at the Savoy, broadcasting nationally and making a long series of records for Decca, quite a number of them with Ella. Most of her Decca recordings were reissued by the GRP label at the time of her seventy-fifth birthday, thirty-nine of them, including *Oh, Lady Be Good, Lullaby of Birdland, Black Magic,* and *My One and Only Love.* She was one of the few singers who *could* sing *My One and Only Love.*

"When she wasn't singing," George T. Simon wrote in his book *The Big Bands,* "she would usually stand at the side of the band, and, as the various sections blew their ensemble phrases, she'd be up there singing along with all of them, often gesturing with her hands as though she were leading the band."

But Webb's health was fragile, and he went home to Baltimore to die of tuberculosis on June 16, 1939. He was thirty years old. Ella took over the band and was its leader for the next three years. Then she disbanded and embarked on a solo career, making many records for Decca, including three with the Ink Spots, one with Louis Jordan, and even in 1946 a calypso number called *Cold Stone Dead in the Market.* She also made an unforgettable early LP accompanied only by pianist Ellis Larkins.

Then, in 1946, she began to tour with Jazz at the Philharmonic. Norman Granz became her manager and career guide. When her Decca contract expired, she signed with Granz's Verve label and launched the series of records—including the songbook albums—that would secure her place in history.

Fitz—as the Jazz at the Philharmonic veterans called her—became an integral part of that touring family, and the musicians seemed to encircle her protectively. Granz was particularly protective. And always, he fought to defend his performers from racism. One of his battles involved the Bell Telephone Company. At that time, guitarist Herb Ellis was in the group that accompanied Ella. When she was booked on the Bell Telephone Hour, the show's producers told Granz as delicately as they knew how that it would not be appropriate for a black singer to be seen on camera with a white musician. Granz insisted that Ellis and Fitzgerald be seen together.

The producers got around their problem by covering the lenses with a filter coated with vaseline, which creates a haloed, misty effect around the central figure. It was impossible to tell who was accompanying her. Granz took a full-page newspaper ad to denounce Bell Telephone for this evasion.

One of his stands against racism came close to costing him his life. On a visit to Houston, Texas, he ordered his ticket sellers to advise buyers that the concerts would not be segregated. Later, during the first of two evening concerts, he noticed three strangers backstage, men in business suits. They told him they were off-duty police detectives who just wanted to listen to the music, and Granz relaxed one of his cardinal rules by allowing them to stay. Oscar Peterson was performing while Gene Krupa, Illinois Jacquet, and Dizzy Gillespie, in Ella's dressing room, were playing a one-dollar game of craps. The three detectives entered the room and arrested them for gambling. When Granz entered the room to learn the cause of the uproar, he was told that he too was under arrest—for running a gambling game. One of the cops entered Ella's bathroom. Granz, fearful that the man would try to plant narcotics, followed him. The detective asked, "What are you doing?"

"Watching you," Granz said.

The detective pulled a gun and pointed it at him. "I ought to kill you," he said.

Granz later recounted, "I didn't say anything. I did realize there were witnesses, but there were also two other cops. I suppose if he had shot me they'd have come up with some story."

Granz, Dizzy Gillespie, Jacquet, Gene Krupa, and Ella were taken to a court house and charged with gambling. "Curiously enough," Norman told me long after the event, "there were newspaper photographers present. That's when I knew they'd set us up to smear us." Granz posted bail for all of them. "Ella was fit to be tied," he said.

The next morning there were pictures of the JATP group, Ella among them, in the newspapers. Granz could have forfeited the bail, which amounted to $50 for all them, but Ella's embarrassment disturbed him. "I decided to do what no one in his right mind would do," he said. "I decided to fight them."

He did. It cost him $2000 to get the $50 back. But Ella and his musicians were vindicated.

On another occasion, British customs officials held up the arriving JATP group to search them for narcotics. They found none, and as a last resort were about to conduct a body search of Ella. Granz threatened to cancel the tour there and then, and the customs officials relented.

Scandal has come no closer to Ella Fitzgerald than these incidents. She was married from 1948 to 1952 to bassist Ray Brown, with whom she worked on the Jazz at the Philharmonic tours. They adopted a little boy, the son of her half-sister Frances, and named him Ray Brown, Jr. Even after her divorce from Ray Brown, she remained on warm terms with him. They worked together often in the later years.

She was notoriously shy, and her private life was kept private indeed, and quiet. When she was home she indulged her love of children, including a grand-daughter and several nieces, her sister's children. She seemed startled that I knew she maintained the Ella Fitzgerald Day Care Center in one of the black ghetto areas of Los Angeles, for the children of working mothers. Was it true that she funded it entirely out of her own money? "We try to," she said, slipping shyly into the on-stage royal We. "I don't like to feel like I'm bragging for what I am doing.

"It's for kids of that neighborhood. It's down in Watts. I haven't been able to go down there in the last two years, after I became ill." She suffered several illnesses, including diabetes, and her thick glasses compensated for cataract surgery.

"I'd usually be there when they had the Christmas celebrations. I'd sing for them. They give little shows for the kids. The last time I was there, there was a little Spanish boy, and he had a great big sombrero. And he was supposed to dance around it. But he was so small, he was falling down. It was the cutest thing. He would get up and start all over. I miss that from the kids.

"There are kids there of all languages, and they sing in all the languages." Val Valentin said the children sent her huge cards covered in signatures.

Ella Fitzgerald on stage always seemed an incredibly assured performer, pouring forth melody with consummate rhythmic force. Thinking of her terror at the Apollo, I said, "Have you ever had stage fright since?"

"Yes! I stayed that way! I still have stage fright. I think, if you really are sure of yourself, that nothing happens. You can't work. I don't think I could go on that stage, walk out there and go, *Well here I am!* and go ahead because you never know what that audience lacks."

At the height of her career, Ella was rather plump, matronly looking, but when I saw her that day she was thin. Her doctor, she said, had made her take off weight to lower her blood pressure. She appeared to have recovered a little of her health. Still, I didn't want to tire her, and insisted it was time for me to go. I asked her a final question:

"If you had your life to live over, would you do anything but sing?"

"No. Because I found out that I couldn't be a dancer."

Not long after that, the circulatory problems caused by her diabetes advanced to the point where her legs had to be amputated. Toward the end, she slipped into a coma. Her adopted son, Ray Brown, Jr., was convinced she could hear, and saw to it that music was played constantly in the house.

The sweet voice of Ella Fitzgerald was silenced forever on Saturday, June 15, 1996.

Phrasing
Julius La Rosa

Years ago I wrote a magazine column examining the influence of Frank Sinatra on other singers, among them Jack Jones, Tony Bennett, Vic Damone, Steve Lawrence, Matt Monro, and Julius La Rosa.

Probably the record that jolted me into awareness of the quality of La Rosa's work dated from a period when he recorded for MGM, with charts by the wonderfully fertile and inexhaustibly musical Don Costa. Further, I suspect it was *Spring Can Really Hang You Up the Most.* It is a song I had admired for its craftsmanship but never really cared for. It had been recorded for the most part by relentlessly "hip" girl singers indulging in its 1950s affectations of language. Indeed, the only record of it I had ever liked was Jackie Cain's, for its inevitable musicality. La Rosa's approach to it is dramatic, as if it were a costume drama. The song is of its time and place, and so is the "character" he becomes in singing it. In La Rosa's reading, it takes on a different coloration and genuine beauty, the natural expression of someone living in that time, and as such it is surprisingly poignant rather than cute.

I wrote that La Rosa was the most brilliant singer of the Sinatra school. Someone showed that column to him, and he wrote me a thank-you letter that initiated a friendship. We talked on the telephone, and exchanged long letters. I have had long conversations about singing with all sorts of friends and acquaintances among singers, talks about vibrato, vowels, intonation, the pitch problems of diphthongs on high notes, talks about intervals. But the most extended discussion of the subject has been with Julie. He has all our correspondence. Typed, single-spaced, it is a pile a foot and a half high, he tells me.

Julius La Rosa was born in Brooklyn, New York, on January 2, 1930.

"My father was born in Sicily—right in Palermo," Julie said. "My mother—her name's Lucia—was born in a little town called Castel Buono, which is outside Palermo. My father was born in 1906. He came to America when he was fourteen. My mother came with her family when she was about eleven.

"He was a self-trained radio repairman. My mother was married at fifteen and a half and by the time she was eighteen, she had three kids. I have a sister who is a couple of years older than I. A little boy born between me and my sister died when he was about four months old. My mother had another baby a couple of years after that. She died at two and a half of spinal meningitis. It had an incredible effect on my parents, and through them on me and my sister. I found out, when I was in shrinkdom, that I felt an element of responsibility in her death, because she died falling downstairs. My whole life I was afraid I might have pushed her down the stairs. Her name was Angelina, and we referred to her as Baby Angie. Talk about old-country superstition! My parents would say, 'Swear on Baby Angie.' 'Mama, I didn't take the peanuts out of the jar.' 'Swear on Baby Angie!' It compounded the guilt.

"You *know* me. You *know* the effect it had."

"Was the family musical?" I asked.

"Well," Julie said, "my father, though he was unschooled, liked music. You remember the old Victrolas? Always I was hearing either classical music or excerpts from operas. Not the whole opera, just excerpts. I heard a lot of old Caruso records. I guess from that I developed a love of music and ultimately singing. In the beginning, I wanted to be a baseball player. I wanted to be Pee Wee Reese with the Brooklyn Dodgers.

"Pee Wee Reese came up about 1940, about the time Sinatra started to make a lot of noise. I started to sing and I loved it.

"My Uncle Tony used to tell a story. My father would have those big radio consoles in the shop, for repair. When I was small, I would stick my head in the back where the speaker should have been and sing, and I'd say, 'How do I sound coming out of the radio, Uncle Tony?'

"Everyone said I was bashful. I wasn't bashful. I was scared to death of any kind of authority. I would be asked to sing at parties, but I would never do it. I would fail at it. I could never please my father.

"The first time I ever heard him praise me, and it was indirect, was when I was doing the Arthur Godfrey show. I was singing some Patti Page hit. My father was in his store. He had a relatively new thing, a Webcor tape recorder. He taped the show with a microphone. In the middle of the song, he said, 'Attaboy, Julie.'

"The awful thing was that when I learned all that, I was unable to rid myself of the unconscious effects. That's why it took me twenty-five years to feel comfortable on a stage. It's a matter of 'My God, they *do* like me!' But there's always that fear on the first show, 'They're not going to like me.'"

I said, "Henry Mancini was never able to please his father. Hank went into military service and never completed his degree at Juilliard, and his father always said to him, even when he was a huge success and many times a millionaire, 'If only you'd got your degree, you could teach.'"

"That's uncanny."

"You always said that Hank was what you call in Italian *superbia*. He really wasn't that way. He was just one of the cats,"

"That was probably his defense," Julie said.

"Hank told me that when he was a kid in school, his mother would make him salami sandwiches, and it was really greasy salami. The grease would seep through the bag and eventually left a spot in his desk."

"Yes!" Julie said, with a laugh of recognition. "And it would smell when you took it to lunch. You don't get over those things. I once *built* a five-tube super-heterodyne radio. In my father's store. When I finished it, and the thing was playing, we were listening to it, listening to Martin Block. The radio *worked*, and he looked at it and said, 'Bad soldering.'"

"I must have been fourteen or fifteen."

"Most opera singers don't sing words," Julie said in a conversation the next day. "They sing notes."

"And a lot of them," I said, "sing out of tune. Including the famous three tenors."

"Yes they *do*!" Julie said.

"Mario Lanza, for one."

"He was *terrible*. He probably had the same kind of immigrant background as I do."

"Sinatra had a stupefying impact on a lot of us."

"Oh yes. He came out of the era of dance bands, and the singer had to sing within the framework of the meter. Despite the restrictions, he was still able to put a period here, a comma there, to heighten the meaning. It came to be known as phrasing. And all he was doing was telling the story as he believed those words should be spoken. But it was revolutionary and it was what made him Sinatra. Nobody did it before. And so those of us who grew up listening to him didn't copy him but recognized the intelligence of that kind of interpretation.

"Today, coming home in the car," Julie said, "I was listening to Natalie Cole. She was singing one of my favorite songs, *When I Fall in Love*, but there's a mismatch of words and music in that song, the lines 'the moment that I feel *that* you feel *that* way too ...' The way to phrase it is 'the moment that I *feel* ... that *you* feel that way too.'" He sang "feel that way" as a triplet.

"Sinatra started all that. He could take a thirty-two-bar song and turn it into a three-act play. He is number one, and the second guy in line is number thirty-six. That's the gap between Frank and whoever is the next best singer."

"When was the first time you sang in public?" I asked.

"The Grover Cleveland High School senior chorus. My friend Joey used to get time off. He'd get days off from school. He'd say, 'We've got to rehearse for the concert next Wednesday.' I joined the chorus so I could get those days off.

"I then get a mad crush on Jeanette Caponegro. She was in the All-City chorus. I figure I've got to get into the All-City Chorus so I can spend Saturdays with her. This is 1946. I'm a fast sixteen years old. So I go to try out for the All-City Chorus. Remember *Just a Song at Twilight?* Well I sang that for the audition. Mr. C., as he was always called, hit a couple of chords on the piano and you had to sing them. And I sang them. I had a curious thing: I would hear the third first.

"And he said, 'Why hasn't Miss Brown sent you to me sooner?' She was my glee club teacher at Grover Cleveland High School. He said, 'Well, young man, I'm going to break a rule. We usually don't tell the students who try out for us until we send a postcard to the teacher, and normally Miss Brown would tell you. But I'm telling you right now, you're in the All-City Chorus.' I'll never forget that. In my whole life. That's when I began to sing. I was in the All-City Chorus! Three hundred voices.

"Now the head of the chorus was P. J. Wilhousky. A mad Russian. A strict disciplinarian. We were rehearsing the summer concert of 1947, which was the year I graduated high school. We were doing *Begin the Beguine.* We get to 'I'm with you once more . . . ' It's a cello line. The baritones ain't gettin' it right, the first basses ain't gettin' it right. I'm in the third row. And of course I'm doing Frank!

"And P. J. Wilhousky says, '*That's* the way to do it! What's your name, young man? Julius La Rosa? That's the way everybody should sing it!'

"Two years ago there was a piece in the *New York Sunday Times* magazine by a man who is a professor of zoology at Harvard, about his remembrance of singing in the All-City Chorus with one of the great people he's ever known, the stentorian and dictatorial Peter J. Wilhousky. And he related the time when Wilhousky said to one of the singers, 'Young man, you're singing *flat.* And do you realize, *Julius La Rosa* used to sit in that chair?'

"I wrote to him and we had a nice correspondence."

After singing with the All-City Chorus, Julie joined the Navy for a three-year hitch. "I was two months under eighteen," Julie said. "I joined the Navy to learn electronics so I could go into the radio business with my father. While I was in the Navy I was in the glee club.

"After boot camp, I was sent to aviation electronics school for twenty-eight weeks to become a radar operator and learn Morse code and basic electronic theory.

"In Pensacola, Florida, I was ship's company on the *USS Wright*. That means you are part of the ship's crew. The *Wright* was an aircraft carrier, a converted cruiser. I did twenty-six carrier take-offs and landings–as a crewman, not a pilot.

"Between July and September, we would go to a joint outside the base called the Town Pump. I would get up and sing a couple of songs, and the owner would be feeding me and my buddies beers, on the arm.

"Arthur Godfrey came to Pensacola to take training for his Navy wings. He was a pilot and a big Navy-phile."

Godfrey was a Navy veteran. He had been what is called in the Navy a white hat, an enlisted man. He was flying private planes by the 1930s, when he worked in Washington as a disc jockey. Godfrey would smash records he didn't like over his microphone, which is not exactly good for the health of the microphone, and abandon advertising copy to improvise his own versions of it. He graduated in the post–World War II years to his own five-mornings-a-week radio show on CBS and a weekly television show called *Talent Scouts* on that company's burgeoning television network.

Godfrey spoke in a low, unhurried, unctuous, and perfidious voice. He liked to sing, and did so a notch or two below the mediocre, playing strum-strum-strum ukelele. The mothers and grandmothers of America adored him and he was a huge success in those early days of snowy black-and-white television.

Godfrey was, as Julie said, a Navy buff. Godfrey went to Pensacola to get his flier's wings. This required six take-offs and landings from an aircraft carrier. Veteran Navy fliers have likened the experience to landing on a postage stamp. There are those who suggest that Godfrey's experienced navy "co-pilot" actually made his landings. In return for granting Godfrey his wings, the Navy got exposure on network radio and television.

Julie said, "One of the kids I used to buddy around with–to this day, I don't know who it was–snuck into BOQ, Bachelor Officers Quarters, and left a note for Godfrey saying, 'Why don't you come to the Enlisted Men's Club and hear our buddy Julie sing? Maybe you'll want to put him on *Talent Scouts*.'

"The next day I got a telegram saying, 'Be at the enlisted men's club tonight and Mr. Godfrey will audition you, as your shipmates requested. Lt. So-and-so.'

"I sang *Don't Take Your Love from Me.* Godfrey said, 'Young man, we took a kinescope of this, and when I get back to New York, I'm going to put this on my television show.' I say to him—and I'm not a smart-ass kid—I say, 'Mr. Godfrey, if I give you my mother's telephone number, will you call her up to be sure she's watching?' I swear on my children, I did that!

"He goes back to New York. The admiral gets a telegram. 'I've told my audience about that young sailor, but the kinescope didn't show up. Can you send him up to do the show?' I had some leave accrued, but I'm sure they'd have sent me anyway.

"I get up there, I think it was Monday morning. Archie Bleyer set the key. I think it was *I Only Have Eyes for You.* That and the duet I was supposed to do with Godfrey, the one Crosby did with his son, *Sam's Song.* I rehearsed it with him.

"The show went on. I waited and waited and Godfrey never called me. And then the show was over. I stomped out of the green room. The producer stopped me, he said, 'Julius, where are you going?' 'Home,' I said. 'My mother was watching, my friends were watching, and I wasn't on.'

"He laughed. It turned out that Godfrey saw I was not ready at all. He called the admiral and said, 'Can you extend the kid's leave? I'll put him on the show next week. I can put him on the radio Monday and Tuesday and he'll get a little experience and I can put him on the television show Wednesday night.'

"That was the paradox of the man. He was a sick man.

"Finally I did the Wednesday night television show. And he said on the air, 'Young man, when you get out of the Navy, you come right here, and you've got a job.'

"That year he called on me to do his Christmas show. As a result of the Godfrey show, the Navy transferred me to Washington, D.C., to sing with the U.S. Navy band. I sang with that band for a year.

"I got discharged November 11. I went up to the Godfrey office and said hello. Two days later I got a call from Archie Bleyer. 'Can you come up tomorrow and set some keys? You're starting Monday.' I started on the show November 19, 1951.

"Godfrey said, 'Here's the fine young lad from the Navy.' He liked that word 'lad.' And you remember that kindly avuncular attitude he could affect? He says, at one point, 'Do you miss your buddies in the Navy?' Now I've been out of the navy about five fucking minutes! I said, 'Sir, I haven't been out that long yet.' And the audience breaks up. He gives that low chuckle of his." Julie imitated it perfectly. *Heh, heh, heh, heh, heh.* "In retrospect, I realize I was probably just a nice kid."

Archie Bleyer, Godfrey's music director, had been a writer of stock arrangements in the 1930s and a bandleader. Bleyer started a record label called Cadence, and had big hit records with the Chordettes and the Everly Brothers. He signed La Rosa to Cadence and got a hit with him on the Frank Loesser song *Anywhere I Wander* from the film *Hans Christian Andersen.* It reached number four on the charts in early 1953.

La Rosa told Bleyer about a Sicilian folk song that he and his friends would sing on the subway on their way to Coney Island, *Eh Cumpari.* It is about a country band, and the participating singers have to imitate the instruments in it. Julie says it occupies a place in Sicilian folk culture akin to that of *Old MacDonald* in ours. Bleyer said, "Let's record it." *Cumpari* means companion, friend.

The song was a boon in that it sold a million copies and reached number two on the charts, and a curse that haunts La Rosa to this day: audiences still want to hear it. "Sooner or later, whenever I perform," Julie said, "somebody calls out, '*Eh Cumpari.*' I've given up. I just do it."

Julie drew fan letters from his first days on the Godfrey show, eventually 7000 a week. His youthful innocence was part of the appeal and he was featured as one of "all the little Godfreys," as Godfrey referred (somewhat patronizingly, one realizes from this distance) to his regular cast of talent. In a profile of La Rosa in the September 28, 1987, issue of *The New Yorker*, Whitney Balliett described them as "that oppressed band of entertainers that ... Godfrey had gathered around him.... Most of them were mediocre, and all of them had a basic purpose, to pamper Godfrey's ravenous and famous ego."

La Rosa is one of the few persons to whom fame actually did come almost overnight. One day he was an unknown, and within weeks, even within days, he was a star. And he was terrified. Nothing had prepared him for this.

He was playing a theater in Chicago. Girls mobbed the place. He went to his hotel room. There were girls gathered even in the back alley. He was alone in his room, wishing desperately he had someone to talk to. Fame was completely disorienting.

"Now," I said, "what was the story about you and one of the McGuire Sisters? Rumor always had it that you were having an affair with her. Were you?"

"I was *in love* with her. I'm twenty-three years old, and these three really pretty girls come onto the show. The one on the right, as you looked at them, was Dorothy, the one in the middle was Phyllis, and the one on the left was Christine. And Dorothy and I fell in love. She was married, but she and her husband were separated. We dated for a couple of years.

"And Arthur didn't like it. Christmas of 1954. I'm working at the Chicago Theater. Godfrey is going to take the McGuire Sisters to Thule

Air Force base in Greenland over the holidays. So I tell Dorothy, 'Don't go.' But she went. And that was the end of it. There was stuff in the papers that Godfrey was able to get her and husband back together again.

"Phyllis was the real engine of that trio, even though the other two were older than she. She was the boss, she gave the orders."

"And wasn't Phyllis the one," I said, "who was Sam Giancana's girl-friend?"

"Yeah. Sure."

"Rumor always had it that Godfrey resented you because he wanted to knock off Dorothy for himself. Was that true?"

"Maybe. It could have been Phyllis."

"*Drama in Real Life,* as they say in *Reader's Digest.*"

"There's a lot of that goes on," Julie said.

"No kidding," I said. "You amaze me. I didn't know that!"

"And it doesn't go out of style."

"And what happened?"

"New Year's Eve. Dorothy and I are now history. Marion Marlowe was the semi-legit soprano on the Godfrey show who used to sing the duets with Frank Parker. She was opening at the Plaza. She called and invited me. I didn't have a date. So I called my press agent, who was Perry Como's press agent. He said there were some starlets in town. He said, 'But you don't want to go with any of them. Rory, Perry's secretary, is a beautiful girl. She's a Catholic.'

"I said, 'I don't care *what* she is. I'm not looking to get married. I just need a date.'"

Their first date was in January, 1955. They were engaged the following New Year's Eve and married in 1956. She was born Rosemary Meyer of a German-Czech family in Milwaukee, and called Rory.

"And what about Godfrey?"

"Well, I'd become friends with the secretary to the producer. Her name was Amy Bullett, and we're still friends. She saw I was this raw kid. We'd have lunch.

"After a couple of months, it was in some famous restaurant where the song-pluggers hung out, I said, 'Amy, he's really not a nice man, is he?'

"She said, 'You know it. But don't let anyone else know you know it.'

"We used to have what we called prayer meetings. After the Wednesday night show, we would go over the show and start preparing for next week's. Here is a verbatim quote: 'Remember, some of you are here over the bodies of people I have personally slain, and I can do it again.'

"Toward the end of the summer of 1953, Godfrey started dancing lessons for the members of the cast. But none of the other guys on the show, the Mariners, Frank Parker, went. Only the girls. And I said, 'Forget it, I ain't gonna go either.'

"On a Thursday, there was a note on the bulletin board. It said, 'If you're not at today's dancing lesson, don't bother showing up for the show tomorrow morning.' That day, after the show, I got a message, 'Call your folks.' My sister was having a problem with her husband. Could I come home and help straighten it out? I went up to the office and asked if I could go in to see him. I said, 'Mr. Godfrey, I have trouble at home.' He said, 'Well, if you can get back, get back.'

"So I went home. Well, you know, Italian arguments never last an hour and a half. So I didn't show up. Next morning there was a note on the bulletin board saying, 'Mr. La Rosa, since you felt your services were not required at the dancing class yesterday, they won't be required on the show today.'

"I was astonished, because he'd given me permission. I walked over to the Lexington Hotel, where he lived, three or four blocks from 52nd and Madison where the studio was. I get on the house phone. I asked for Mr. Godfrey. The girl asked who was calling. I said, 'Julius La Rosa.' She said, 'Oh, Julius, I'm such a big fan.' Thirty seconds later, with a different tone in her voice, she said, 'I'm so sorry, Arthur isn't in.' I know the poor lady's lying, because right in front of the hotel is his Rolls Royce, license plate AMG 1, Arthur Morton Godfrey.

"Some months before that, Tom Rockwell, who was the head of GAC, General Artists Corporation, had approached me. One of the unwritten rules was that you didn't need an agent or a manager while you were on the Godfrey show. With *Anywhere I Wander* and *Eh Cumpari* I was making $60,000 a year, which was a lot of money in those days. I had a luncheon with Tom Rockwell, because I was scared. He said, 'If you'll sign with us, I'll guarantee you a minimum of $100,000 a year.'

"When Godfrey lied to me, I signed with Rockwell and he wrote a letter to Godfrey, saying, 'Dear Mr. Godfrey: In future all dealings in regard to Julius La Rosa will be handled through GAC.' I have been told since that Godfrey went to Bill Paley, who was the head of CBS, and said, 'Do you believe this little shit? I've got to get rid of him.' So Paley said to him, 'You hired him on the air? Fire him on the air.'"

On the evening of Wednesday, October 19, 1953, Julie was to perform in the first half hour of the show. The show was nearing its end when at last Godfrey announced him. This is a transcript of what followed. Whitney Balliett described Godfrey's voice as "homey, drawling, glutinous, sinister."

Godfrey: Except for the McGuire Sisters and Luanne, who came after him, Julius is our youngest member. Yeah. How long ago did you come?

Julie: It was November 13th, no, November 17th, 1951. Be two years next month.

Godfrey: Not quite two years.

Julie: Yes sir.

Godfrey: It was about three years ago, then, when I first met you.

Julie: October 4th, 1951.

(There is audience laughter at this.)

Godfrey: When I first met Julie . . . I'll never forget when he first came up here, and I said to him, I told him, he came up and he did a couple of guest appearances with us, if you remember, he was in uniform. And I said, "Well when you get out of that man's navy, if you don't want to stay in for thirty years, come on up here and I'll give you a job." And he took me at my word. And he came and I put him to work. And immediately everybody loved him. And it always has done my heart good to see that you people saw the same quality in him that I saw. Which, if you have noticed, and I'm sure you have, is the same quality that I have in everybody in my cast. I pick them all that way. Sure he's got a good voice, but lots of people have good voices. There's something else that you like, which is a wonderful quality that it's hard to get. So, I'll never forget when he first came here and went to work steadily, he said, "Gee," you know he used to go, *Gee*. "I don't know, with all those stars on the show!" And I said to him, "Julie, you don't know it, but I don't have any stars in my show. In my show we're all just a nice big family of very nice people. Like yourself. And you hold on to that quality, and you'll never have to worry about a thing. You're just as big as anybody else, you just go on, try to improve yourself all the time, and one day you'll be the big star, see?"

And this boy in two years time has done this. In two years time, he has . . . he and Archie have their own recording company now, and he's, he's, gotten to be a great big name. I would like Julie, if he would, to sing me that song called *Manhattan*. Have you got that?

Julie: Yes, sir.

La Rosa sings *Manhattan*.

Godfrey: Thanks ever so much, Julie. That was Julie's swan song with us. He goes now out on his own. As his own star. Soon to be seen in his own programs, and I know you wish him godspeed, same as I do. This is the CBS radio network.

(Crossfade to theme: *Seems Like Old Times*.)

The incident remains the most famous firing in the history of television or popular music. And it made headlines, of course. Some of the reports were so critical of Godfrey that he was forced to concoct an explanation of his actions. Obviously he couldn't say that he wanted Dorothy McGuire for himself, or that he had punished La Rosa for failing to attend a dance class, or that he was outraged that a rising young star should have the temerity to engage an agent. So, in what remains one of the more bizarre lines of that year, he said he'd fired La Rosa because he had "lost his humility." Humility, of course, being part of the job description for a career in show business.

The incident served to reveal to the public something of Godfrey's true character. The little old ladies who loved him also loved the boyish La Rosa. The resulting bad press may have been the start of Godfrey's decline, and ultimately would lead to the 1957 Elia Kazan movie *A Face in the Crowd* in which Andy Griffith played a hobo with a lovable personality who is promoted into television stardom. He evolves into a ruthless, egomaniacal, and vicious figure who still maintains his façade to the public. It was widely recognized that the character was based on Godfrey.

"To this day, I have mixed emotions about getting fired that way," Julie said. "A lot of people said it was the best thing that ever happened to me. But it put a stigma on me, and just about every disc jockey or interviewer to this day asks about it. It's often the first thing they ask. I've become gun-shy about answering questions about it. I have said, 'Arthur Godfrey was the father of my career, and I will always be grateful. But he wasn't a very nice man.' Bingo. Sound bite for television: 'He wasn't a very nice man.'

"After the show that night, I went back to the green room. The cast was offering condolences, saying 'Everything's going to be all right' and that sort of thing.

"And then I went up to Godfrey's office and said, 'I want to thank you for the opportunity you gave me.' I swear to God. And later on, he was quoted in a piece about him saying that the only son of a bitch who ever thanked him was that little La Rosa."

Two or three days after the incident, Julie got a call from Ed Sullivan's office. Sullivan had a television show as big as or bigger than Godfrey's.

"Ed put me on the show the first Sunday after I was fired," Julie said. "That show drew the highest rating of any Sullivan show up to that time, and it wasn't exceeded until the first appearance of Elvis Presley, and then, later, the Beatles.

"There was a booking at the Metropolitan Theater in Boston. And Ed tells America, 'Julius is going to be arriving at 2 o'clock,' or whatever it was, 'on Monday, to perform for five days,' and there were *thousands* of people at Logan Airport!

"And then I went out and, literally, learned my job.

"You can't learn it from a book, you can't learn it any way but to go out on a stage and get your face bashed in. Which is what happened to me a lot of times.

"In the spring of 1956, I got my first booking in Las Vegas, the old El Rancho Vegas. I was bad. I didn't know what I was doing. Saloon audiences! One guy at a front table can't wait to get to bed with the broad, two other guys are drinking, there are two pretty girls over there and they're trying to pick them up, and unless you've got some real authority, they'll kill you. And I got killed a lot of times. I didn't know how to handle it.

"I worked at the old Chicago Theater. The man who ran the place had an acerbic sense of humor, and after two or three shows he said, 'Hey, kid, can't you sing more fast songs? You're slower than Perry Como.'

"But I was filling joints like mad during that period. I worked at the Steel Pier in Atlantic City, eleven, twelve, thirteen shows a day between the news and the shorts on the screen.

"But I really can't tell you when I began to feel a little confident on a stage."

One of the things La Rosa did to learn his "job" was to continue serious vocal studies with the late Carlo Menotti, begun when he was still on the Godfrey show, in New York. He worked with Menotti on and off for fourteen years.

It is interesting, therefore, to go back now and listen to his first two hit records, *Anywhere I Wander* and *Eh Cumpari,* to see what kind of instrument he was working with. The voice is wonderful, the more so when you remind yourself you are listening to a twenty-three-year-old kid with no training other than choral experience. His range is big, the consistency of sound up through the registers startling. There's simply no break in the voice. He has what I think of as sharp-shooter intonation. There's no groping for the pitch. The chops are formidable. That this is coming from a neophyte, essentially a young Navy radarman without prior aspirations to show business, is amazing. And, incidentally, except for the intelligence of the phrasing, he does *not* sound like Sinatra. In fact, he sounds a little like the late Andy Russell, and Julie may well have listened to him.

"You know," I said, "Tony Bennett told me it took him ten years or something to learn to walk on a stage properly."

"Well," Julie said. "In 1954 or '55, I was working at Loew's State in Times Square. The star was, if you can believe this, Julius La Rosa, and the extra added attraction was Ella Fitzgerald. And I was in awe of her. And between shows, you talk, you rap. And one day I said I knew I was brand new and had a lot to learn. And Ella, she was so sweet, said, 'Julius, it took me fifteen years to learn how to walk onto a stage.'"

"One of the concert pianists," I said, "said that the longest distance in the world was that between the wings and the piano."

"Oh, that's wonderful!"

Even as Julie went about learning his craft, the contretemps with Godfrey haunted him: "I had a very strong feeling that the publicity that came after it placed a strong negative stigma on me.

"I was no longer the young guy who sings but the kid who got fired."

Julie and Rory were expecting their first baby. Something went wrong and she was rushed to Mount Sinai Hospital. She was delivered of a boy, premature and still-born. Julie told the doctor he wanted to see the baby. The doctor advised against it. "Just think of a pound of butter," he said.

After sitting with Rory, Julie got into the elevator, dazed and disoriented, to descend. A woman recognized him and asked for his autograph. For once—he has almost saintly patience in dealing with the public—he declined the request. She persisted. He tried to explain that he was distraught, saying, "Please!" And finally he told the woman he had just lost a baby son.

She said, "Hmm. Arthur Godfrey was right. You've got no humility."

After his departure from the Godfrey show, Julie worked in theaters that still presented live shows between the movies, fast becoming fewer. He played in clubs, made appearances on television, began to act in summer stock, playing among others the role of Billy Bigelow in *Carousel* and Sky Masterson in *Guys and Dolls*.

In 1968, he got a call from WNEW in New York, asking if he would be interested in doing a disc jockey show from one to four in the afternoon. WNEW at that time was a good-music station. The hours left his evenings free to do whatever gigs came along. And the money was good, eventually $100,000 a year. And of course the job permitted him to spend far more time at home with Rory and their two children, Chris and Maria. He would do his show at WNEW for eight years.

By then he and his family were living in a four-bedroom split-level home in Irvington, up in the glorious Ichabod Crane-Rip Van Winkle region of the Hudson River Valley. They still live there.

Whitney Balliett described Julie thus: "La Rosa is a handsome, stocky, medium-sized man. He has widely spaced eyes, and he often pops them when he is emphasizing a word or phrase. He has double parentheses on each side of his mouth. His fingers are thick and powerful, his teeth are small, and he has a firm, rocky chin. When he sings, his expression flickers between bemusement and outright smiling. His work bears little resemblance now to Frank Sinatra's. His voice, a pleasant baritone, has a slightly mystifying quality. This quality is not in its timbre or its texture;

it seems to encase his voice. It gives it a cheerfulness, a hello-sunshine sound. La Rosa's gentleness is reflected in long connective single notes and in a self-effacing vibrato. He can shiver the timbers and buzz like a bee. He uses his acting abilities cautiously and well: he likes to lift an eyebrow, dip his head and close his eyes, and be regal with his hands, in the manner of Mabel Mercer, whom he first saw in the fifties. . . .

"La Rosa has a singer's power-in-reserve speaking voice, and although he is a delicate and tightly controlled performer, he talks in startling bursts and shouts. He sounds like surf on rocks, like thunder in flat country. Sometimes he shouts the opening syllable of a word and whispers the rest, and sometimes it is the other way around."

Julie shares the inferiority complex common to New York City Italians. This quality, which I have seen in both men and women, baffled me for a long time. You don't find it in New England Italians, and not in all New York Italians. You didn't find it in the cocky Bobby Darin, for example, but then Bobby was a special case: he suffered rheumatic fever as a child, knew he didn't have long, and rushed with the abandon that only impending death can inspire to achieve all his ambitions in a life that in fact ended when he was thirty-seven.

It was explained to me by a New York native of some perspicacity that the Irish got to New York first, and were cruelly abused. And the Irish in turn took it out on the arriving Italians.

This lack of a sense of personal worth is something I saw even in Tony Bennett, in a vivid incident. Tony paints, and in recent years an amateur talent has blossomed into a superb one. Tony *knows* painting. One day Tony was explaining Picasso to me. It was a revelation, and I listened raptly. And all of a sudden, the cloud came over him, and he said, "But who am I to be talking about Picasso?"

I couldn't get another word out of him on the subject.

I told Julie about this, and named this phenomenon in New York Italians "the Picasso syndrome." It has become one of our code terms. He'll be slipping into that lack of faith in himself and I'll say something like, "Oh, don't give me the Picasso syndrome."

Another New York–area Italian who doesn't suffer from it is Frank Sinatra, born in Hoboken, right across the river: you can see Manhattan from Hoboken. I cannot help reflecting on how Sinatra would have reacted had Arthur Godfrey done to him what he did to Julie. Even in his youth, Sinatra was volatile, as witness his fights with Buddy Rich in the Tommy Dorsey band. What would he have done to Godfrey? One way or another, Godfrey would have regretted the incident, not Sinatra.

La Rosa, however, intelligent, gentle, witty, alive with laughter, solicitous, polite, and truly humble—Arthur Godfrey to the contrary notwithstanding–comes across even on a bandstand as someone you would like to have for your best friend, which is of course why he is one of mine.

We can all cite the injustices of show business, the talent that went unrecognized, the fools and egomaniacs who rose to the top. I can think of two or three instances of gifted performers who committed suicide over their failure.

When in 1996, Julie recorded a new album, it was his first in eleven years. I know his work as well as I do primarily from live performances. It's a dark comment on the music business that one of the most brilliant vocal talents in the history of American song has been so little documented on records.

Arthur Godfrey is the perfect illustration of Marc Antony's observation in Shakespeare's *Julius Caesar*:

> The evil that men do lives after them,
> The good is oft interred with their bones.

I spent the early part of 1984 in Northern Italy, writing the lyrics for an album for Sarah Vaughan. I began to learn to speak Italian, and indeed was getting to function, if primitively, in the language. And I was becoming accustomed to Italian manners and gestures, including a peculiar habit of grabbing you by the arm to seize your attention when the person wishes to say something he considers important. It began to annoy me.

When I returned, I was walking up Seventh Avenue in New York when who should I encounter on the northeast corner of Seventh and 59th Street but La Rosa. There was laughter and much hugging and a decision to go somewhere for coffee. We were headed along 59th to the coffee shop at Sixth Avenue. Every few feet La Rosa would seize my arm to say something. And I thought I had escaped this.

I told him about this recently, adding, "You're lucky I didn't belt you one."

"You know, you're right," he said. "It's a very, very Italian thing to do. In fact I'll tell you a story about that."

Over the years, of course, Julie came to know Frank Sinatra. Julie said, "Some years ago," he said, "I was doing a telethon. On the opening night, late, Sinatra was going to be a guest. It was about a quarter to twelve. I was coming out of the so-called green room. Frank walked in with two elderly men, seventy-ish. I said, 'Nice to see you again, Frank.' I said, 'You sonofabitch, you put me into the business and you put me out of it.'"

"How did you mean that?"

"Well. He put me into the business because I learned to sing from him.

And he put me out of the business because I never learned to sing as good as he."

"Neither did anyone else," I said.

Julie laughed and said, "I don't *care* about everybody else. I just care about *me!*"

"How did he react to that?"

"Well he got the point. And now what he did was a typically Italian thing. He *grabbed me* by the elbow. He turned me to the two gentlemen and said, 'Tell them what you just told me.'

"It wasn't from ego, it was from pride.

"And I'll never forget it. That's the last time I saw him, and I'll remember it for the rest of my life."

A Family Affair
Jackie and Roy

Roy Kral was one of two children in his family, Irene the other. He was born Roy Joseph Kral on October 10, 1921, in Cicero. Cicero is a city unto itself, but it abuts Chicago to the east—it is twelve or so miles from the lakefront. Cicero had a reputation for being the headquarters during the 1920s of the Capone mob, and the Capones indeed held sway there. Ralph Capone, Al's brother, gave Roy his first break in show business.

Roy's background is Czech. He spoke the language a little until he was three, but his parents gave up speaking it at home. I think I detect an influence of the language on his speech even to this day. There are no definite and indefinite articles in the Slavic languages. Roy in his speech not infrequently omits the articles. He has a beautiful speaking voice, which is one reason that he for a time did a lot of voice-over work in television commercials.

"When I was five years old," Roy said, "my parents had me study the piano. My feet didn't touch the pedals. But I was playing scales, and practicing, and getting into classical music. Then I started school, and it was difficult to continue playing. So I dropped off for a while. Later on, more lessons. I studied maybe five years, six years. I wasn't fascinated by this classical music, although now I love it. But I had studied enough to be able to read music. Then I started to hear bands. I didn't go into the high school orchestra or the music department. I was playing football. But then I started playing again, because I could go to a party and play a song. It was marvelous.

"I remember, even before this, getting into bed and waiting for midnight. I had this little radio under the covers, and I was supposed to be asleep. But I would hear Earl Father Hines broadcasting from the Grand Terrace Ballroom in Chicago, and I thought, 'I'm in heaven.' 'Cause the drums would go. . . ." And Roy sang a drum pattern. "And a man would call out, 'Earl Father Hines,' and Earl would do his piano runs! Great! The next morning, I'd get up and go over to the piano. And I discovered that my piano didn't have those notes on it.

"I'd think, How do you do that?

"Then I was copying Teddy Wilson's runs. It was like an F minor sixth run, that you can use on B-flat seventh. And I said, 'Oh that's how he does it!' And I finally got that down. And I got some descending runs, and I thought, 'This is great!' Some of my friends and I formed a little group. We started playing Elks' Clubs, and I thought I was king of the world.

"We lived on Austin Boulevard near 16th Street in Cicero–1634 Austin Boulevard. Al Capone, the Organization, had a huge three-story apartment building on the corner of 16th Street and Austin Boulevard, big yellow-brick building.

"When I was about seventeen, we were rehearsing our dance band in my basement. Four brass, four saxes, three rhythm."

His sister, Irene, would always remember this. She said, "I was always fascinated by my brother rehearsing in the basement with different bands and singers, and they were having so much fun, I just knew that I wanted to do that too." Born January 18, 1932, Irene was eleven years Roy's junior and so must have been about six when that band was in rehearsal.

Meanwhile, Roy said, "The guys started saying to me, 'Hey, get us some work.' So I said, 'Maybe Mr. Capone can help me.' I didn't know Al or anything, but I'd seen his brother, Ralph, around. So I'm hanging around the corner, and finally I see him. I say, 'Ralph! We've got a real good dance band and we're trying to get some work. And I was just hoping there was some way you could help me.' He said, 'See me in about a week. Maybe I can tell you something.'

"Went back there in a week. Didn't see him. Ten days go by. Finally I see Ralph again. I said, 'Ralph, I was talking to you last week about getting some work for our dance band.' He said, 'Yeah, I remember. Look, we got a place up on the North Side called the Campus. It's west of the Northwestern University campus, and we need a band up there. If your band is any good, you've got a job. If it's no good, you're out. Friday and Saturday.'

"Great! So we went. We had a good band. We started getting bookings all over the Midwest. It was a cooperative, but they elected me the leader. I'd do announcements. I was writing maybe half the charts for the band. We traveled a great deal, young guys seventeen or eighteen years old. All the local ballrooms everywhere. Bare essentials and making no money to speak of, but having a great time and the orchestra was excellent. It would be good today. It was billed as Roy Kral and His Orchestra.

I thought it sounded too Czechoslovakian, we should change it to something classy.

"But traveling on the road, I was having a hard time keeping everybody together. Finally I took the book and a few of the players and joined a good Midwestern band by the name of Charlie Agnew. He was good and we played a lot of hotels and so forth.

"But the war was on. It became a matter of enlist or be drafted, so I enlisted in the army in 1942. I went into a military police band. We lived in a tar-paper barracks up in Skokie, Illinois. Not only were we bandsmen, we were also on K.P., and walking guard duty at night carrying rifles. All of it. Four years later, I was in Battle Creek, Michigan, guarding German prisoners with a shotgun.

"Military Police for four years, first in Skokie, then in Fort Sheridan, Illinois, which was a cushy job. I had gotten in trouble with my sergeant in Skokie. Well, we had a fight. He had me shipped out for combat duty. So I took all the charts for our army dance band and said, 'Look, these belong to me. This is *my* book.' And I took it with me.

"When I got to Fort Sheridan, I ran into a Sergeant Papandrea, a career army man. He said, 'You're from the MP battalion band.' I said, 'Yeah. I ran into some trouble over there and I'm sent for combat.' He said, 'You play piano, right? You're an arranger?' I said, 'Yeah.' He said, 'We're forming a band. So hang on.' Two days later, I get a call. I go over to this beautiful building–they called it The Hotel–on Fort Sheridan base. I had my own room, I had a piano in it, it was warm. I went from tar-paper barracks to heated heaven.

"He got me a pass for my car. I could drive my car up from Cicero, put it on the post. And he said, 'You're free to do anything you like. Just show up for formations and if you want a leave, here's a permanent pass.'

"It was really sweet. We would play the officers' club, play a lot of USO dances. Finally that broke up and I was sent to Detroit. The Detroit band did a lot of broadcasting over WWJ, the Detroit News station. A huge auditorium. We were the star band in the area. It was a concert band, forty-five or fifty men. I wrote for that, I wrote for the dance band, I did all kinds of things.

"Then I went to Battle Creek, a huge hospital facility for wounded veterans. We would push a small sixty-note piano on wheels through the wards. There'd be a guy carrying a snare drum, a bass player, maybe an alto and a trumpet. We'd go through the wards, playing for all these guys. I saw what a basket case really means. No arms, no legs. They were in wicker baskets.

"Some of them, poor guys, part of the skull was missing, and you could see the gray brain showing through transparent skin. These guys were really beat up. But damn! they enjoyed having somebody come around and play some music for them. We went through all the wards almost every day. Then we would play for dances at night. I was discharged after four years. That was 1946.

"I went back to Detroit, to WWJ, because the announcers, the producers, the music directors, knew that I was the arranger for that army band. I said, 'I'd like to have a job here at the station as an arranger.' I was hired. I lived in a hotel room. I had a little pump organ for a keyboard, and I started doing charts for the WWJ orchestra, which had violins, the whole thing. It was very nice. Finally I realized that here I am, head down writing arrangements, and I never hear them because they play them too early in the morning and I stay up all night long writing. I said, 'Wait a minute, I'm going home.' I quit, packed up my stuff, and went back to Chicago, no prospects in sight. I couldn't take just arranging.

"Got to Chicago. I met George Davis. He had a group. He'd just lost his piano player. He had a great bass player, a great drummer, and he played very nice alto. He said, 'Join us.' They played at a little place on the South Side called Jump Town, which became quite famous. Western Avenue and 47th Street. Played there maybe a year.

"Finally, my friend Bob Anderson from seventeen-year-old dance-band days, brings a young blonde singer in to hear our group. He said, 'Let her sing. She's a great singer.' I said, 'Oh man, don't be bringing your girls in and asking me to let them sing. And you want me to play for 'em?'"

The girl's name was Jacqueline Ruth Cain.

Jackie was born on May 22, 1928, in Milwaukee, Wisconsin, a workaday city north of Chicago best known for shoes and beer. It was also the home town of Woody Herman, Bunny Berigan, and Hildegarde, who was a year or two ahead of Woody in their high school.

Like Woody Herman, Jackie's mother is of German and Polish stock, a common mixture in Milwaukee. Jackie's late father was of mixed German, Irish, and English stock.

"My mother and father were divorced when I was very young," she said. "I only saw my father maybe once a week. But I was close to him. I admired him so much. He had a great personality. He was funny, he loved music, he loved to go to theater. He was a salesman. He sold office furniture, which was not really what he wanted to do, because he was quite a good artist. But at that time, the Depression, he couldn't continue. He had to make a living, so that's what he did. I think that's the reason he later became an alcoholic. My dad could draw. He had a special talent for it. My family on my father's side, several of them are artists. My cousin is a staff artist on the *Milwaukee Journal.*

"I guess frustration is what drove my father to drink, and being a sales-man, you tend to drink anyway, with clients and lunches. I think he was just a very disillusioned man. He shot himself when he was about sixty-two years old. It was about the same time Jack Kennedy died. It was a big blow to me.

"I was, I guess, a natural singer. We never had a piano. My mother liked to sing, and she would teach me songs by singing them to me. My father was the manager of a little neighborhood theater. They always had amateur hour on Monday nights. One Monday, they didn't have enough amateurs, so my dad wanted me to do it. I was about six years old, but I knew a couple of songs. So they entered me in this amateur contest, just to fill out the program. And I won. And that of course started it.

"My mother taught me more songs and helped me to do more, wher-ever there'd be an amateur hour. I started singing at places like the American Legion post when I was very, very young.

"By the time I was fourteen or fifteen, I wanted to sing very badly. I just loved listening to the radio and learning songs. We didn't have a phonograph. I learned from Jo Stafford. She must have been one of my earliest influences.

"I was a very shy person, not secure in it at all. But I got up the courage to ask bandleaders, 'Could I sit in?' I went to the Eagle's Ballroom, and if they had a good band, I'd say, 'Could I sing a number?' And they'd say, 'Are you any good?' And I'd say, 'Yeah, I'm good.' I don't know how I got the nerve to do that. I had to screw up my courage even to approach the guy. I sang with Horace Heidt's band at the Riverside Theater at fourteen. I got up and sang one tune and they asked me to come back and sing at every show. They put me on a chair, because I was very small.

"After that, I started working with local bands that played for dances on Saturday night. We played the then-current big band stock arrange-ments. I sang with that band all over Milwaukee. I finally graduated from high school and I got a job for a full week at a club in downtown Milwaukee with a band.

"Jay Burkhardt was up, visiting his aunt, I think. He said, 'You sing well. I'd like you to come down to Chicago and work with my band. We have three or four jobs a week.' He gave me his phone number and his card and said, 'Please talk to your parents and see if you can make it.' Chicago is only ninety miles away, but I'd never been out of Milwaukee. In the meantime, I'd also met Bob Anderson, who was playing with a band at the Schroeder Hotel. He was also an arranger. Was he in the army with you, Roy?"

"No, he was in my band when we worked for Capone."

"The musicians in Milwaukee," Jackie said, "had been turning me on to other singers. They'd say, 'Have you ever heard Billie Holiday?' They'd give me records to play. By then we had a phonograph. I liked Peggy Lee, Anita O'Day, Billie Holiday, Ella Fitzgerald, and the Andrews Sisters.

"I asked my mother if I could go to Chicago and work with the Jay Burkhardt band, and of course she said, 'No. I can't let you go down there and live in a hotel by yourself. You're too young. You'd have to have supervision and everything.'

"So I cried and carried on and stayed in my room, and my stepfather said, 'Let her try it. She'll be back in a month.' So I called Jay Burkhardt. My mother spoke to him, and they arranged for me to stay at his house with his family.

"I lived with the family in Hegewisch. It's right near Gary and Hammond. A real working-class area.

"Jay's parents had a little grocery store. They lived behind the store, and they owned a house. And they were wonderful people. I enjoyed that time so much, because I never had a real family life like they did. Everybody sat down at the table together. My folks had a grocery store too, and we lived behind the store. My mother or stepdad, either one of them had to get up and answer the doorbell every time someone walked in. It was a real Mom and Pop operation. Somebody always had to leave the table, and we never really had a meal together.

"Bob Anderson was, like, a real buddy of mine. He wrote arrangements for me with Burkhardt's band. I had a couple of really great charts. Kind of dissonant. Boyd Raeburnish. Lou Levy played piano on that band. Jimmy Gourley, the guitarist who lives in Paris now. Cy Touff. And Joe Williams. We sang the same charts, but I was an octave higher. Irene"—she referred to Roy's sister—"sang with the band. A lot of people started out with that band." (Eventually, in 1957, Irene would join the Maynard Ferguson band and leave Chicago permanently.)

It was during Jackie's period with Burkhardt that Bob Anderson took her to Jump Town to meet Roy. When Roy showed the usual pianist's reluctance to have a girl singer sit in, Anderson drew him over to the bar. "We had a couple of drinks," Roy said, "and he talked me into it. And Jackie sang. And she was *good.*

"The owner of the club was there, and he said, 'Hey, she's great. You guys need a vocalist on the weekends.' 'We do?' 'You do.'

"We had a vocalist on the weekends, Jackie. She was seventeen, something like that. Voluptuous and beautiful!"

It is a judgment with which musicians have concurred ever since. There is a long line of musicians who at one time or another have had distant crushes on Jackie. Aside from her cool beauty, they love her intonation.

"Pretty soon we had some things going, some nice charts. Then she was singing with us every night of the week. We started to do broadcasts on WBBM radio, remotes. We became very hot around Chicago, and we were proud of it."

Jackie said, "I sort of had a crush on Roy, but I was quite a bit younger, and he had a girl who was older, very sophisticated. If he was interested in me, he didn't look it. One New Year's Eve, we were working at Jump Town. Midnight came, and I thought, 'Here's my chance!' I was waiting to kiss the guy. After we sang *Auld Lang Syne*, I gave him this big wet juicy kiss. Suddenly he started looking at me differently. So then he started driving me to the train. I was still living with Jay Burkhardt's family in Hegewisch.

"The last train was at 2 A.M. If I missed it, we had to sit in a restaurant until 6 in the morning.

"Dave Garroway had his radio show, the 1160 Club. He talked about us all the time. He'd say, 'You ought to hear this group at Jump Town.'"

Roy said, "And Garroway would present us in his concerts at the Morrison Hotel. Name groups and local groups. We had heard Dave Lambert and Buddy Stewart with Gene Krupa singing *What's This?* We'd heard Louis Armstrong"–Roy imitated Armstrong's scat style–"and Bing Crosby, and we added it all together and said, 'We can *do* that.' So I wrote some things for two voices and the alto.

"We were on one of Dave Garroway's concerts opposite Charlie Ventura's group. Buddy Stewart, Kai Winding, Shelly Manne on drums, Lou Stein on piano, Bob Carter on bass. A hot group."

Jackie said, "Buddy Stewart was the first one I ever heard sing *Try a Little Tenderness*. He was singing ballads, then he also did the stuff with Kai and Charlie, the three-way thing they did. If he had lived, he would have been a big star."

Stewart, who was from New Hampshire, had sung in a quartet with the Claude Thornhill vocal group called the Snowflakes, and, after service in the army, joined the Gene Krupa band. The Dave Lambert–Buddy Stewart *What's This?* with Gene Krupa was the first recorded bop vocal. But Stewart was equally effective as a ballad singer. He died in a New Mexico car crash in May, 1950, about two years after Jackie met him. He was twenty-eight.

"Shelly Manne was such a gas," Jackie said. "I remember I had *never* heard a drummer play so beautifully behind a singer. When I would do a ballad, he would play all these brush strokes and these little touches, nuances and color. I almost forgot what I was singing, sometimes, because I'd be listening to him, and I'd say, 'Where am I?'"

"Once in a while that will happen with Roy, too. He'll throw a chord in there and you almost forget your lyrics. Yeah!

"Buddy Stewart was just so good. It was nice getting to know those guys, working with them. And of course after that was when we started to work with Charlie. He came to hear us at a Dave Garroway concert. He liked Roy's writing."

"We were a well-rehearsed group," Roy said of the Davis band. "Tight. We just poured it on. Three days later, Charlie Ventura came out with his manager, Don Palmer, and listened to us at the Beehive, where we were playing now. Next day they called us, and said to Jackie and me, 'We're forming a new group, and we'd like to have the two of you join us. We're going to open at the Blue Note in Chicago in three weeks. Will you write the book for us?'

"I did nothing but write charts for the Charlie Ventura group."

"It was a smash," Jackie said. "The charts sounded good, and we got all kinds of rave reviews, and the band just took off.

"Actually, I joined Charlie first. He hired me alone, because he had a job at the College Inn at the Sherman Hotel. He had a ten-piece band. And I worked with Buddy Stewart and Shelly Manne and that group. They only needed a girl singer for that particular job. They had air time every night from the College Inn. I just did my little tunes, and Roy wrote my arrangements. The announcer was in the studio and couldn't see us. So he thought Kai Winding was the girl and Jackie Cain was the guy. And he'd say, 'And now the lovely Kai Winding.' Kai was teased about that one for a long time."

Roy said, "Then Charlie got Bennie Green on trombone, Ed Shaughnessy on drums, Conte Candoli on trumpet, Boots Mussulli on baritone, Charlie on tenor, Gus Cole on bass, and me on piano. We started recording, doing concerts all over, traveling, we won all the polls, *Down Beat, Metronome.* It was a very hot group."

"What was the first record you made with Charlie Ventura?"

"*Lullaby in Rhythm* was one of them," Jackie said, "but I don't think it was the first."

As we were talking, I heard in my head Jackie's voice singing the verse of the song, so long ago: "When the day is done and the sun is red, out in the western sky. Then you la-ay your head on your tiny bed, and you close your sleepy eyes." I sang it back at her, with the dropping-fourth melisma on the word "lay."

She said, "I remember going into the other room at the record date, and thinking, 'I don't like this straight. Let me think about this a minute.' I thought about the phrasing for a minute, how to do it a little differently. And I made it up.

"I sang the first chorus, and Roy came in on the vocalese. By then we had started hanging out together."

"Romance in Chicago," Roy said sardonically.

"Romancing a little," Jackie said. "And then when we were on the road with Ventura, we actually started living together."

"Shocking stuff, in those days," I said.

During this period, Jackie was studying with a voice teacher named Don Maya. Then Irene Kral studied with him and, at Irene's suggestion, so did I. He was a short, barrel-shaped Mexican who had a wonderful gift of teaching.

"Don was good at teaching technique," Jackie said. "There are a lot of teachers who know how to coach and how to work with songs. But I don't think that's what you want. You want to develop your own style and the way to do that is by doing it. It's an evolutionary process. In the beginning, you always emulate whom you admire.

"Early Sarah is what I really admired. And so I tried to sing like her, and I sounded a little like her at that point. I used to do all those slurring things. And one day I realized it was silly to try to sing like somebody else, because you had to develop your own sound. You had to be original to be anybody. And I said, 'I'm not going to try to be anything I'm not. I come from Milwaukee, I'm American, I'm white. I'm just going to sing straight ahead with a good sound and try to make the lyrics mean something.'

"But the midwestern *r* is detrimental in singing, really. People to this day can still peg that I'm from the Midwest, because I have those very hard *r*'s, and the broad *a*'s. The broad *a*'s are okay for singing, because you *want* to have the broad vowels. But the *r*'s are a give-away."

"Did you study voice, Roy? Ever?"

"Nope."

Jackie said, "In fact Roy always hesitated singing. He never really wanted to sing. I started to coax him as we went along, and he had to do a couple of things where we sang lyrics. I guess it was hard at first to do both. When you're a piano player, it's difficult."

"Nat Cole told me *he* found it difficult," I said. "If anybody should have been at ease, he should have. He said it divided your attention. He said he sang better when he didn't play."

"And you play better if you don't sing," Roy said.

"Roy never really wanted to sing because he didn't think of himself as a singer. In the beginning, he had kind of a funny little fast vibrato ..."

"It was a Skinnay Ennis vibrato," Roy said. "Jackie told me, 'Listen, why don't you use this Don Maya approach? It'll help you.'

"So I started practicing. We'd warm up together. Play the chord on the piano. Like Don Maya did. And then sing the long tones. Then sing the scale going up and coming down a few times. Then half step up, right up for two octaves."

"Well," Roy said, "all of a sudden it was much easier to sing. I could control it, I had breath control, I could hit the notes where they were supposed to be. And it fixed my vibrato."

"The thing about scales that's important," Jackie said, "it's not so much singing—it's a question of becoming really comfortable and familiar with your voice. The more you sing, the more you feel natural doing it. And when you sing scales and sing long tones, you're actually building your diaphragm. That was Don Maya's main thing, to sing on the breath. Remember when he'd say, 'On the breath'? Because you have to build up the diaphragm so that it can support the tone. For example, when we do clinics and talk to kids, you're not telling them what they want to hear. You say, 'Look, what you really have to do is learn a little about technique and sing long tones and do these things.' It's like being a weightlifter. You have to build up the musculature necessary for singing, if you want to be really good at it.

"And it's better if you play an instrument, and really understand chords and the way chords move, and so forth, to be able to do improvisation. And they don't want to hear that. They want to get up and sing off the top of their heads, but it's never going to be very good if they do that. You have to have more knowledge and more experience with vocalizing."

Jackie's work with Don Maya came to an end: she and Roy went on the road with Charlie Ventura. First stop: New York.

Jackie said, "That first time in New York with Charlie Ventura was a very special thing. To drive to New York, to come through the Lincoln Tunnel, to see this big city, to be working at the Royal Roost—opposite Bird, and Tadd Dameron's group—was thrilling. Such an exciting time. The images of the city. We stayed in a hotel at 49th and Broadway, and worked at the Royal Roost, which was right nearby . . ."

Roy said, "First we were opposite Tadd Dameron's group, then Dizzy's. Then Billy Eckstine was there. Then Charlie Parker. And another singer was there, Kenny Hagood."

"I remember he used to eat an onion like an apple, before he'd go on," Jackie said.

"Said it was good for his voice," Roy said. "When Charlie Parker was there, opposite Charlie Ventura, occasionally when it was time for Charlie to go on, Al Haig would be delayed, for one reason or another. Or not show up. And Bird would say, 'Hey, Roy, come on!' And I would play the first tune, and that would be it. A few days would go by and Al wouldn't be there again. Bird would say, 'Okay, Roy, you be Al now.'"

"Were you nervous?" Jackie asked.

"Sure I was nervous! Are you kidding? Coming to New York? Working at the Royal Roost? Opening a set with Charlie Parker? Oooo! Look out!"

Jackie said, "There's one scene I have always remembered from that time. We were working opposite Mingus. One time we worked there, Mingus was there, working with Bird. And for some reason—well, I know the reason—Bird was late and he didn't show up. And Mingus got on the microphone and delivered a tirade about how this kind of musician gave the music a bad name, and gave us a bad reputation. And he was talking about Charlie Parker.

"And I remember at that time too, we'd loan Bird a lot of money. Hey, got five, got ten? He nickeled and dimed us to death, and he was doing that to a lot of people. You knew what he was doing, but you couldn't say no to him. He was a wonderful guy."

"He was so *brilliant*," Roy said. "And charming! A *nice* man, a lovely man. And so eloquent."

"I used to love to sit and watch him play," Jackie said, "because of the way he used his hands on the saxophone. His fingers hardly moved from the keys. Minuscule movements. He kept his fingers sort of open. They weren't real bent. He was just so technically proficient on that instrument, it was amazing, and I just used to sit and watch his fingers, because I couldn't believe all these notes were coming out and the way he was playing—so effortlessly. Total focus."

"This was 1948, '49," Roy said. "With Ventura at the Royal Roost, we were doing live broadcasts with Symphony Sid. He would come on the air and ... " Roy sang the front strain of *Jumpin' with Symphony Sid.* "And one night, I remember, he said something like, 'And now Jackie Cain and Roy Kral are going to join Charlie Ventura. They've been doing a little light housekeeping around New York.' I thought, 'You son of a bitch!'"

"He was probably stalling," Jackie said. "He probably couldn't think of anything else to say. He was kind of a goofy guy."

"Blurted to the world?" I said.

"Well, on the radio," Roy said. "Cat's out of the bag."

"I'm glad it wasn't being broadcast in Milwaukee, that's all I can tell you," Jackie said, laughing. "But I wanted to get to know Roy better. We were living together, and getting along very well."

"Well it worked," Roy said, "because here we are. We'll be celebrating our wedding anniversary in June. We got married June 19, 1949." This alone makes Roy unusual: one of the few men who can remember the date of his wedding anniversary.

Jackie said, "We were only with Charlie a year and a half."

"Yes," I said, "but it had a considerable impact. Then you went on your own. But as I recall, the billing wasn't Jackie and Roy, it was Jackie Cain and Roy Kral."

"Jackie and Roy was catchy, and it was easier," Roy said.

"We left Charlie Ventura and got married," Jackie said. "We were having problems with Charlie. He was a wonderful guy and we loved him. But he was very, very jealous. Whenever we would do something that would get a lot of applause . . . If I sang a solo, and got a lot of applause, he wouldn't let me sing the next set."

Roy said, "Newsmen would come up to us if we had been doing something unique with the unison voices or voices and horns, and they'd want to talk to us. He forbade us to talk to anyone until he okayed it. Or they had to go through him before they could talk to us."

"One time," Jackie said, "the whole band was supposed to be interviewed for a New York paper, I think the *Mirror*. It was a feature story for the Sunday magazine section. We all went to this meeting and he didn't show up on time. In the meantime, the photographer and the guy who was going to write the piece started asking questions. And so we started answering. Finally Charlie arrived. Then the band got up and they took pictures of us. When the article came out the following week, it was mainly about us. Which was not our fault. The article was all about the voice-horn thing."

Jackie said, "Charlie got very angry about the article, and we had a big fight about it. It happened quite often. And we thought, 'Do we need this?'"

"It was quite upsetting," Roy said. "Actually we were stupid to leave that early, because the band had just reached a pinnacle. We were named the best small band that year by both *Metronome* and *Down Beat*. We were at a crest of popularity. The last concert we did, the Gene Norman concert in Pasadena, they still sell that record. And it still sounds good."

"And the way it was presented," Jackie said, "the way Charlie would introduce the guys as they came out, it had a certain quality about it. But it got uncomfortable, and when we decided to leave, the bass player, Kenny O'Brien, who was also unhappy with the job, decided to come with us. His wife, Elaine Leighton, was a drummer. And so we said, 'Let's use Elaine on drums.' So we formed a group with cello. We made four sides on Atlantic."

Roy said, "It was amplified cello, tremolo guitar to sustain long notes, and arco bass, and then the drums and piano and voices. For ensemble work, it was an unusual sound, among other applications."

"We had it for about a year," Jackie said, "but the world was not ready for that kind of a group. It was ahead of its time. It was the first time I ever heard of a group having a cello. It blended well with the voices. Roy wrote some nice arrangements. Finally we had to disband, because we weren't making any money. Then we started doing a duo. Sometimes we worked with bass."

"We worked around Chicago," Roy said. "Little odds and ends jobs. We wound up with some group. . . . You were pregnant, and it was the last of the engagements because you were going to retire to have the baby. We were at the Stage Door in Milwaukee. The following week Anita O'Day was coming in, and she needed a pianist. She talked to me and said, 'Listen, would you like to travel with me for a while?' Jackie said, 'Well, I'm going to be home, I'm not going anywhere.' So I did that for about nine months. Traveled with Anita as pianist and conductor, rehearsed all the groups we'd pick up in Kansas City and Denver and wherever."

"She had nice things to say about Roy in her book," Jackie said. "One of the few nice things she said was about Roy."

"Anita was going to Hawaii, and I didn't want to be that far from Jackie. I got a job working at some little joint in Chicago, just playing solo piano. And occasionally singing a song. A woman owned the place. And she was a singer. And she would always want me to accompany her. And she sang like, well, like a hysterical Judy Garland. It was loud and poignant . . . and super-adequate. And the bartender, Sammy, would also sing, but he was Mario Lanza!" Roy sang in a Lanza voice: "See the pyramids along the Nile. . . . Same song, every night. I didn't hate it. I was making a living.

"That was 1951. Nickie was born in 1952.

"I continued to work at this place, the Casbah, on Rush Street. Then I worked at the Black Orchid, playing intermission piano. They had class acts, and I would accompany different acts when they needed it. Once again, I was making a living, but it was not what I wanted to do."

"And we didn't want to start anything until Nickie was at least a year and a half old," Jackie said.

"Then, all of a sudden," Roy said, "out of the blue we got a call from Charlie Ventura. He said, 'I've bought a jazz club, it's in New Jersey, outside Camden. I'm starting up the group, and I'd like you guys to join us.' It was called Charlie's Open House, and it was really great. He would have acts, we played for dancing, and we also did the show. Here was a marvelous way to get back into the business, be together, and have employment. Start over again.

"We stayed with him about a year, traveled, played theaters, did more recordings.

"We were in New York doing something. One of our friends we'd known in Chicago, Rogers Brackett, who was an advertising man, introduced us to Alec Wilder. He said, 'Alec Wilder is a very important man.

He has a lot of connections and I'd like to have him hear what you do, because I've been talking about you.' I had admired Alec Wilder early on. I heard his octet in 1938. On my Victrola! He was one of my early heroes. We finally met him. Our friend set up a meeting in someone's apartment on Central Park South, twentieth floor or something like that, just Jackie and me, piano and the two voices.

"The piano was a spinet. Alec went over to a couch and sat down with his back to us. I understand why. He didn't want to have to register like or dislike. We go into our stuff. We were doing some very good things. We were very well prepared. We'd finish a song, like we were doing a *Lover* at breakneck tempo. And it was all working. And we'd hear Alec going"—Roy imitated Alec's growl—"'Oh no! Oh no!' and I thought, 'Oh shit, we're dead.' But he meant, 'Oh my God! I don't believe it.'

"We finally knew that, and we went on and on. We finally started looking up at the pictures on the piano. I see Winston Churchill, seated with a young woman and his wife. I said, 'Where are we?' And Rogers said, 'This is Sarah Churchill's apartment and I'm sort of taking care of it while she's out of town.' I thought, here we are looking at a picture of Winston Churchill and at the same time we're performing for Alec Wilder. What a day!

"Alec got us an audition with Max Gordon at the Blue Angel on 55th Street near Third Avenue. It was a very famous cabaret. We were hired. Bart Howard was playing in the show room. We got to know him; we got to know all the acts. Andy Griffith, Orson Bean. We stayed and stayed and stayed. The pianist in the barroom was Bobby Short. He was just wailing.

"It was a really slow, slow time for jazz. But we were able to work, with just piano and two voices, all over the country. We were out in Los Angeles in a supper club, up in San Francisco, the Purple Onion in New York, Boston, Toronto at the Town Tavern."

Jackie said, "We often worked opposite people we liked. We worked opposite Lenny Bruce quite a few times, or near him. We'd be at the Interlude in L.A., and he'd be at the Crescendo, downstairs, and we got to hear him a lot. We got to meet people."

"Then after doing enough work that way," Roy said, "we had a circuit we could go on. We were making more money so we could take a rhythm section with us. Or we'd get out to California and give Shelly Manne a call. He'd work with us and Leroy Vinnegar on bass. A lot of recording with Creed Taylor."

I said to Jackie, "Are you aware that you're Creed's favorite singer?"

"Noooo!" she said.

"Yes. He told me so."

"You know," Roy said, "it's a *treat* for me to play behind Jackie. I take great pride in accompanying her, and of course I love listening to her. To this day, after working all these years, I'm still thrilled. Certain songs she finishes, I wish I could go out in the audience and applaud. Sometimes I'll do what I've seen the symphony musicians do. I'll knock on the corner of the piano when she finishes something that just knocks me out."

While they were working in Los Angeles at Gene Norman's Crescendo, Jackie learned she was pregnant again.

"Having a second child was perfect," Jackie said, "because it was four years after Nickie and we wanted them to have each other."

"At that time," Roy said, "we were living at Barney Kessel's house in L.A., remember? And we didn't know what we were going to do or how we were going to work it out. We came back to our apartment in New York, which we hadn't seen for a year. We'd been traveling that much. Meanwhile the water has been turned off, the gas has been turned off, and pushed through the mail slot is a mound of mail about three feet high. We took care of that, we lived there for a while, then decided to move to Milwaukee and live in an apartment above Jackie's mother's. And Dana would be born in Milwaukee."

Jackie said. "It was perfect, because my mother had just bought this house, and we could have the upper apartment and do what we wanted with it."

"However, before we left," Roy said, "we did the *Tonight* show. Steve Allen still had it. They put Jackie behind the piano so they couldn't see she was pregnant. Then we got to Milwaukee. There was a big IGA supermarket that Jackie's mother and father had by now. One morning one of the helpers doesn't show up. Jackie's dad, Ted, says, 'Hey, Roy, could you help out at the store?' I said, 'I'd be happy to.' So here I am stocking shelves, loading coffee cans up, putting the price stamp on them, take the old ones from the back and put them at the front, dust them off, and there's a woman walks by with a cart. She hesitates a moment and looks at me. She goes about ten feet past me, and she backs up and she says to me, 'Excuse me, weren't you on the *Tonight* show four or five days ago?' And I say, 'That's right, Ma'am.' And I keep moving those coffee cans.

"We stayed in Milwaukee about six months. Associated Booking was nice enough to advance us some money, and then they got us some jobs. We went to California and played some jobs out there. We were carrying a governess with us and two kids with high chairs. We were gypsies."

"We had a buggy in the back seat of the car," Jackie said. "We used a sterilizer every night in the hotel to sterilize bottles."

"We were coming back to Mr. Kelly's in Chicago," Roy said. Mr. Kelly's, in the Rush Street area of the Near North Side, was an exquisite presentation room owned by the Marienthal brothers, George and Oscar, who also owned the London House, a major room in the jazz circuit and an excellent restaurant. Mr. Kelly's was a perfect room for singers, with a good piano, good sight lines, and excellent sound system.

"That's where we were headed, Mr. Kelly's," Roy said. "We stopped in Las Vegas to see a friend who was playing trumpet in one of the bands. And who do we run into but Don Palmer, Charlie Ventura's manager. He says, 'Hey! What are you doing?'

"I said, 'We're going to Mr. Kelly's in Chicago for two weeks.'

"He said, 'Wait a minute. One of my groups fell out. They're not going to open tonight at the Thunderbird. Fill in!'

"I said, 'Oh no. I don't even have a rhythm section.'

"He said, 'I'll get you a rhythm section. You open tonight!'

"We got a rhythm section, we rehearsed, we opened, it was very successful. They loved what we were doing and it was nice. When our two weeks were over and it was time to go to Mr. Kelly's, the people at the Thunderbird said, 'You can't leave.'

"We went to Mr. Kelly's, and came back and stayed at the Thunderbird for about eleven months."

Jackie said, "That started a new thing for us, working the gambling circuit. Once we played the Thunderbird, we got work at different hotels. Each hotel had more or less its own clientele, so you could do that. We worked about a year at the Sands. We worked at the Dunes, then we went up to Reno and worked at Harrah's and the Wagon Wheel."

"We worked a great deal during the summer at Lake Tahoe," Roy said. "Took our kids with us. And one of my friends lent me his ski boat. We'd have a marvelous time, bippin' around, work San Francisco, then get back to Las Vegas and book another job for another year. We bought a house, lived there for four or five years. The kids were in school, great school system, and we had a marvelous time."

"I must say it was hard at first," Jackie said. "Because the audiences there couldn't care less about what we did. It was basically a gambling crowd. But we worked in the best lounges that existed at that time. At one time we were at the Sands, opposite Red Norvo and his group. And that was the hotel that had Frank Sinatra, Lena Horne, Sammy Davis, Nat King Cole, all the good acts. I met Nat Cole there. It was the one place that had some good music, so you did get a better clientele. Nevertheless, it was still a gambling place. But it taught me that you had to have a little bit more showmanship. I used to just stand there with my hands at my sides and just sing. I found that I had to get into it more. I don't do it much, but it makes you aware of it.

"I have noticed that the best work we do is where we're shown well and have good lighting. It all helps. It enhances what you're doing. It puts a lot of drama in it when you're singing a song that tries to tell a story.

"At first I didn't like working there. You didn't get the applause at the end, you didn't get the attention that you would in a jazz club. And so I'd go home feeling very depressed. But as we worked there, we learned to play to the audience more and finally we started to get a reaction. And more people who heard about our being there started coming in when they were in town. Especially opposite Red Norvo and his great group."

"We recorded a number of albums with Columbia," Roy said. "And then we got with Creed Taylor. The gem of the ocean."

"Look," I said, "you must get asked this question all the time. But how does a marriage survive when you are *always* together?"

Roy said, "This way, being together all the time, we have more time to argue." And they both laughed. "Well," he continued, "we like the same things. We like music, we are friends."

"We do everything together," Jackie said. "We even cook together. We sleep together, we walk together, we talk together. Everything is a sharing. I was an only child. I would never be in this business if I had to be alone on the road. I have to have a companion. And Roy is my companion, as well as my lover, my husband, my daddy, everything. We get along. We've had our rough periods. We went through a couple of years when we almost broke up. But I guess that's the test of our having a strong relationship, because we got back together and it's been tighter than ever ever since."

"That was when we were working on the gambling circuit—Las Vegas, Reno, Lake Tahoe," Roy said. "We'd shoot out to San Francisco, then down to L.A., then back to Las Vegas. For eleven months straight we worked at the Thunderbird, at the Sands for nine months. Then we got into all the temptations of Las Vegas. Booze, broads, gambling. I'd be walking down a hall somewhere, and one of the chorus girls would come by with her fur coat on, so there'd be no clothing marks when she'd go back onstage naked, and she'd go: Tah-dah!"

"Were you falling victim to this?"

Roy sighed, then said, "Yes!" and then laughed.

"Yes, Father," Jackie said in a mock respectful voice, as if I were their confessor, laughing too. "Then there was a lot of tension, because we had to work such long hours. Like, our shift was generally from midnight till six in the morning. They wanted to get people into the lounges after the second show. We would do at least four or five sets, forty-five minutes to an hour long. I started to resent this. There isn't enough money to make you work that much, especially as a singer. My voice was starting to give me trouble. I began to become very lax about being on time, and that drove Roy crazy, because he's a very punctual person. He likes to be there early, and be set up and comfortable. And I felt they were taking advantage of us, and I felt, 'Oh, ten minutes late, fifteen minutes.' And that would get him crazy."

"But the management," Roy said, "would not complain to Jackie. I would get it."

Jackie said, "And I'd say, 'Tell 'em to come to me!' When I thought of it later, I wondered why I was doing it. And I think that was the reason. Because I resented that we were working that hard and not making that much money."

Roy said, "That was 1957, '58, '59, '60."

Jackie said, "The reason we settled there in the first place was that we had a chance to work in one place, and the kids were just of school age. We wanted to be with them. We didn't want to send them away to school or have someone else take care of them all the time. We wanted to raise them ourselves. So we stayed there and we made enough money to get a down payment for a house. We had a nice little place."

Roy said, "The hours were perfect. We'd finish at six in the morning. The desert sun is shining. It's beautiful. We'd get home, have some breakfast, get the kids to school, putter around, water the rose bushes, and then finally say, 'Wow, I'm tired.' Go to sleep, like 10:30 in the morning."

Jackie said, "Roy would get up and pick the kids up and bring them back. After they had dinner, they'd go to bed, and we'd lie down and take a nap. We slept in broken-up hours like that.

"And then one day, after being in Las Vegas for five years, Nickie came home from school and said, 'What's a stripper?'

"It started us to thinking: What future is there for them in Las Vegas? What influences will they have, growing up? It was a nice little hick town when you lived away from the strip, but I got thinking, This is too easily accessible to young kids."

Roy said, "We'd been working, and making money. We'd bought a house, we'd developed equity. But there's no future here. They call it the entertainment capital of the world. But nobody else *knows you're there*. We've disappeared for five years."

"Being from the Midwest, we liked the East Coast a lot. To me, L.A. never seemed like a real city. We had memories of New York being exciting and wonderful and stimulating. We discussed it and finally decided to move to New York. That was in 1961.

"We rented our house in Las Vegas to a bass player. We had a little trailer. We put our mops and our paintings and our brooms and our luggage in the trailer and the kids in the station wagon and we drove to New York City."

Jackie said, "We had no idea where we were going to live. But a very good friend of ours who had worked with Tony Bennett, a bass player named Don Payne, had written to us saying, 'If you ever want to come to New York, come to my house and use it as a base until you get situated.' When we got to New York, we stayed in a motel on the other side of the river before coming into New York. We phoned and said, 'We're here.' He said, 'Fine, come on over to my place tomorrow.'

"We got up, left the motel, and went to his place in Riverdale." Riverdale is a lovely hilly and leafy section of the city just north of the island of Manhattan. Now much of it is covered with red-brick apartment buildings, but in those days it was all single homes; some of it still is. It is on the east bank of the Hudson River, which is grand and regal at that point. Across the river the palisades of New Jersey rise steeply from the water.

Jackie continued: "We got the local paper and found a motel for several nights. We put the kids in school from a motel room, making sandwiches in our room. In the paper we found a house for rent in Riverdale that sounded too good to be true. Roy didn't even want to check it out. He said, 'It's too good, it's going to be too expensive.' The ad said *Private Drive. Use of swimming pool.*"

Roy said, "Five and a half acres overlooking the Hudson River. I said, 'Oh God, Jackie, I don't even want to see it. It'll break your heart.' Then we looked at some of the beehive apartments in New York, the honeycombs. Finally I said, 'Let's take a look. What can it hurt?'"

They pulled up in front of an estate with two big sculptured dogs at the driveway entrance. Jackie said, "This old Victorian house looked like a horror-movie house, scary. A Charles Addams Victorian house. It was Elie Nadelman's house. He was a famous sculptor who died there twenty-five years before. We moved into this house after being investigated by their legal department, who accepted our children when they saw how well-behaved they were, and we got this place. Don Payne went over with us. It was only $300 a month! Seven rooms, with two bathrooms, kitchen, living room with shutters that closed and a little gas fireplace. Marble busts, wooden busts. Beautiful things. We're caressing these things."

Roy continued, "And the house is fifteen minutes from midtown Manhattan, with a private driveway. We moved in. We were overjoyed. There was a 300-year-old copper beech tree in the front yard. It cost a hundred fifty bucks to join the swimming pool across the driveway. We had a sledding hill.

"And we were in New York! We went back to Vegas in 1962 and sold the house we had, then came back to New York. Then a friend of mine, as we were about to leave for a job, said, 'Listen, I'd like to have you sing on a Halo shampoo commercial.' I said, 'We can't do it. We're leaving town.' He said, 'It will probably mean a lot of money to you. Delay it a day.' We did it, it was an easy thing, a bossa nova vocalese." He sang a fragment of it. "We leave town. We're in San Francisco. We start to get checks in the mail. We open up an envelope. There'd be seven checks. Nine hundred dollars. Seven hundred and fifty dollars. Five hundred dollars. I said, 'What *is* this? Here is more money than we make for singing in a club for a whole week, and it's all for the half hour we spent in the studio.'

"When we finally got back to New York, I set up a music production company. I started to go to meetings. I did Cheerios, Plymouth automobiles, Fritos, Borden's instant coffee, Dr. Pepper. Those were the big ones. I'd do the creative work, read the story boards, write the music to fit it. Time everything. Hit all the highlights. We'd be in the studio for three or four hours every two weeks. The money was coming in beautifully. We'd take the kids to lunches at Voisin. We were having a party. We rented a house for the season out at Fire Island. Just having a great time. We were doing this for, what, about four years?"

"Yeah," Jackie said. "And it was the first time that we *ever* had the money and the time to enjoy New York City. We took the kids to the theater. We saw many shows. We had dinners and lunches."

"We also did singing in commercials for other people. Then one day we finished in the studio and we were in the car on the way home and I said to Jackie, 'Hey, what did we just sing?' She said, 'Hmm. God, I can't remember it.' I said, 'This isn't very important stuff, is it?' She said, 'No.'"

"Boring," Jackie interjected.

"I said, 'Well, let's get a group and go on the road.' She said, 'Okay.' And we did."

"It's very seductive," Jackie said. "Because you start making that easy money, after you've worked so hard all your life. When you're raising kids you've got to do something. But after four or five years of it, we said, 'Hey, let's not do it any more.'"

Roy said, "We'd made some money. We bought some real estate in California. We bought ITT, we bought Ford. I didn't know what we were doing at the time, but today, I'm so happy that it went that way.

"It must have been around 1965 or '66 that we went back on the road."

Jackie said, "One day when we were out at Fire Island, we called

Creed Taylor and said, 'We'd like to talk to you, Creed.' We came in from the beach. We said, 'We'd like to make an album. We haven't done anything for four or five years because we've been doing commercials.' We were all ready to give him a big sales talk, and he said, 'Okay.'

"As it turned out, he had something in mind too. He wanted Don Sebesky to write some charts for us. That's when we did the *Time and Love* album."

Roy said, 'For one of the tracks, Creed called Paul Desmond to play the solo on a composition called *Summer Song*."

"There are a lot of other people on it," Jackie said. "Billy Cobham and Hubert Laws and Ron Carter and Bob James. It was fun! Working with strings! We had a seventy-piece orchestra. They did the tracks first and we overdubbed. I don't really like that."

Roy said, "Your ears are covered with the earphones and what you're hearing is coming back to you through the system. It tends to make you sing flat. We've learned to cover just one ear. Wearing earphones and recording in the studio is an alien feeling."

"An unnatural atmosphere," Jackie said. "And if you're recording with orchestra, and they goof, and you do more takes, then it starts to get kind of tired."

Roy said, "And the good part of the song, the place where you had no trouble, all of a sudden a little chink falls out."

"It's the domino theory," Jackie said. "If you don't get a thing in the first take, it's better to leave it and come back to it, I feel. But we did the album, one of the first things we did when we decided to get out of the jingles business. It got us back singing. And then we started to take some jobs."

"We traveled everywhere," Roy said. "I remember we went up for two weeks at the Colonial in Toronto. I've got to tell you about Oscar Peterson's piano! We get onstage at the Colonial, and here is this little five-foot grand piano that sounded like it was strung with rubber bands. We did opening night on it. And I remembered in the back of my head that Oscar said one time, 'Listen, if you're ever in town and need a piano, give me a call.' Bam! The light went on. I called all around and finally got him in Cleveland or Cincinnati or Kansas City or somewhere, and I said, 'Oscar, we opened at the Colonial last night and the piano was terrible.' He said, 'Say no more. Just go to work tonight and don't worry about anything.' Went to work early. And that little crappy piano is on its side in the hallway and up on stage is Oscar's own Steinway B from the warehouse, set up, cleaned up, tuned, ready to go. It was gorgeous! I'll never forget it, and I'll always be grateful. There was only one problem with it. For two weeks I played like Oscar Peterson!" He laughed.

"You *wish*," Jackie said.

"Yeah. I wish!"

"Then what?" I asked when the laughter subsided.

"Well, let's see. In 1971 we went to Europe. We were still living in the house in Riverdale. That year, Creed Taylor was sending a bunch of guys to Europe on a tour he was sponsoring. He said, 'Would you guys like to go?' Were we gonna say, 'No'? He had Hank Crawford, Stanley Turrentine, Freddie Hubbard, Jack DeJohnette, Ron Carter, Joe Farrell, Grover Washington. Come on! We'd never seen Europe, except London."

After that tour, Jackie and Roy moved to the house in Montclair, New Jersey, where they have lived ever since. It is a beautiful big Colonial home on a street of leafy big trees. On a really clear day, you can see the distant spires of Manhattan.

"We had to get out of the house in Riverdale," Jackie said, "because the owner was coming back from Europe. We started looking around and found this house and moved to Montclair. That's when we had the experience with Nickie. . . ."

"You know," I said, "it's a subject I've avoided with you. For years. I never wanted to ask. But if you want to talk about it now, maybe it's time."

"Absolutely," Roy said. "Well." And he paused. "We were living out of suitcases. We had just moved in here. May 1, 1973. There are suitcases open on the floor. We don't know where to put anything. Nothing's settled. And we have this weekend gig. Friday, Saturday, and Sunday. We do Friday night, and everything's terrific. We're overjoyed. We get home and get into bed and about five in the morning, six in the morning, the phone rings. I say, 'What is this?'

"And it's Marshall Mechanik's mother or father. He was Nickie's boyfriend. They were living together. And his mother, or his father, I can't remember, said that they had just heard from Jersey troopers that Marshall's automobile was in a wreck on the highway. They told her Nickie was in the car and she's in the hospital down in Tom's River. And we'd better get down there.

"So we jumped up and got dressed, just praying, thinking, Oh God, I hope she isn't injured too badly, and that nothing is broken. It took an hour and a half or two hours to drive down there.

"We get to the hospital, and we're *waiting*. And the doctor comes out finally, and he says, 'Sit down.' And he said, 'She just passed away, fifteen minutes ago.' I think I grabbed him, I'm not sure. He said, 'Take it easy, take it easy.' I said, 'No, no!' And he said, 'I'm terribly sorry, but she passed away fifteen minutes ago.'"

Jackie said, "We wanted to see her. But he said, 'You wouldn't want to see her.' Later we heard that she had hit her head so hard that even some of her hair was still in the car. She must have had a terrible injury, and if I had seen that, I probably never would have forgotten it."

"And then we were asked where we wanted the body sent," Roy recalled. "Then and there we had to make arrangements. We were just dumbfounded. And we said, 'She wanted to be cremated.' And we arranged for that.

"Then we got back into the car. We were sobbing and crying."

Jackie said, "I don't know how Roy drove."

"I think the car drove itself," Roy said. "We were just wiped out. We walked in the door and Dana said, 'How is she?' And how do you tell her?"

"She idolized Nickie," Jackie said. "Nickie was twenty and Dana was sixteen. And she just started crying and she ran up the stairs, inconsolable. We couldn't touch her. I wanted to hold her, and she just wouldn't have anything to do with it. She had a friend who had been here, staying overnight, which was a good thing. It was just dreadful. We just fell apart.

"Nickie was a singer. She wasn't working at it, but she was very good at it. She loved horses. She was on her way to the Monmouth race track, because she liked to walk the horses to cool them down. I think she had ideas of eventually having a horse and learning more about them. She had ridden a lot in Vegas. She was partners with a friend named Nina Bergman in their own business."

Roy said, "She and her partner the night before had just gotten a big order for chamois bikini bathing suits from some boutique. They were just overjoyed, and so they stayed up late, and she got up early, and didn't have enough sleep. And here she is, driving along. We went to see the road, a two-way road, just pine trees, narrow road, very boring. It just drones on and drones on. She fell asleep, went off the road and into a tree."

Jackie said, "She hadn't been driving more than two or three months. In fact, the last time we had seen her was when we went to the Felt Forum to see Eumir Deodato. And Nickie met us there with her boyfriend Marsh. She brought a big log as a gift for Roy. It had shells on it shaped like hearts that she found on the beach."

Roy said, "Dana just disappeared. We were sobbing, couldn't think. We did call a few friends. They came over and brought us food. We're supposed to go first. Not one of your kids.

"This was on May 5. We were still living out of suitcases. Then it was hard to even care about organizing. The third floor was going to be Nickie's place. Dana would have the guest bedroom, and we would have the master bedroom. Everything was all figured out. Well it was all wrong.

"So then we couldn't put a record on the turntable, because we couldn't stand to listen to music. We'd break out in crying again. I couldn't perform any music. We left the piano and all our stuff at the club, and eventually somebody packed it up and brought it to us. After a week or so, friends started coming by."

Jackie said, "Our best friends, Gerry and Sharon Freeman, who lived right here in town, would bring food over, all ready to eat, salad with the dressing already mixed. And one day they were driving by and they rang the doorbell. I went to the door. Sharon said, 'C'mere,' and we went out. There was a rainbow in the sky, and they wanted to make sure we saw it."

I said, "When was the next time you laughed?"

Jackie said, "I don't remember laughing at all."

Roy said, "Yeah. At some point something was said, and we had to laugh, and I think we were almost hysterical. In the meantime, I'd been digging in the mud in the yard, scraping the walls of the basement, anything I could do to keep my hands busy. Slowly we started to work through it and unpacked. We had to go and pick up her ashes. We did that. We had them here. We waited until one night of the full moon. I thought about her wishes."

Jackie said, "She used to run outside and howl like a wolf. She liked to be mischievous and devilish. And when there was a full moon she'd go outside and ..." Jackie gave an eerily accurate imitation of a wolf's howl. "She'd make a lot of wolf noises at midnight. I used to say, 'Nickie, don't *do* that, the neighbors are going to think you're crazy.' She said, 'I just like to do it.'"

Roy said, "At the full moon, we went out to Fire Island, which was her favorite place. We took her boyfriend and her best friend and Dana. We walked along the beach to the point that reached furthest out to the ocean. And I said, 'Okay, everybody take a handful of these ashes and put them into the ocean.' That's what Nickie wanted. That's what we all did. There was some left, and I said, 'Marshall, you have to take the rest and dump them in.' And he waded out into the ocean, waste-deep in his clothes, and it wasn't warm at the end of May. And he took the ashes and threw them out into the air and a gust of wind blew some of them back on him, and he said, 'That's just like Nickie.'

"After we did this, I was going to read something Alec Wilder had written in his book *Letters I Never Mailed.*"

Jackie said, "He called her Vicky in the book. It's about a little girl who came up to him and said, 'I'm all in pink.'"

"But I couldn't read it," Roy said. "I couldn't talk."

Jackie said, "Alec sent it to us and said, 'Please take this note out to the beach and bury it beneath a shell, with my love.' So we did that as Nickie's ashes were being put into the ocean."

Roy said, "Then we went back to the Freeman's beach house. We had a feast and wine . . ."

". . . and a fire, and told stories about her," Jackie said. "That felt better. Finally, we talked to Creed. It was after quite a few months. He said, 'Look, the best thing you could do is go back to work. You're not going to pull yourself out of this unless you start doing something.' We said, 'Well, maybe he's right. We won't be thinking about it all the time. And we've got Dana to think about. Thank God we've got her.'

"We had some songs we wanted to record, and Creed said, 'We'll do an album.' It turned out to be very strange, all original material, all our material. There was a lot of anger and angst in that album because of what we'd been through."

"Claw music," Roy said.

Jackie said, "People put it on and said, 'What is *that*?' It sounded so harsh, but for us it was cathartic, and Creed allowed us to do it."

Roy said, "Creed said, 'I want you to go into this club. And I'll get you a rhythm section." He got us Ron Carter on bass, Jack DeJohnette on drums, and a vibes player named Dave Friedman. So that was the group. We rehearsed. We played the Half Note, which was then on 56th Street. Later on we did a concert with that group at Carnegie Hall. And we were back into it."

"How do you handle it?" I said.

"You never get over it," Jackie said. "You carry a scar on your heart. Anything that happens that makes you identify with that date. I get a little sad on May 5, but I don't go boo-hoo. The crying wells up at funny times. One day I walked up and saw a pair of her boots in the closet, and you could almost see her feet, because of the way they were worn. And I fell down crying."

Roy's sister, Irene Kral, moved to Los Angeles in the mid–1960s. She married trumpeter Joe Burnett, lived in Tarzana, and had two daughters. For a time she languished in obscurity, then made a series of albums with Alan Broadbent.

In the mid–1970s she began to get the recognition she deserved. Then she discovered that she had breast cancer. I remember visiting her during that time. She remained uncannily optimistic, and whatever fears she felt, she never put her burden on anyone. She died on August 15, 1978. Thus Roy and Jackie lost their daughter, and Roy lost his sister, whom Jackie saw as her own sister, within five years. Irene was forty-six.

One of Irene's daughters, Jodi Burnett, is a cellist. A rather sweet coincidence has occurred. Clint Eastwood used records by Johnny Hartman in the sound track of *The Bridges of Madison County*, giving Johnny a degree of recognition he rarely got when he was alive. Eastwood also used some of Irene's work in the film. Jodi is in the orchestra playing the underscore of that film. Thus she and her mother, seventeen years after Irene's death, are in the soundtrack of the same picture.

Jackie's mother and stepfather are still alive. She and Roy went out to Milwaukee to visit them and got caught in Newark Airport in the blizzard of '96, then caught in a Milwaukee airport fog as they tried to return to New Jersey. It was a long journey home. I was talking to them on the phone a few days later. As you may have noticed, you don't talk to one without the other. Their paragraphs flow together as smoothly as their music. One of them will begin a thought and the other will complete it.

"How would you want to be remembered?" I said.

"One thing I want," Roy said, laughing. "I want to be mentioned as an accompanist."

Jackie said, "And I'd like to be mentioned as a soloist! Because we're a duo, and that's the unique thing about what we do. And that's all they talk about or think about."

And that's how they undoubtedly will be remembered, as a remarkable vocal duo, unique in American musical history, the serene, flawless and exquisite blend of two voices lifting the melodies they have chosen, giving them a new character.

There are, I suppose, no perfect marriages. But theirs comes as close as one is likely to find. Jackie and Roy have lived the story in the songs they sing.

The Sparrow
Edith Piaf

Americans never really knew Edith Piaf. When she died, the *New York Times* said in its obituary, "Strangely, Miss Piaf was perhaps best known in the United States for her *La Vie en rose*, a song of happiness and love." There may have been something ironic about it, but there was nothing strange. Her act was bowdlerized and glamorized for her appearances at the Versailles and the Waldorf-Astoria in New York. Her songs about prostitutes and their *marlous*, about the murders that often ended the search for love, were thrown out or cleaned up for Americans raised on a diet of sexless love in songs and happy endings in movies and *Saturday Evening Post* fiction.

To anyone who really knew her work, death added no unexpected dimension to her legend. Death was in her life and in her songs, gritty realistic ballads about the Paris streets and the outcasts who prowled them. Her songs—and her life—were filled with the desperate faces one sees fitfully in the poems of Villon, the novels of Balzac and Hugo, and the erotic fantasies of Jean Genet.

One of Piaf's classics, *Un monsieur me suit dans la rue*, is about a little girl who dreams of the day when a man will follow her in the street. When at last one does, he is "*un vieux dégoûtant*," a disgusting old man. Later another man follows her in the street—she is now a prostitute. In the final verse her childhood dream is fulfilled for the last time: a sexton follows her coffin.

She sang songs of this kind in the era before rock, when you assuredly did not mention death or prostitution or juvenile sexuality in American songs. *Un monsieur me suit dans la rue* was about all three. Even when rock had become pornographic, satanism filled the grooves of records, and drug use had been chronicled and condoned for more than twenty years in American pops, we heard only a sophomoric rebellion against the

Puritan tradition, bad little boys writing bad little words on walls. We heard nothing—nothing whatever—to compare to the songs of Edith Piaf. Rap of course has changed that somewhat.

Cole Porter dealt with prostitution in *Love for Sale* but not for the mass audience. Porter knew about as much about the harsh life of a whore as Paul Whiteman, by his own honest admission, did about jazz. The song is a soft one, the prostitute's life seen through a misted long lens from the luxurious penthouse apartment on top of the Waldorf-Astoria, where Porter lived in the cushioned comfort of inherited wealth, the same Waldorf where Piaf presented herself with a scrubbed face to the New York chic set. And at that, *Love for Sale* was barred from radio broadcasting for years. *Un monsieur me suit dans la rue* was never played on American radio either, not even in French.

Though the American misrepresentation of Piaf was to some extent corrected in the early years of the LP by the release on the Angel and Capitol labels of collections of her songs, you still could not get *Un monsieur me suit dans la rue*. Nor could you get *Paris-Mediterranée*, a song about a girl who meets a man on a train bound for the Riviera and beds with him. On their arrival in the railway station the next morning, she sees him arrested. She shrugs and says, "You just can't trust the people you meet on trains these days."

Her real name was Edith Giovanna Gassion. She was given the name Piaf by the cabaret owner Louis Leplée. It is Parisian slang for sparrow. (Or at least it was in her day; who can keep up with the slang of Paris?) No name ever suited an entertainer better. Her voice was neither pretty nor melodious. It had that rapid French vibrato that is obtained I know not how—or why. (Even housewives sing that way in France.) But that voice was filled with an intense and urgent energy that could not possibly, it seemed, be coming from so tiny a body. She stood four feet eleven inches tall and, when she was in good health, weighed ninety-nine pounds.

In her work she always wore a simple black dress with a sweetheart neckline. As she stood in a stark spotlight, she seemed all head and hands. And the hands were marvelously expressive. They floated disembodied in the air, open and at ease. As a song progressed, they became more agitated. At last, at the peak of a song's drama, they curled into trembling claws, at once imploring and ominous. In the last months of her life, those wonderful hands, gnarled now by arthritis, looked more than ever like talons. But they never lost their eloquence.

Her songs were, in effect, rhymed short stories of pain, irony, and compassion for the human condition. Occasionally the blues and some country-and-western songs give a hint of a similar flavor. But the blues by their very twelve-bar construction are structured for quick aphoristic snapshots of life, not for long-form story-telling. And country-and-western songs, even those that do deal with comparable subject matter, are almost always compromised by sentimentalism or a maudlin self-pity. Nothing in all the songs of the English language approaches the vinegar imagery of the French *chansons réalistes*, in which the narrative has primacy. There is a tunelessness about many of these songs that no doubt derives from the fact that the lyrics were written first. In all history, only a few composers have been capable of creating fluid contoured melodies for existing text. When lyrics are written first, composers almost always come up with melodies that have a slightly stiff and recitative quality. Thus it was with Piaf's songs, but they worked for her to intense dramatic effect. American songs, in the golden age of Kern and Gershwin and Youmans, put a primary emphasis on melody; French songs, at least of the kind Piaf sang, put it on drama, and must be listened to in a different way. (There is another kind of French song that is gloriously melodic.)

Piaf wrote almost nothing. But no singer was ever more truly defined in her songs. The best of them were drawn from her life by the writers who worked with her, such as Raymond Asso, who created the bulk of her early repertoire. *Paris-Mediterranée* is a case in point.

Traveling to Nice with her half-sister Simone Berteaut, Piaf was smitten by a handsome, well-dressed man who shared their compartment. She leaned close to him, he took her hand, she put her head on his shoulder. When the man stepped into the corridor for a smoke, Piaf told her sister she was mad for him and would never leave him. At Marseille, the man got off the train to stretch his legs. The girls watched in astonishment from a window as two cops clapped handcuffs on him. The man turned and gave her a last smile before being led away.

Piaf later told the story to Asso, who turned it into *Paris-Mediterranée*.

When Piaf was about sixteen, singing in the streets near Porte des Lilas, she became enamored of a little blond delivery boy and sometime bricklayer named Louis Dupont, known as P'tit Louis. They lived together, along with her sister, in a scabrous hotel in the the rue Orfila, where they slept three in a bed. Piaf sang and Louis made his deliveries and on Sundays they went to the films of Tom Mix, Rudolph Valentino, and the little tramp the French call Charlot—Chaplin. She gave birth to a girl she named Marcelle. She soon tired of Louis, resumed her infidelities, and got a job singing in a sailor's suit in a dive called the Juan-les-Pins. Simone was hired as a stripper although she was as flat in front as she was behind, stood only four-foot-eleven, like Edith, and was not yet fifteen. P'tit Louis objected to Edith's working there because she was surrounded by prostitutes. She left him.

Having no need for full-time lodgings, as the two girls now saw things, they moved from one shoddy hotel to another, dragging Marcelle along with them. Piaf had no idea how to wash baby clothes. When Marcelle's got dirty, she and Simone would throw them away and buy new.

Much of the time the baby was left untended at their hotel. One day Edith and Simone returned to find that P'tit Louis had come on his bicycle and taken the child away. When the two girls went to the old hotel in the rue Orfila, he told Edith that she could have her daughter only if she would return to him. She shrugged and walked away. The child had been a nuisance anyway.

A few months later, P'tit Louis sought her out to tell her Marcelle was in hospital with meningitis. She rushed there with Simone. The child died the following morning. Edith was eighteen.

She was ten francs short of the eighty-four she needed for the funeral. She had lived all her life on the edges of prostitution: abandoned by her parents, the Italian street singer who was her mother and a father who was an itinerant street acrobat from Normandy, she had been raised in a bordello by her grandmother, who was its cook. So, after getting drunk on Pernod, she did the natural thing: she accosted a man on the street, the boulevard de la Chappelle. In a hotel room, he asked her why she was doing this and got what must have sounded like one of the tiredest of the hard-luck stories told by whores since time immemorial. Yet the man gave her more than the ten francs and left.

She continued singing in the streets by day, with Simone, two and a half years her junior, collecting the cash, and at the Juan-les-Pins at night, living in a succession of shabby Pigalle hotels. Their friends were pimps, prostitutes, burglars, pick-pockets, con men, and hoodlums. Piaf liked tough guys. They were her preferred bed companions. And they protected her when she worked the streets. All her life she had a taste for the company of pimps. It was a bent she shared with Billie Holiday. The difference is that Holiday's early history was totally hidden from the American public; Piaf virtually trumpeted hers.

Americans for years saw Pigalle as a place of naughty fun, but the French knew it as a sinkhole, the haunt of gangsters and their girls, of weary *putes* and their vicious "protectors." In recent decades it has been repopulated by gangsters from Algeria. It was easy to get your throat cut in Pigalle.

Piaf fell in love with a pimp named Albert. She refused to whore for him, however, and begged him to let her continue working as a street singer. He at last agreed, providing she handed him thirty francs a day. In due course she broke with Albert, as she did with all her men when boredom set in. Some of her friends gathered to protect her when he came after her. He pulled a gun and demanded that she return to him.

Piaf said—one of the great lines—"Fire, if you're a man!" All ninety-odd pounds of her.

He did, too. But one of her friends struck his arm and the shot only grazed her neck.

Edith—the French pronounce it Ay-deet—took to singing in the area between l'Etoile and La Place des Ternes. She was singing for a small crowd in the rue Troyon one autumn afternoon in 1935 when a well-dressed man stepped forward, gave her ten francs, wrote his name and address on a corner of his newspaper, and told her he owned a cabaret called Cerny's in the rue Pierre-Charron. She auditioned for him the next afternoon. Louis Leplée said he could use her. But that name, he said, her real name, half French and half Italian, Edith Giovanna Gassion, would have to go. He named her *La Môme Piaf. Môme* means brat, urchin, waif, but the connotation is affectionate. Edith Piaf, then, made her nightclub debut as the Sparrow Waif, or the Sparrow Kid.

Louis Leplée was the first person to start teaching her her profession. She and Simone began immediately to call him Papa Louis. He made her learn new songs. He began an advertising campaign for her. He planned every detail of her opening, including the lighting. That first night the place was full of celebrities, including Maurice Chevalier and Mistinguette. Terrified, Piaf began to sing, " *C'est nous les mômes, les mômes de la cloche . . .*" The audience talked on. And then they began to fall silent. "She's done it!" Louis Leplée cried. She was invited to tables. Gentlemen addressed her as "Mademoiselle." She was astounded. Chevalier praised her.

It was not, however, Chevalier's praise that emplaced Piaf in the national awareness. It was Louis Leplée's murder.

Leplée had become her manager, mentor, and father figure, building her career, arranging for her to perform in galas as well as his club. Under his direction, she got her first record contract, cutting *L'Etranger* for Polydor. One night, with a record date scheduled for nine the following morning, she went on one of her periodic benders with Simone, dragging back to their hotel at 8 A.M. Knowing how angry Papa Louis would be, she phoned to tell him she couldn't make the session. The voice on the phone told her to come immediately to his home on the boulevard de la Grande Arme. As she sobered up in the taxi, she began to think it was not Papa Louis who had spoken to her. A crowd stood about in front of his house, into which Piaf was escorted by a cop. During the night four young men had come to Leplée's house, tied up his cleaning woman, and shot him where he lay in his bed. Piaf was arrested as a material witness, which, in view of the company she kept, is hardly surprising. She was soon released for lack of any evidence of complicity in the killing, but not before photographers and newsreel cameraman had made her face famous. (There were several theories about the death, but the case has never been solved.)

Years later a French critic wrote that his first awareness of her had come from a Paramount newsreel in which she was seated on a bench, telling the police, *"Je ne sais rien, je ne sais rien"*—I know nothing. Such was the power of her personality, he wrote, that he was fascinated by her without ever having heard her sing a note. Some people have that kind of presence.

Again, Piaf made use of her life's experience: The song *Browning* that she sang several years later describes a little hole in a man's head and the other little hole, in a gun barrel, out of which comes Madame Death.

After the Leplée affair, Raymond Asso became the next important figure in Piaf's life. She'd met him through Leplée. He was a slim, intelligent man-about-show-biz in his early thirties, and a veteran of the Foreign Legion, which was not without its appeal to Piaf. She had a taste for Legionnaires and sailors. Simone said, "It was Leplée who discovered Edith, but it was Asso who made her." Asso took her as a mistress, then became her manager, coach, and teacher, an incarnation of the Henry Higgins character in Shaw's *Pygmalion.* She was barely literate, having had only a year of school. Asso taught her to sign her autograph without errors; all her life she did so using phrases he had written out for her to copy. He pounded a measure of education into her and also Simone, forcing them to learn such names as Baudelaire.

But he also listened patiently, smoking a pipe, as she told him her tales of the streets. He decided that she would have to have a repertoire entirely her own, drawn from her own experience, and began writing the first of what would be a long list of her most famous songs, such as *Elle fréquentait la rue Pigalle, Mon Légionnaire, Le Fanion de la Légion, Je n'en connais pas la fin, C'est lui que mon coeur a choisi, Le Grand voyage du pauvre nègre,* and *Le Petit monsieur triste*—the very core of her early repertoire. It was Asso who introduced her to Marguerite Monnot, who had written *L'Etranger.* Monnot, an extremely well-schooled musician—she'd made her piano recital debut at the age of three and a half, playing Mozart, and had been trained by Nadia Boulanger—became his collaborator of choice and one of the most important composers in Piaf's life. Asso would write a lyric, Piaf would recite it, and the dreamy Monnot would go to the piano and start playing, gradually fitting melody to lyrics. It was a unique professional relationship.

A genuinely tough young man, as well as a refined one, Asso cleared out the crowd of pimps and hoods who hung around Piaf. And the minute he thought she was ready, he got her her first important booking at the ABC, the best of the major Paris music halls, on a bill with Charles Trenet. Asso next introduced her to Raoul Breton, the music publisher, and his wife, whose support was critical to the success of a singer in those days. It was Mme. Breton who suggested that she henceforth bill herself as Edith Piaf, not La Môme Piaf. And Piaf worked. She studied Marie Dubas, a singer she admired all her life—how Dubas walked on a stage and left it, her gestures, her inflections, the way she sequenced her songs.

She was a smash at the ABC. Raymond Asso had made her truly famous. But her affairs usually lasted about eighteen months, as Simone has noted, and his days as her lover were numbered.

In 1969, six years after Piaf's death and a year after Asso's, Simone Berteaut published a book about her half-sister, titled simply *Piaf.* (They had the same father, Gassion.) It is a remarkable book, both in its unconscious self-portrait of the archetypical gofer, namely herself, and for the insights into Piaf's character. It is one of the finest studies of a singer ever written. It examines the egotism, the compulsion, the hunger, the ingenuous self-involvement—and the drive. It is all the more compelling for being a naive rather than a clinical portrait. And Berteaut hardly even questions her own utter devotion to her half-sister.

She quotes Piaf as saying, "A woman who gets herself dropped is a poor sap. There's no lack of men—the streets are full of them. But you have to find a replacement first, not after. If you wait till after, you're the one who's been cheated on; but before, it's him. And that makes one hell of a difference."

Berteaut says, "Edith always applied this principle with a clear conscience. No man was ever able to make her change. She'd cheat first, and then see what happened. Sometimes she'd tell them; other times she'd just laugh watching them. And if any man thought he'd cheated on her first—boy, was he wrong! She'd already beaten him to the punch. As long as the new guy wasn't ready to shack up with her she didn't say anything; she kept the old one. She had to have a man around the house."

Piaf had the sexual rectitude of a starfish. Of all the famously libidinous show business ladies, not even excluding that English actress long known in Hollywood movie circles as the British Open, Piaf appears to have been the most voracious and the most casual. She must have had thousands of men in her life. Berteaut tells how, when they were living at one Paris location and found themselves without a man of an evening, they would open a window and put themselves on display. When a cop arrived with a complaint, they'd grab him. Both of them. Indeed, although she never says so, Berteaut gives the impression in her book that when a man took on Piaf, he might get two for the price of one. Charles Aznavour called the endless succession of men "Piaf's boys."

Raymond Asso's successor was the singer and later actor Paul Meurisse, an urbane man whose cool polish and perfect manners impressed her. War was pending and ex-Legionnaire Asso had been called back into military service. Born in Dunkerque, son of a bank manager, Paul Meurisse had come to Paris as an insurance investigator who really wanted to be a singer. He'd entered an amateur contest, won it, become a chorus boy, and was singing in cabarets when she met him. Pierre Hiégal, who supervised her recordings for the Polydor label, later wrote, "When one evening Paul said to her, 'Come over to my place for a glass of champagne,' she accepted quite naturally—and stayed two years."

This time, her life's adventures became the material not for a song but for a play. Her new friend Jean Cocteau wrote a one-act drama about Piaf and Meurisse, who fought incessantly and bitterly, which he called *Le Bel Indifférent*. Piaf and Meurisse starred in it, playing characters based on themselves. The success of the play launched Meurisse as an actor.

They continued their battles, offstage as well as on, and finally parted. Singer Tino Rossi tried to effect a reconciliation, but Piaf had decided to make Meurisse jealous. Knowing Meurisse was following her, she met a man in a cafe. Meurisse dragged her home. In the ensuing battle their apartment was wrecked. And Piaf left for good. She was twenty-five.

By now Paris was under German occupation. Piaf and Simone took up residence, along with the secretary she had acquired, in a high-class bordello frequented by Gestapo officers in civvies, out for a little fun between torture sessions at their nearby headquarters; incognito members of the French underground; and big-time gangsters, both French and German. The conquerors were constantly after her to perform for them in Germany. She never did. But she did do performances in various stalags for French soldiers still held by the Germans. During one of these, her secretary, Andrée Bigeard—unbeknownst to her employer an active member of the French underground—told her to ask permission to have her picture taken with the German guards and their French prisoners. Back in Paris, the faces in this photo were carefully blown up and attached to false identity cards and travel documents, which Piaf slipped to the prisoners on a second visit to the camp. Many of them escaped with those documents.

In the spring of 1944, on the advice of one of their pimp friends, Piaf and Simone checked out of their brothel. A few days later the house was closed and its owners jailed.

When the war began to go badly for the Germans the atmosphere in Paris grew grim. Black-bordered posters bearing the names of hostages appeared on walls. From time to time, the Germans would shoot a batch of them, often in the ruined old castle in the Bois de Vincennes. Piaf sang a song called *Où sont tous mes copains?*—Where Are All My Pals?—against the projected backdrop of a French flag. The audience was full of German officers. The next day Occupation authorities told her to take it out of her act. She refused. Her only compromise was to drop the flag from her staging.

Paul Meurisse's successor, aside from the casual lovers, was Henri Contet, of whom she said to Simone, "We've never had a newspaperman; it'll be a change for us." Contet was a writer with *Paris Soir*. Piaf seemed to have an instinct for taking up with men who could educate her, and Contet was no exception. She in turn affected their lives just as deeply. She had made an actor of Meurisse. And now she turned Contet, as she had Raymond Asso, into a lyricist. If Asso had created the body of her first repertoire, Contet—working with Marguerite Monnot—created that of the second, such songs as *Y'a pas d' printemps, Coup de grisou, Monsieur Saint Pierre, Histoire du coeur, Mariage, Le Brun et le blond, Bravo pour le clown*, and the great *Padam ... Padam*. Contet went the way of all her lovers, but, like Asso, continued writing for her.

She had long since lost count of her lovers. At one point she decided to file them by period: the streets; the sailors and colonial troops, the pimps, the flings. She referred to the time of Asso and Meurisse as her professor period. Contet she listed in the brothel period. After Contet, she went into what she called her factory period. She'd made Asso and Contet into famous songwriters. Now she began manufacturing singers.

The first was Yves Montand, a six-foot 180-pound "dream," as she called him, born in Italy and raised in Marseille. She met him when he was assigned on a bill with her at the Moulin Rouge. She promptly vivisected his act, telling him it was corny and out-of-date, and mocked his Marseille accent. She told him that when he was ready to accept it, she would train him. And train him she did. She developed a new repertoire for him, some of it written by Henri Contet. She taught him gesture and movement, sometimes rehearsing him for fifteen hours at a stretch. In two months, she created the Montand the French public was to know, the dramatic figure in simple brown slacks and shirt. Then she made a movie with him, about a singing star who takes a lover and turns him into a famous singer only to lose him to the stardom she has herself created. Montand was in love with and wanted to marry her, but when his name became as big as her own she threw him out.

She next took an interest not in one but nine singers, Les Compagnons de la Chanson, who had begun singing together in the French resistance. She coached them and took them on tour with her, as she had Montand.

In the mood of francophilia that saturated the United States in the years right after the war, Piaf acquired an American reputation. In

November 1947 she toured the U.S. with Les Compagnons. The tour was a failure for Piaf, although Les Compagnons, whose act was all sweetness and light, went over well, with songs such as *Les Trois Cloches* (The Three Bells). Piaf decided to leave the tour and go home. The critic and composer Virgil Thomson wrote a newspaper column explaining the character of her work, ending it with, "If we allow her to leave on the heels of this undeserved failure, the American public will have given proof of its ignorance and its stupidity." On the strength of that review, she was booked into the Versailles. Charles Boyer, Marlene Dietrich, and Jean Sablon were in the high-society audience that came to cheer her. She had been booked for a week; she stayed twenty-one. She and Dietrich would become close friends.

A few months earlier, toward the end of 1946, when she was thirty-one, she had met, in a Montmartre cafe, Marcel Cerdan, the boxer, born in Casablanca, billed as the Moroccan Bomber, the French contender for the world middleweight championship. Cerdan was a handsome roughneck with a heart of utter simplicity.

Piaf was intensely lonely during the Versailles engagement. Then she got a call from Cerdan, who happened also to be in New York. He took her to dinner, then to Coney Island after midnight. Some of the sports fans in the crowd recognized him; and some people recognized her, begging her to sing *La Vie en rose*, which she did, on the spot, old street singer that she was. She saw Cerdan fight for the first time. And she was in love again. But Cerdan was married. Marriage to Piaf was impossible.

The relationship with Cerdan was unlike any she had known. She had always bought gifts for her men and dressed them. Cerdan would not allow this. He, on the contrary, bought her gifts, a mink coat among them.

Cerdan went into training for his title fight with Tony Zale in New York. Piaf was booked into the Versailles during that time. She arrived early, and Cerdan, against the rules, smuggled her into his training camp at Lake Sheldrake. Despite the supposedly debilitating effects of sex on prizefighters (and tenors), Cerdan, in Madison Square Garden on September 21, 1948, took the title from Zale at the end of the fourth round. A euphoric Piaf left the arena to sing at the Versailles. The crowd cheered when she went on, and cheered anew when Cerdan entered.

The next autumn she again played the Versailles. Again Cerdan was to fight in New York: Jake LaMotta had challenged him for the title. Cerdan was to travel by boat but Piaf phoned to urge him to take a plane instead.

On October 28, 1949, the Air France Constellation in which Cerdan was a passenger plowed into a mountain peak of the Azores. Cerdan died in the crash, along with the brilliant young French violinist Ginette Neveu. Piaf believed she had killed him, and nearly went mad. She entered onto the most bizarre period of her life. After trying to starve herself to death, she induced Simone to obtain a three-legged table with which to conduct seances. The tapping table told her to resume eating. From then on she consulted it daily. What she did not know is that her half-sister was moving the table, which Berteaut revealed in the 1969 book. She constantly asked it for advice, advice that a terrified Berteaut was forced to give.

It was during this period that she discovered Charles Aznavour, singing in the duo of Roche and Aznavour. The other member of the team was Pierre Roche, who later would emigrate to Canada. Piaf was taken by one of the songs they had written, *J'aime Paris au mois de mai*, (I Like Paris in the Month of May), a very attractive tune with a charming lyric. Though he was tiny and had a large nose that Piaf immediately criticized (and which later was altered), she thought Aznavour had big talent, and took him into her entourage. He went to live with her at Boulogne, where he slept on a sofa. He became her secretary, chauffeur, handyman, and general factotum.

Berteaut says that Aznavour's relationship with her was purely professional. Aznavour's own attitude to Piaf seems to substantiate this. In any case, her bed would not remain empty for long. In still another nightclub, she met a big, rough-looking American, with a pock-marked face, named Eddie Constantine. Constantine's looks, which would stand him in good stead when, later, he became a sort of Humphrey Bogart tough guy in French movies, were at odds with his background.

Born in Los Angeles in 1915 into a family of Austrian opera singers, a prize-winning voice student at the Vienna Conservatory, he had been an L.A. studio singer, doing commercials for cigarettes and chewing gum, work that he—like so many others before and after him—disliked intensely, as profitable as it was. He went to Paris to take his chances, working for a time as a production singer. Then Piaf found him. The factory began to hum as Piaf relentlessly rehearsed Aznavour and Constantine.

Cerdan remained her great love, no doubt because he had died at the peak of the romance, before she could grow bored with him. This time *le grand amour* could be preserved forever in the shrine of her illusions. Cerdan could never be lined up with her other trophies. Once she had a party for eight of them, all of whom turned up in the blue suits she always bought her men, along with the cigarette lighters and watches.

Piaf flew with Simone to Casablanca, effected a reconciliation with Marinette Cerdan, brought Marinette and Cerdan's children back to live with her at Boulogne, bought Jacques Fath clothes for her lover's widow, and undertook the education of his children.

And then the bad days came. With Aznavour at the wheel, her car went off the road and was destroyed. They were unharmed. Three weeks later, asleep with Aznavour in the back seat of a car driven by the bicycle rider who was her current lover, she was in a second accident. This time she got two broken ribs and a broken arm. The doctors eased her pain with morphine, to which she became almost immediately addicted. She took up with another cyclist, a friend of the first. She began to sentimentalize about her lost child Marcelle. Then came Jacques Pills (pronounced Peelse.)

She'd met him in 1939, an elegant man and a gentleman, the husband of Lucienne Boyer and half of Pills and Tabet, the biggest singing team of the time. He'd seemed beyond her wildest aspirations. Now, all these years later, he brought her a song—his lyrics, music by his accompanist, one Gilbert Bécaud. It was *Je t'ai dans le peau* (I've Got You in the Skin), which as always she made her own, in the process helping launch another singer, Bécaud. As for Pills, it was, once again, love at first sight for Piaf. With Pills, she was convinced, she could kick her morphine habit, a habit Pills didn't even know she had. He thought she was on cortisone. Berteaut recalls her crawling around the floor looking for a lost syringe. And the pushers were both supplying her and blackmailing her. Pills, who long since had been divorced from Boyer, proposed to her.

"This woman," Berteaut wrote, "demolished by drink and beginning to be corroded by drugs, dreamed of a first communion dress like a ten-year-old." In July 1952 Piaf and Pills were married in a civil ceremony in the town hall of the fashionable sixteenth arrondisement. In September, on her fifth trip to the United States, after a fix, she married Pills a second time at the church of St. Vincent de Paul. Marlene Dietrich was her witness. Piaf wore a long dress of pale blue, and in a photo taken as she entered the church escorted by Dietrich, she looks like the radiant child she thought she was. She was thirty-seven. Pills was forty-six.

Pills was soon to learn his bride was both an alcoholic and a drug addict. Three times he put her in a clinic to take the cure. They parted in 1955 but remained close friends.

Her work was deteriorating. Yet she pulled herself together to make a triumphant appearance—her seventh American trip—at Carnegie Hall at a fee of $3000 per night.

She used to speak of "my pals the Americans." But in France she had acquired a reputation for unreliability and bad work. Nonetheless, Bruno Coquatrix, who owned the Olympia theater, decided to take a chance by giving her a one-month engagement. She was a smash. Coquatrix canceled other contracts to keep her for twelve weeks. Her record sales soared.

She suffered an attack of delerium tremens. Again she was hospitalized. And again she left for the United States, to perform in New York, Los Angeles, Las Vegas, and Chicago. The tour lasted eleven months, and she was paid a higher fee than anyone in American history to that time, excepting Bing Crosby and Frank Sinatra.

In the fall of 1959, on her way to the airport to leave on her ninth tour of the United States, she was in her third automobile accident. Her face was badly cut, but she recovered with little scarring. In February 1960, she collapsed onstage at the Waldorf-Astoria, vomiting blood, and was taken to Columbia Presbyterian Hospital for stomach surgery. Jacques Pills came to her bedside.

A young American fan, a twenty-three-year-old painter named Douglas Davies, sent her flowers. When she left the hospital, she took him back to Paris with her. She collapsed onstage in Stockholm and returned to Paris for more surgery. She broke up with Davies, who–like so many of her lovers–remained her friend. He died in June 1962 in a plane crash near Orly Airport.

Simone Berteaut records that in the twelve years from 1951 to 1963, Piaf survived four automobile accidents, an attempted suicide, four drug cures, one sleep treatment, two attacks of d.t.s, seven surgical operations, three hepatic comas, a spell of insanity, two attacks of bronchial pneumonia, and one of pulmonary edema. She had ulcers, arthritis, and jaundice.

She had been blind in childhood. Whether the blindness was hysterical or caused by cataracts, as she believed, is problematical. Considering that she had been hideously neglected and half-starved by her mother before being taken to the Normandy bordello, the former seems likely. The nature of the cure further suggests it. The prostitutes were very good to her. They scrubbed and scraped away her encrusted filth. They made rag dolls for her during her blindness. They mothered her. In August 1921, according to her legend, after the ladies of the house had become aware that she could not see, they shut up shop for a day, dressed like housewives, and paraded through the streets to the basilica of St. Thérèse de Lisieux to burn candles and urge divine intercession for Edith. Four days later she could see. Or so Piaf told Simone, who presumed she must have heard the story from her father, since Edith had been seven at the time of her "miracle."

After that, Louis Gassion took his daughter on the road with him, making her sing in the streets and cafes and teaching her to con money from the gullible. It is hardly a wonder that she hated bathing (when she acquired her luxurious home at Boulogne, she filled the bathtub with goldfish), liked whores and partook of their morality, manipulated people with uncommon skill, was most at home in cabarets and the streets, and sustained a pathetic belief in the supernatural.

The ravages of hard living had taken a toll. Yet she worked in spite of her ill health, touring in France and other countries until one of her periodic collapses would force her to cancel. She had very little money, having given far too much of it to musicians, vagabonds, sycophants, and parasites of various styles and stories.

In the fall of 1962, Piaf opened once more at the Olympia. She was terribly weak by then. A doctor watched from the wings as she tottered toward the microphone, so thin that the cords of her neck and the tendons in her hands stood out conspicuously. Her hair had thinned to a reddish fuzz.

The recording made during that engagement is an incredible testament not only to her talent but to raw courage. There was a new kind of rasp to her voice, the rasp of physical pain. And yet that recording is one of the best she ever made. One of its songs is *Le Billard électrique*, about a boy who plays a pinball machine as he waits in a bar for a girl. The song is rhythmically punctuated by a hysterical ding! ding! She had recorded the same song some years before. The early version was great Piaf. The latter is even greater Piaf, for her energy had become demonic. At the end of the song she screams "Dinnnng!" The sound is frightening in its intensity.

A male voice is heard in one song on that final album from the Olympia—that of Théo Sarapo, a hairdresser of Greek parentage who was half her age. They had recently been married and she was trying to turn him, like others before him, into a singer. It was as if she could imagine nothing else that one might do with one's life. The French snickered at her and Sarapo, who was seen as a gigolo opportunist. Berteaut says that, on the contrary, Sarapo (Piaf gave him the name; it is Greek for *I love you*) loved her desperately and stood to inherit from her only her debts. He came from a comfortable family to whom he very properly introduced Piaf before their marriage. The doctors had told him her life was nearing its end; he married her anyway. Berteaut recalls him hovering by Edith's sickbed, in a house on the Riviera, combing her hair, putting eau de cologne on her face, and washing her hands.

She had had a concerto grosso of illnesses in those last years, but it was cancer that finally killed her at forty-seven. Told she was dying, her close friend Jean Cocteau said, "Piaf had genius. There will never be another Piaf." On October 11, 1963, four hours after he learned she was gone, Cocteau, who had suffered a stroke early in the year, was himself dead of a heart attack. No one doubted that Piaf's death caused his.

The Church at first refused Piaf a religious burial on the grounds that she had lived "in a state of public sin." A few hours later, however, the official position softened, purportedly in consideration of Piaf's deep piety. Her friends no doubt concluded, with French cynicism, that someone had put in the fix.

Mourners at her burial in the cemetery of Père Lachaise included Marlene Dietrich, Gilbert Bécaud, Jacqueline François, the faithful Jacques Pills, and Aznavour, along with a very large crowd of very little people: 40,000 of them, mostly from the working class. As Piaf had requested, the souvenirs she treasured most were buried with her. The inventory: three fluffy toy animals, a green silk cravat, some religious pictures, a plaster statue of St. Thérèse de Lisieux, whom she believed had restored her sight, a silver medallion of the Virgin, the épaulette of a Legionnaire, a sailor's beret, and a postcard from the chapel of Milly-la-Forêt with a dedication from Cocteau.

Sacha Guitry said, "Her life was so sad it seems almost too beautiful to be true." That's a cute little oxymoron. There is nothing beautiful about arthritis, drug addiction, alcoholism, or cancer. But it is in accord with the general view of her life as tragic. I do not share it. Born literally on a sidewalk from a slut of a mother who had no interest in her, this indestructible child of the streets climbed with cunning and courage to the highest levels of the international entertainment world. She had sung for Princess Elizabeth, the soon-to-be Queen of England, who invited her to her table, an honor Piaf could not quite believe. When she was awarded a Grand Prix du Disque in 1952, she was photographed with the Président de la Republique and Nobel Prize–winning novelist Colette. Her friends included the rich, the famous, and the fascinating of two continents, actors, playwrights, composers, poets, and politicians.

Only a few months before her death, she sang from the top of the Eiffel Tower for the world premiere of the movie *The Longest Day*, the film about the bloody but successful Allied landings at Normandy in 1944. Her audience, gathered for dinner in the gardens of the Palais de Chaillot, included Winston Churchill, General and former President of the United States Dwight D. Eisenhower, Viscount Bernard Law Montgomery of Alamein, Lord Louis Mountbatten and General Omar Bradley, the very architects of Germany's defeat, the King of Morocco, Don Juan of Spain, Queen Sophia of Greece, and movie celebrities such as Elizabeth Taylor, Sophia Loren, Ava Gardner, Robert Wagner, Audrey Hepburn, Curt Jurgens, and Richard Burton, not to mention all the people of Paris who heard that fierce voice ringing out from the sky such of her songs as *Non, je ne regrette rien*–No, I Regret Nothing.

If in the early years she collected lovers who could help her career, she repaid the debt in the later years by gathering around her men she could–and did–help. She earned and threw away fortunes. She had a remarkable ability to get people to do exactly what she wanted, including the half-sister who lived through her. Although she had a dumpy little body, men were mad about her, one after another, and she lived a sex life far beyond the wildest fantasies of any bored housewife. If she burned her candle at both ends, for a long time it burned exceeding bright. Cocteau said she was like "a terrifying little sleepwalker who sings her dreams to the air on the edge of the roof." Ah, but her father was a juggler and acrobat who had taught her the rudiments of his trade; she had a spectacular sense of balance. If the last years were hard, so they are for many people who have known nothing of the heights she attained. And singing your dreams to the air beats life in a Normandy whorehouse.

A year or two after she died, I got a call from Paris from the New York music publisher Howie Richmond. He had published some of the Antonio Carlos Jobim songs I had translated from Portuguese. He asked me if I knew French. "Better than I do Portuguese," I said. Howie said he was planning a one-man Broadway show for Charles Aznavour and wanted to know if I would come to Paris to write English adaptations of the Aznavour songs. I left the next day. The first song I did was *J'aime Paris au mois de mai*, which I called *Paris Is at Her Best in May*, as a sort of brand-X refutation of *April in Paris*. I had no idea at the time that this had been the first of Aznavour's songs to catch Piaf's attention.

Aznavour was playing the Olympia, working on the same stage where Piaf had made that last album. We talked in the dressing room, probably the same one she used—the star's dressing room. At the end of each show he would put a table across the door of that room and sit behind it, signing autographs with a star's conditioned automaticity for the long lines of people who came by and discussing with me the pending New York show. Naturally, during those weeks, I asked about Piaf. There is much about him that is like her. He is tiny, and works in simple attire. The songs he writes are in her tradition, though not as harsh. He has that same quick vibrato.

He told me that Piaf had a rich and raucous sense of humor, that she was always surrounded by friends, and that she would have liked to sing comic songs, had her public been willing to accept her as anything but a tragedienne.

One of the songs that bears her name, he said, is actually his. When he showed it to her, she said, "Charles, that song is me!" She begged him to let her put her name on it as its writer. She said she would make it up to him if he did.

"And did she make it up to you?" I asked. "Of course," he said. "She gave me my career."

Um Abraço No Tom
Antonio Carlos Jobim

Some time in the 1960s, I interviewed Robert Russell Bennett in his office in New York. He was then, I would think, about seventy: he was born in Kansas City on June 15, 1894. Bennett was one of the countless American composers trained and shaped by Nadia Boulanger, whose influence on American music is inestimable. He was for a long time the premier arranger and orchestrator of Broadway musicals. Bennett talked of George Gershwin as if he were some sort of idiot savant. He said that Gershwin had a peculiar capacity to pick up any musical thought that was in the air and use it. He came just short of calling him a plagiarist.

I said, "But Mr. Bennett, how is it that you can hear only two or three bars of a song and know that it's a Gershwin tune?"

"Ah," he said, "but that's genius."

Not talent. Genius.

I have had cause to reflect on this since the death of Antonio Carlos Jobim.

The gift of writing melody is a mysterious one. Not every educated musician has it; Nelson Riddle didn't. Nor does lack of education preclude it.

What is fascinating about Jobim is the range and depth and power of his ability to make new, fresh, distinctive music out of conventional materials. Jobim gave us some of the most exquisite melodies of the twentieth century, and, when he wrote with poets of the stature of Vinicius de Moraes, truly magnificent songs—that wedding of words to music that remains the favorite and most enduring of musical forms.

The decline of melodicism in American popular music dates from approximately the mid-1950s, although the omens were evident in such examples of Tin Pan Alley trash as *Papa Loves Mambo* and *Hot Diggity Dog Diggity*. But in Brazil, in the late 1950s, a new birth of melodicism was occurring, a movement that would become known as bossa nova. The central figure was Jobim.

My first encounter with his music came in the fall of 1961, in an album issued on Capitol by one João Gilberto. Something on its cover mentioned the samba. My knowledge of samba was limited to the performances of Carmen Miranda, singing and dancing giddily under a headdress of tropical fruit in movies. When at last I got around to listening to the album, I was electrified by the music. It was far from Carmen Miranda, or at least the Carmen Miranda who was exploited as a sort of joke in Hollywood movies. Jobim had arranged it; he also wrote a number of its songs, including one called *Corcovado*. The harmony in all the Jobim songs was thoughtful and skilled, reflecting Jobim's taste not only for jazz but for the French Impressionist composers.

The Brazilians had solved the problem of the ballad. As the song form evolved in the United States, the harmonic content became more sophisticated, nowhere more so than in the music of Jerome Kern. But whereas this new Brazilian music was harmonically interesting, the composers did not depend so heavily on this factor for motion. This was due to the nature of the rhythmic pattern.

The music was largely notated in 2/4 time, unlike American ballads, most of which are in 4/4. (When these Brazilian songs were brought north, publishers had them re-notated in 4/4.)

The bass player used an eighth-note pickup just before the first beat of each bar, setting up a da-boom, da-boom pattern. And the drummer played a pattern of eighth notes over this, often with other percussion instruments added. This gave the songs motion, even in cases where the composer chose to sit on one chord for a comparatively long time. The rhythms were complex and incredibly stimulating, even in the gentlest ballads, such as Jobim's *Outra Vez* and *Meditação*.

Not long after I began to be familiar with this music, I was approached about making a State Department journey as tour manager through all Latin America (except Cuba) with the Paul Winter Sextet. It was in part my interest in this new music that impelled me to go. We left Chicago on February 1, 1962.

We traveled down the west coast of South America, then crossed to Argentina. In Buenos Aires I began to hear still more of João Gilberto and Jobim, including two albums that had not yet been issued in the U.S. Since I spoke French and Spanish, I was able to deduce—sometimes with the help of new friends—the meaning of the lyrics, and I was beginning to memorize them.

After stops in Paraguay and Uruguay, we entered Brazil—a nation even larger than the continental United States—from the south, first landing in Porto Alegre. Samba seemed to be everywhere. The country really seemed to swing—*balançar*, as they say in Portuguese. I remember a young man in an elevator playing a samba rhythm with a set of keys on a ring. I saw a donkey pulling a two-wheel cart; even that animal seemed to swing. I was already familiar with a song that João Gilberto had recorded: Dorival Caymmi's *Samba de Minha Terra* (Samba of My Land). The release says: Whoever doesn't like samba isn't a good guy. He is bad in the head or sick in the foot. I was born with the samba, in the samba I was created. From the damned samba I have never separated.

We played a concert in some small town, I no longer remember where. And then we were to go to Rio de Janeiro (River of January), the place we all wanted to be and see. We flew above high white clouds, and then at last came in between two billowing banks of them to see Rio lying in the sun in front of us—Sugar Loaf; Corcovado, with the statue of Jesus, arms outstretched as if to embrace the world; Guanabara Bay; and the spreading ocean beyond it. I once told Charles Aznavour that I thought Paris was the most beautiful city in the world until I saw Rio. Charles said, "Paris *is* the most beautiful city in the world. But Rio has the most beautiful setting."

We played our concert, and, the next day, I searched out a man named Enrique Lebendiger, who owned a company called Fermata do Brasil. Fermata published a lot of the Jobim songs. I arranged a meeting with Lebendiger. I said I wanted to try my hand at translating some of the bossa nova songs and therefore would like to meet Jobim and some of the others. Lebendiger urged me to have nothing to do with Jobim. He said he was crazy and difficult. He said I should go ahead and make translations without seeing him. I told him I couldn't do that. Finally he gave me a telephone number for João Gilberto.

I called the number and reached what seemed to me to be a very shy housewife named Astrud Gilberto. She was completely unknown in music; within eighteen months she would be internationally famous. She spoke a little English and told me that her husband was rehearsing that evening at Jobim's house, and she gave me a phone number. I called Jobim and, somehow, managed to communicate that I wanted to meet him. He invited me to a rehearsal.

It was raining heavily that night; I took a taxi out to the Ipanema area. Jobim lived in a modest little house on a street not far from the beach. I knocked at the door. I suppose something about the dignity of his name, Antonio Carlos Jobim, had led me to expect someone much older. It is odd how we build impressions around names, and how often they turn out to be inaccurate. He turned out to be only a year older than I.

Jobim was born in Rio. "Brazilian" was literally his middle name: Antonio Carlos Brasileiro de Almeida Jobim. His birthdate was January 25, 1927, and thus he was an Aquarian, which became one of the jokes and a faint little commonality between us. Sergio Mendes, too, is an Aquarian. I was born February 8. Sergio was born in the Rio suburb of Niteroi on February 11, 1941. In later years whenever I would encounter either of them he would say something like, "How's the other Aquarian?" or "What do you hear from the other Aquarian?"

But who could foresee that? I stood under a little overhang, out of the rain: I remember the shine of streetlamps on the wet street, patterned with the moving shadows of trees. The door opened, and a very handsome young man stood in the light from his living room. Jobim was then thirty-four. He invited me in.

João Gilberto sat on the sofa, curled around his guitar, singing with a vocal group called, as I learned, Os Cariocas–the Cariocas. (*Cariocas* are the natives of Rio.) I had become fascinated by his singing through the recordings. It was a very fresh approach to singing, infinitely soft and almost devoid of vibrato, yet warm with some sort of hidden passion. But I could not have imagined how truly soft his voice was: you could scarcely hear him five or six feet away in a small living room.

Jobim invited me to the kitchen, which was off the living room to the right as you entered. He opened a bottle of Johnnie Walker's and poured two drinks, the first of many we would share. He spoke only a few words of English, but I had found that a great many educated people in South America, whether Spanish or Portuguese speaking, knew French, and I tried French on him. As it turned out, his family background was French: the name was originally Jobin. I had also come to realize that Spanish and Portuguese are sufficiently similar that if I spoke Spanish very slowly, Brazilians would understand me.

So Jobim and I that night spoke a bizarre mixture of French and Spanish. Years later I told him that Brazilian Portuguese, with all its dentalizations and buzzing sounds, sounded to me like a mixture of Spanish and French as spoken by a Russian. And still later, he told me that he remembered my remark once in an airport in Europe. He observed several men standing together talking, and thought from the distant sound of their voices that they were Brazilians. He approached them only to discover that they were speaking Russian. There is something similar about the rhythm. In later years, one of the things Jobim and I shared was a fascination with language.

I told him that night that I thought his songs could be and should be translated into English. He urged me to try doing it. We had several more drinks; he and I would never have only a few. I always remember the way he pronounced Scotch, with that peculiar Carioca vowel. It came out almost Sco-watch. And then, indicating João Gilberto in the living room, he said, and this was in English, "I am crazy. He is more crazy."

I told him that he slightly reminded me of Gerry Mulligan, and it was then that he told me that Mulligan was one of the inspirations behind the bossa nova movement. He said that the street samba of Brazil was passionate and hot, and his ideal had been to calm it down for the recording studio, after the manner of the Mulligan tentet and quartet records, without losing the swing. "We must not lose important things," he said.

"The samba," he said to me at a much later date, "is basically a Negro–European thing. It has roots very similar to the jazz roots: the Portuguese song with the Negro beat and the Negro feeling. And also samba is not just samba. There are ten or twelve different beats of samba. But that's the main stream. We have other things, like *baihão,* like *maracatu,* many different rhythms.

"But samba is the main stream, the main road. Bossa nova could be called a branch, one of the many branches that samba has.

"The regular samba, the street samba, the Carnaval samba, has all kinds of percussion instruments, and cans and tambours and tambourines, whatever you can think. The bossa nova had this advantage. It was kind of washed, more concise, less noise, less things going on, easier to record in a studio. Because I had tremendous experience recording *Black Orpheus.* With twenty guys playing percussion, it sounds like the sea. The holes are filled, there's no space left. Bossa nova came with a very detached beat, very characteristic, that cleaned the whole thing. It was cleaner. It was easier. And maybe because of that it became more universal."

I listened to the rehearsal. João Gilberto was singing *Só Danço Samba,* which means I dance only samba, a humorous little song about someone who says he has danced the twist too much, has danced calypso and cha-cha-cha, and now wants to dance only samba. It was a matter of months until he and Jobim would record that with Stan Getz in New York.

In the next day or two I wrote English lyrics, remaining as close as possible to the spirit of the Portuguese originals on two of Jobim's songs, *Corcovado* and *Desafinado.*

I had become almost as fascinated by the lyrics of the songs as by the music. I was intrigued by all the fresh (to me) rhymes, failing at first to see that as we have our cliches in English, so do songs in Portuguese. Brazilians endlessly rhyme song, guitar, and heart—*canção, violão* (which means not violin but guitar), and *coração.* For the most part, I found a poetic freshness in the songs, some of which had lyrics by the poet and playwright Vinicius de Moraes. And there was a wistful quality, often a pervading fatalism, as in Jobim's song *Vivo Sonhando*, which means "I live dreaming." He and I would eventually render it into English as *Dreamer*.

Later, when I knew a great many of them by heart, I came to a conclusion about the nature of these lyrics. I think they reflect an influence of the Portuguese folk song known as *fado*, which means "fate," and I have speculated that this in turn may be the consequence of the centuries of Arabic domination of the Iberian Peninsula. A central tenet of Islam is kismet, the fatalistic acceptance of the will of God. Jobim and his colleague Sergio Mendes both thought that this hypothesis was a reasonable explanation of the nature of the bossa nova lyrics.

Jobim had explained to me that the lyric to *Desafinado* (by Newton Mendonça) was a joke, sly gentle fun poked at the criticism to which the bossa nova composers were subject from older singers and songwriters. The traditionalists said that these new songs were hard to sing. They said they were "crooked," and *Desafinado* does indeed contain a melody note that is a flatted fifth, one of the hallmarks of bebop. In F, the second chord of the song is G7b5, with the melody landing on the D-flat. This note drove conventional Brazilian singers crazy, Jobim told me.

I wrote the English lyric for *Corcovado* while crossing town on a bus. It is impossible, of course, to translate any song verbatim: it simply won't fit the music in the other language. What one has to do is to understand the song's essential spirit and reconstruct it as closely as possible in the second language. The first thing that is lost in any translation is humor. Humor, particularly plays on words, cannot be translated at all. And so wherever touches of humor were lost in *Desafinado*, I had to find little byplays in English to replace them.

In the next two or three days, I wrote English lyrics to both *Desafinado* and *Corcovado*. Later, in New York, Jobim and I added a verse to *Desafinado*. The song supposes a girl of flawless character who looks down her nose a little at her suitor, who is singing the song:

> *Verse*
> Every time I sing, you say I'm off key.
> Why can't you see how much this hurts me?
> With your perfect beauty and your perfect pitch,
> You're a perfect (*pause for a silent rhyme*) terror.
> When I come around,
> must you always put me down?
>
> *Chorus*
> If you say my singing is off key, my love (*on the flat five*)
> you will hurt my feelings, don't you see, my love?

> I wish I had an ear like yours, a voice that would behave.
> All I have is feeling and the voice God gave.
>
> You insist my music goes against the rules.
> Ah but rules were never made for lovesick fools.
> I wrote this little song for you, but you don't care.
> It's a crooked tune. Ah but all my love is there.
>
> The thing that you would see if you would do your part
> is even if I'm out of tune, I have a gentle heart.
> I took your picture with my trusty Rolleiflex,
> And find that all I have developed is a complex.

(The reference to the Rolleiflex is in the original. The line is, more or less: I photographed you with my Rolleiflex, and what has developed is your enormous ingratitude. It's funnier in Portuguese, but I couldn't make it work in English.)

> Possibly in vain, I hope you'll weaken, O my love,
> and forget those rigid rules that undermine my dream of
> a life of love and music with someone who'll understand
> that even though I may be out of tune
> when I attempt to say how much I love you.
> All that matters is the message that I bring,
> which is: my dear one, I love you.

Corcovado presented problems, too, of course. The release contains a reference to a window looking on Corcovado, which means the hunchback. But an American audience would hardly know the name of that mountain, and the great panorama of the sea that the statue surveys. So I changed it. The Portuguese lyric is by Jobim, and it is one of his better ones. Again, it contains that fatalism that I find so common in Brazilian lyrics.

I noticed something odd about the Portuguese lyric. It rhymes throughout until the end, when it breaks the pattern. It is almost the opposite of Shakespeare's practice of writing iambic pentameter without rhyme until he reaches the end of a scene, which he signifies by a rhymed couplet. Why did Jobim do that? I was learning the tune on a small guitar I had purchased in La Paz, Bolivia. The song, which is in C, begins with a chord Jobim called D9/A. I've seen that written as Am6, with which it is enharmonic. But its function is that of a secondary dominant, and Jobim meant it that way. It is a very guitaristic song. The bass line descends chromatically from the A to the Em7 open-string chord, if you want to play it that way. It lies perfectly on the instrument.

But—and this is an important but—the song never fully resolves; it never goes to the tonic chord. It ends where it began, on D9/A. And this puts you back at the beginning; you have to start all over. The song is thus circular in shape, like Malcolm Lowery's novel *Under the Volcano*. It is a musical mobius band. I realized that Jobim broke rhyme at the end to make your ear yearn for a resolution; it perfectly fits the setup that occurs with that D9/A. And I decided to retain that effect in English. For all its seemingly simple beauty, that song is incredibly ingenious.

> Quiet nights of quiet stars,
> quiet chords from my guitar
> floating on the silence
> that surrounds us.
>
> Quiet thoughts and quiet dreams.
> quiet walks by quiet streams
> and a window looking on
> the mountains and the sea—how lovely.
>
> This is where I want to be,
> here with you so close to me
> until the final flicker of life's ember.

(In Portuguese: *ate o apagar da velha chama*, which means: until the old flame goes out.)

> I, who was lost and lonely,
> believing life was only
> a bitter, tragic joke,
> have found with you
> the meaning of existence,
> O my love.

Jobim and I had lunch, or more likely, a couple of drinks, at the Copacabana Palace, one of the more luxurious hotels along what is unquestionably the most beautiful urban beach in the world. I still see the white tablecloths in sunlight that flowed in through big windows. I see that gorgeous crescent of sand, the girls in skimpy bikinis, the curved zig-zag of stones along that great sidewalk. I explained the lyrics to him carefully, probably in French. He was delighted with the lyrics and asked me to leave them with him.

At this point, I must violate the time sequence in order that you may know Jobim better. It is appropriate that at this time, you know his background. But the conversation I am about to quote did not happen then. It occurred twelve years later, in 1974, in the Sunset Marquis hotel in Los Angeles, when I was working on the lyrics for *Double Rainbow* with him. By then he spoke quite a bit of English.

"You told me your father was a poet and a diplomat,"

"Yes, that's true," he said. "He was gone very soon. He died when I was eight. And I remember him very vaguely."

"Do you think the poetic instinct was passed on to you?"

He laughed. "I think probably. I'm a musician, but I like words, I like lyrics, I like literature. He was not a musician at all, you know. He had a very bad musical ear. It was not his business. And later on, my mother married my stepfather, and he helped me a lot.

"I was very prejudiced about music. I thought playing piano was something for girls. I liked to play soccer on the beach. A piano came. You know, we rented a piano. My sister was supposed to study. But she didn't want to study the piano, the scales. And I started fooling around with the piano. I was about twelve, thirteen. I fooled around with this old piano, an old Bechstein. My stepfather always, you know, pushed me up.

"He always thought that I would be a good musician. And I was kind of scared. My mother had a school." (The school was the Brasileiro de Almeida Music School.)

"There was a teacher from Germany." Jobim was referring to Hans Joachim Koellreutter, who was one of the early champions of Brazilian dodecophonist composers.

"He was very helpful. He taught me the basic things. Later on he gave me some composition and harmony. He was not the dumb piano teacher. He opened my eyes. If you just memorize little pieces, and don't know what you're doing, it's no use. You scare off the kid from music."

Jobim's guitar was resting on the bed of his hotel suite. The windows were open and the California birds were singing. He was never without a guitar. Although piano was his primary instrument, he played guitar; he taught me quite a bit of guitar, and he used to say that I was the only lyricist he'd ever worked with who knew his chord changes. I said, "You know, I've never met a Brazilian who didn't play the guitar."

"Yes," Jobim said. "All the Brazilians play the guitar. It is quite a national instrument. I also used to fool around with the guitar. I have two uncles. One of them used to play classical guitar, the Spanish repertoire and Bach, these famous pieces for the guitar. My other uncle used to play popular songs and accompany himself. He could sing well. So this was the basic music around me when I was a kid.

"Then I got a harmonica, a Hohner, German. The harmonica that could play all the twelve tones. Chromatic. There was a group of kids that got together and we made a band with a bass, and with harmonicas. We made arrangements. We would distribute the voicings. It was nice.

"I had a tremendous fight, my wife and I." He was referring to his first wife, Tereza. She was in the bedroom of the hotel suite as we were talking. "She was then a kid," he said. "I went to architecture school because I wanted to marry her, and so I should be somebody respectable. Not a musician. I should be a doctor or something. In Brazil, you call doctor an engineer. If you are an engineer they will call you Dr. Something. I went to architecture for one year. Then we had this terrible fight. I thought I was not going to marry her. I quit the whole thing. I said, 'The hell with it, I'm not gonna be an architect.'" (Their son, Paulo, *would* become an architect, as well as a musician.)

"Music had been till then just a hobby. A passionate hobby. I was crazy about music. I decided to be a professional. I tried to study more and more, get deeply involved. Finally we got together again. We got married. And I needed money to pay the rent. We moved from my mother's house. It was very difficult.

"I started to play in nightclubs and in bars, *boites*, as they called them. For years, you know, I played this nightlife very heavy, for dancing. Playing piano.

"I tried to compose. I tried to write. But I would never show anything to anyone. I had a drawer full of songs. Finally I got to the radio and record companies. I used to write down the melodies that composers would write by ear. I was a copyist. I used to write down the Carnaval melodies."

Carnaval, as surely everyone knows, is that celebration in February, just before Mardi Gras, when the streets of Rio go mad with costumed dancers. Rio is unique among the world's cities in that the rich do not live on the high ground and the poor on the lowlands, as in Montreal and Hong Kong. In Rio it is just the opposite. The rich live in glorious houses and apartments at sea level; the poor live in the *favelas*, as the slums are called, that sprawl up its glorious hills. The poverty is grinding and terrible, and there is a shortage of water. Despite all this hardship, residents of these neighborhoods—mostly black—will work for a year making costumes for Carnaval, often spending much of a year's income on them. Somehow they find it worth it, and when Carnaval at last comes, there is fabulous dancing to what the Brazilians call *escola de samba*, school of samba.

"Carnaval is not any more what it used to be," he said that day. "It's changed a lot. Brazil is industrial, and coffee isn't any more the first

income. But Carnaval was a big thing. *Escola de samba*, the street samba.
Everything was very important.

"Also the making of 78s. I mean records. Records that would have a
short life. It was just a hit, a Carnaval hit. And some of them are good,
well done. And it was a big thing. The melodies, and the samba and the
samba cancão, the slower songs. They're called *mediano*. In other words,
mid-year music, every music that is not played during the carnival.

"Before Carnaval—let's say from December—everybody was already
composing and recording for the coming Carnaval in February. Lots of
activity in January. And then in February, Carnaval would come and
take over. You wouldn't listen a mid-year song any more. Radio was very
important, before TV. Radio was the thing, and all the radios were playing the Carnaval songs. And I used to be a piano player for a record
company.

"And later I moved to Odeon. I became the a&r man for Odeon. By
then I had a lot of songs already. And singers started to record them. And
I started to *show* them, which I didn't before. I was very timid, very shy,
very scared. I had lots of sambas. I wrote some scores for movies, and
finally João Gilberto came. And I arranged a record for him. I was basically, before being a songwriter, an arranger. I had the attaché suitcase,
going downtown every day to record, mainly with singers, and, how do
you say, some instrumentalists.

"Then an important fact in my life: I met Vinicius de Moraes." The
Brazilians pronounce it: Vee-nee-syuss duh Mo-rah-ees, stress in both
names on the second syllable.) "He was a poet, a composer. At the time
he was a diplomat. But mainly a poet. He had had several books of
poetry published, good poetry. He was a man educated at Oxford. He
was with the foreign service in Paris."

"Wasn't he at UNESCO for a time?"

"UNESCO. He's been around. He was at Strassbourg.

"He had this idea of writing the *Black Orpheus*. Then he arrived in
Brazil. He had been for a long time abroad. He had that deep nostalgia—"

"*Saudade*," I interjected, laughing, knowing it was the word he really
wanted. One of the first things you learn in Brazil is that the word *saudade*
is ubiquitous and untranslatable. It is pronounced sow-DAH-djee. It
means, roughly, longing, yearning, sadness, something akin to what we
mean by "homesick."

"Yes, *saudade*. Vinicius had the script already made. The play, for the
theater. He was looking for a musician. Someone introduced me to him.
We started to do good things. In '56, I think, we went to the Municipal
Theater, and we did *Orfeu Negro* for the stage. It was a big thing there.
Local, but big. All the society came. We did about two weeks in the

Municipal. Then we went to a popular theater, and we did it for two months, the scenery made by Oscar Niemeyer, the famous Brazilian architect.

"Later the French came and decided to produce *L'Orphé Noir*."

The producer was Sacha Godine, the director Marcel Camus. Filmed on location, the picture made brilliant use of the costumes and dance of Carnaval and of the stunning scenery of Rio de Janeiro, even the *favelas*. The film hewed closely to the Moraes play, in which the Greek legend of Orpheus and Euridyce is played out as the tale of a girl who falls in love with a streetcar conductor. They are of course parallels to the lovers of the Greek legend. Another man falls jealously in love with her and follows her in the costume of Death. The film, which contained music by Jobim and Luiz Bonfa, was released in 1959 and became an international hit, eventually winning an Academy Award as best foreign film.

"We worked on the film. I wrote new songs. Luiz Bonfa wrote the famous *Manhã de Carnaval*. And we worked together. And then the film became very famous and got awards all over the world. And in Brazil I stopped being an unknown. They started to know my name, and they would say Mr. Jobim wrote the music for *Black Orpheus*. It brought a lot of publicity for Luiz Bonfa, for Vinicius, and for me.

"Then João Gilberto came from Bahia in the north. The north is hot. The south is more temperate. So, João Gilberto asked me to make a record with him. And in this record he recorded many of my songs, and it became famous. At first nobody wanted to make a record with him. They thought it was not commercial, you know, the old thing.

"Finally we got permission to make a 78, the old 78s. We did it, and it was a hit. *Chega de Saudade* and *Bim Bom*." *Chega* pronounced shay-ga and it means "enough."

"Then João Gilberto got the permission to make an album. So we did his first album." That was in 1958. "And the second. And the third. João Gilberto became a very famous man in Brazil. And in '62, you came down and I met you."

When the first bossa nova records were heard in the United States, it was bruited about that this music had been influenced by records made in California in the mid-1950s by saxophonist and flutist Bud Shank and Brazilian guitarist Laurindo Almeida. This was ardently denied by the devotees of hard bop in the East: West Coast jazz was so patently effete that this could not possibly be.

But according to Jobim, João Gilberto, and many others, this was indeed the case. Trumpeter Claudio Roditi, born in Rio de Janeiro May 28, 1946, is yet another Brazilian musician who confirms this. Claudio remembers growing up on the Jobim records and listening to West Coast jazz records on the Pacific Jazz label. One of the musicians he listened to, as did Jobim and Gilberto, was Gerry Mulligan. In 1959, Claudio said, the Brazilian label called Musidisc was issuing the Pacific Jazz records in Brazil.

"Everybody was into West Coast jazz then," he said. "These records were issued by Musidisc there. Any other stuff would be imported and harder to find. That's why West Coast jazz influenced the bossa nova people that much. I am quite sure that Chet Baker was an influence. The arrangements of the period all sound as if they were influenced by Bud Shank or Gerry Mulligan or those cats. And mainly Mulligan." Virtually every musician involved in the bossa nova movement attests to this North American influence.

Jobim, however, late in his life, tended to minimize the American influence. He told an interviewer that Debussy and Villa-Lobos were very strong influences on him. He continued: "As for jazz, real jazz, I never had much access. What we listened to here were those big bands. Real jazz here was something for collectors, for rich playboy types. . . .

"I'm not much of a connoisseur of jazz." Maybe. But he liked working with American jazzmen such as Ron Carter and Urbie Green. "Later on, I saw that purists here were saying that bossa nova was a copy of American jazz. When these people would say bossa nova's harmony was based on jazz, I thought it was funny because this same harmony already existed in Debussy. No way was it American. To say a ninth chord is an American invention is absurd. These altered eleventh and thirteenth chords, with all these added notes, you can't say they're an American invention. This kind of thing is as much South American as it is North American. Americans took to bossa nova because they thought it was interesting. If it was a mere copy of jazz, they wouldn't be interested. They're tired of copies of jazz. There's Swedish jazz, French jazz, German jazz—Germans are full of jazz.

"Look, what swings is in the United States, in Cuba, in Brazil. These are places that swing. All the rest is waltzes—with all due respect to the Austrians. There are interesting rhythms in places like Chile and Mexico, but it's not the same essence that we have—the black influence mixed with the white influence. It's a question of nomenclature. Latin jazz, Brazilian jazz, soon you don't know what you're talking about any more. . . . We need to free Brazil from these categories. I faced enormous prejudices. I'd play a ninth chord and people would say, 'Look, Tom's playing bebop.'"

He was quite right, of course, that this kind of harmony was not an American invention. But what he told that interviewer is at variance with what he told me in earlier years, particularly about the influence of

Mulligan. A simple example: Roberto Menescal's charming *O Barquinho* is based on the chord changes of Ralph Burns' *Early Autumn*. And the chart on it in the João Gilberto record, which I have always assumed Jobim wrote, sounds like the Stan Kenton band.

And Dori Caymmi (guitarist, arranger, composer, and son of Dorival Caymmi), said: "Shorty Rogers for me was the inventor of bossa nova because he played the way João and Tom played."

All of this raises some interesting points. Mulligan's California quartet records, issued on the Pacific Jazz label, were among those, according to Roditi, that became available in Brazil. In that case, one is forced to reflect that João Gilberto's soft vibratoless singing may have been influenced by that of Chet Baker. It was also influenced—and he told me this long ago—by the French singer from Martinique, Henri Salvador, as well as some earlier Brazilian singers. And so in the longer genealogy, one is forced to conclude that Gil Evans and Claude Thornhill were among the important influences on bossa nova, because of their influence on Mulligan.

Jobim met Gil Evans just once. Gil's widow, Anita, recalled the encounter. "Gil and I," Anita said, "were at a party at the apartment of a painter we knew. Jobim was there. When he saw Gil, he got down on his knees and walked across the room on his knees and kissed Gil's feet.

"Gil was blown away."

As for Shorty Rogers, he came from a somewhat different direction. Shorty was married to Red Norvo's sister. Shorty, a product of the famous High School of Music and Art in New York, joined Red's group when he was still in his teens. Red at that time was playing xylophone, an unamplified wooden instrument of very low volume. Thus the whole group had to be scaled down to a kind of general pianissimo to balance with it. Shorty said that when he settled in California, he tried to continue in that softer style. And he, along with Mulligan, became one of the formative influences on West Coast jazz and, thus, on Brazilian music. It is possible, even likely, that Shorty, who died about the same time Jobim did, never knew of his influence in Brazil.

I stayed in Rio for a number of days more, seeing Jobim, learning about the culture. Brazil and Canada have something in common: they are the only two nations of the Western Hemisphere that parted from the parent European countries without violence. The culture is unique. King Pedro IV of Portugal, who was also King Pedro I of Brazil, granted Brazil its independence in 1822.

Juscelino Kubitschek was voted out of office on October 3, 1960, a little over a year before I reached Rio de Janeiro. Many Brazilians still con-

sider him the greatest president the country ever had, and insist that had
he continued in office, the cycle of corruption, exploitation, and brutality
that has characterized the country since then would never have happened. The new president was Jânio Quadros, and João Goulart was vice
president.

I began to learn something about the Brazilian sense of humor. It was
widely said that Goulart's wife was screwing half the upper echelon of
army officers. In all the Latin countries, including Italy, where a form of
sign language is common, the upheld fist with index and forefingers
extended is the sign of the cuckold, the fingers indicating horns. And
Goulart was known to be one. The trolley buses of Rio, as elsewhere,
drew electric power through two upraised antennae in contact with over-
head parallel wires. Because of this resemblance to the sign of the cuckold, the trolley lines and buses of Rio became known universally as the
João Goulart. And it passed beyond the joke: the Cariocas casually
referred to it that way: "Yes, I'll tell you how to get there. You go down to
the next corner and you take the João Goulart."

At one point, a rumor swept the city that the police were throwing
winos and the homeless into Guanabara Bay. In the next day or so, it
seemed, half the bums in Rio turned up on the streets wearing life jackets.

Far the most popular car in Rio was the Volkswagen Beetle. The people referred to it as *a bunda*, the ass, because everybody has one.

I had begun to hang out of evenings in a little club near the beach called
Bottle's Bar. There I met many of the Brazilian musicians, including Sergio
Mendes and, I think, the guitarist Baden Powell, and probably the com-
poser and guitarist Oscar Castro-Neves, later to be a very close friend.
Johnny Alf was playing there the first night I entered the place. Most of
these musicians were, and still are, unknown in the United States.

I found that the Brazilian musicians, like their North American coun-
terparts, held critics in contempt. One critic, who wrote for one of the
big newspapers, affected sunglasses, even at night, like the American jazz
musicians he knew only from photos. He would come into Bottle's wearing these black shades. The light in Bottle's was dim to begin with, and
he would enter with his knees a little bent, like Groucho Marx, feeling
his way among the tables but never for a moment removing the shades.

I do not remember his name. But I do remember the name the musicians had for him. They called him Flavius the Vampire.

I was becoming entranced by the language, which contains some locu-
tions and constructions not possible in English, including a widespread
use of the diminutive suffix *inho*, pronounced ee-nyo, or, in the feminine
form, *inha*. It seemed you could attach it to almost everything, including
people's names, as we call someone Johnny. A small coffee was a *cafez-*

inho. A *barquinho* was a small boat, as in Roberto Menescal's song *O Barquinho.* The word for afternoon is *tarde*, which is related to our word *tardy.* The diminishing end of the day was *tardinha*, literally "little afternoon," one of the loveliest words I know in any language.

I didn't want to leave Rio. I loved the city, the people, the language, and the music. But the days leaked away, and the Paul Winter group and I traveled to Belo Horizonte, north of Rio, and on to Belem, British Guiana, Venezuela, then home. We reached New York in mid-July.

Among the American musicians who had discovered the bossa nova movement, besides Dizzy Gillespie, were Bob Brookmeyer and guitarist Charlie Byrd. Byrd persuaded Stan Getz to collaborate with him on an album of these songs for the Verve label. Creed Taylor produced the album, titled *Jazz Samba*, and one cut, *Desafinado*, became a hit in the United States at the very time I was seeing Jobim in Rio. By the time I got back to New York in July, 1962, there was a craze, in part stimulated by the film *Black Orpheus*, for this new music from Brazil. Jobim would be in New York before the year was out.

Rising in the ranks of jazz was arranger Gary McFarland, then twenty-nine years old. He'd had his first important break with some compositions he had contributed to the book of Gerry Mulligan's Concert Jazz Band. Though Gary was then still comparatively unknown in the jazz world, Creed Taylor assigned him to write a follow-up Brazilian album for Getz. On August 27 and 28, 1962, Creed recorded Getz with a superb big band and McFarland charts. It was released on Verve as *Big Band Bossa Nova*. It, too, was a success. These albums shot the career of Stan Getz to the level of a pop-music star.

"Do you remember," I said in 1974 as Jobim and I reminisced about our first meeting in Rio, "you didn't speak much English and I spoke a very weird combination of Spanish and French to you?"

"Yes, I remember that night very vividly," Jobim said. "Yes, I do remember too. That leads us to the Carnegie Hall concert and the bossa nova fiasco."

It certainly does. Suddenly, in New York, everything was bossa nova. It was a craze, a frenzy. (A few months later, Eydie Gormé would record a travesty called *Blame It on the Bossa Nova.* Even more egregious was *Bossa Nova Baby* recorded by the Coasters and, of all people, Elvis Presley.)

Meanwhile, in Brazil, a member of the Brazilian diplomatic corps named Mario Dias Costa had a vision that this was the time for Brazilian music on the world stage. He was the force behind the organization of a concert to be held in Carnegie Hall in New York. He persuaded Varig, the Brazilian airline, to fly the prominent bossa nova musicians to New York. The concert would be produced by Sidney Frey, the owner of Audio Fidelity Records, with co-sponsorship by *Show* magazine (which has long since died). Jobim flew to New York on November 22, 1962, arriving barely in time for the concert that night.

I had begun by then to habituate Jim and Andy's, a restaurant and bar on West 48th Street a few doors east of Sixth Avenue, which lingers in fond memory of just about every jazz musician who lived in New York at that time. And one of my increasingly close friends of that time was Gerry Mulligan. I had told Gerry what some of the Brazilian musicians had told me of his influence on their music. And so when the Carnegie Hall concert was announced, Gerry and I attended it together. We went backstage just before it started. I found Jobim and introduced him to Gerry.

The concert was indeed a fiasco. It presented just about every Brazilian musician Sidney Frey could lay his hands on, including Bola Sete, Carlos Lyra, Sergio Mendes, and Lalo Schifrin. Lalo was not Brazilian, but he knew this music. The average *norteamericano* didn't know the difference between an Argentine and a Brazilian anyway. Nothing went right on that concert. The sound system was disastrous, the balances dreadful. Sometimes you couldn't hear the players at all.

The night was traumatic for the participating musicians, and some of the reviews in the New York papers the next day were contemptuous of this new music from Brazil. Many of the Brazilian musicians turned to me for solace. Gerry Mulligan and I sort of flanked Jobim, trying to protect him. He and the other Brazilians seemed so naive, so vulnerable to the vultures of the New York record and music publishing industries. "In Brazil," Jobim later said to me of these people, "I met the sorcerer's apprentices. In New York I met the sorcerer." Many of the musicians, completely dispirited, went home.

The one who seemed least likely to succeed in America was Sergio Mendes, with whom I had dinner the night after the disaster. He was not a bossa nova musician at all. He was a jazz pianist, much inspired by Bud Powell and Horace Silver. Interestingly, like Horace, he shared African and Portuguese antecedents. Much later, Sergio said of his Brazilian colleagues: "They left Brazil at that time, but they never really left, if you know what I mean. They were always thinking about going back, and when they went back all they were talking about was the United States. But I went to the United States with the idea of having a career, of having a group and developing a sound.

"Wherever they were, the others were always thinking about the other reality. I was always thinking about this reality."

He soon played a gig at the Village Vanguard, and would succeed fabulously.

In 1974, recalling the Carnegie Hall concert, Jobim said, "I wouldn't have come. It was too late for me to make America. I didn't have any intention of coming. I was scared of airplanes, and I didn't want to travel very much. But! That was a foreign service thing, you know. We had practically all the bossa nova guys. We had João Gilberto, we had Carlos Lyra, we had Sergio Mendes, we had Luiz Bonfa, Bola Sete. About twenty-five to thirty guys. The whole batch. Then we went to Washington and we gave a concert there. Then we went to the Village Gate in New York, and then we were free, and everybody went home, because nobody had the permission to stay. So they went back. And I was going to go back too. And I thought, 'You know, I've never left Brazil.' I was thirty-five. 'And I think it's time to see what it's like, these great musicians I'd heard since I was a kid. And I should say hello.' They were all around. Stan Getz wanted to do an album, and things like that. Everybody went home, but João Gilberto and I decided to stay.

"I had many songs that the publishers wanted, so they gave me some advances and I could rent an apartment. And I got my union card, I got a visa and everything. Creed Taylor, who was working for Verve, very much wanted to do an album with Stan Getz and João Gilberto. You wrote the liner notes. I arranged the album, and played on it. It did very well."

The winter closed in. It was harsh enough on those of us who were accustomed to cold, but for the Brazilians left lingering in New York after the Carnegie Hall disaster, it was worse. They would shiver in something close to pain on their way to a little Brazilian cafe on West 44th Street, just east of Times Square. There, finding solace in the Portuguese chitchat, they would linger over *cafezinho*, their faces long with *saudade* for home, reluctant to exit into that cruel winter. On New Year's Eve, Lalo Schifrin threw a party for them at his apartment in Queens. I remember Baden Powell arriving there with his guitar wrapped in a blanket to protect it from the cold. He played duets with the late Jimmy Raney.

Jobim had given my lyrics for *Corcovado* and *Desafinado* to the original publisher in Brazil, apparently Lebendiger. By contractual arrangements I still do not understand, these songs were subcontracted to two U.S. publishers, Leeds Music, which has long since been absorbed into MCA, and the Richmond Organization, owned by Howard S. Richmond and generally known as TRO. Someone at Leeds decided that I had made a "mistake" in failing to rhyme the last lines of *Corcovado*, and turned the song over to Buddy Kaye, whose best-known piece of work was a lyric transforming a Rachmaninoff theme into *Full Moon and Empty Arms.* Kaye changed my opening line from "quiet nights of quiet stars" into "quiet nights *and* quiet stars." This ignored the allusion to a Van Gogh painting. But more to the point, it made it far less singable. With "of quiet," the soft fricative *vvvv* sound passes easily back to the throat and the *k* sound of "quiet." But with "and quiet" you get a sudden and awkward motion of the tongue after the *d* sound from the ridge above the upper teeth back to the *k* sound in the throat, which produces an ugly glottal click and is awkward for a singer. Equally dismaying, Kaye introduced the sentence "my world was dull each minute until I found you in it," which I considered banal and a truly dumb rhyme. More to the point, it vitiated the subtle *triste* quality that I think lies rooted in Arabic kismet. Jobim later was to say—many times, in fact—that he thought that Brazilians had derived the *triste* from the Portuguese. Altering the ending of my translation butchered all that.

Meanwhile, Howie Richmond had assigned *Desafinado* to Jon Hendricks, who came up with an idiomatically American, rather than Brazilian, lyric called *Slightly Out of Tune.* I warned Jobim of what was happening, but he did nothing. It was then that I discovered that he was a rather weak and often vacillating man, for all his brilliance. Sal Chianti, then president of Leeds, once said that Jobim held the opinion of the last elevator operator he'd happened to talk to. (He also said that Jobim made the mistake of thinking he understood English.) Only later, when recordings of these "other" lyrics had come out, did he take action, raising so much hell that Leeds finally republished *Corcovado* with the English lyric I had written, and TRO republished *Desafinado* with my translation and the title *Off Key.*

Jobim wanted to make a demo with my lyrics to both songs. He asked if I could find a pianist to do it with us. Yes, I said. Bill Evans. Bill said he'd be glad to do it. We laid down *Quiet Nights of Quiet Stars* without incident. And then we turned to *Desafinado.* To amuse Bill and me, Jobim, playing guitar, sang all the wrong ways he'd heard Brazilian singers do it. We were laughing helplessly by the end of it. And then, when we came to do a take, I had the wrong versions so firmly fixed in my ear that in the end we had to abandon it. I just couldn't get it right.

I treasured that tape, because it had both Bill and Jobim on it. It was destroyed in a fire around 1972.

Creed put João Gilberto, Jobim, and Stan Getz together for an album called *Getz–Gilberto,* recorded March 18 and 19, 1963. One of the songs was to be *The Girl from Ipanema,* with a lyric by Norman Gimbel. The opening line in the Portuguese lyric contains five notes; Gimbel reduced this to three ("Tall and tan ... "), which completely destroys the swing. Creed wanted to use the English language version of the song. Astrud Gilberto, who was in the studio, harbored secret dreams of singing. So she sang it. The lyric was written for a man. And for the line "she looks straight ahead, not at me," she invented the grammatical horror "she looks straight ahead, not at he."

But it was a hit. Astrud hadn't been paid a penny for the session, though of course her husband had. And within days, the record was on the charts. It was at this point that Getz called Creed's office. Betsy, Creed's secretary, took the call; Creed was out of the office. When he returned and she told him Stan was anxious to talk to him, Creed thought Stan must be calling to see that Astrud got some share of the royalties. On the contrary, he was calling to make sure that she got nothing.

The story of this soon made its way to Jim and Andy's, prompting one of the more famous wisecracks about Getz. Al Cohn, one of the great wits, who had been in the Woody Herman Four Brothers band with Getz, said, "It's nice to see that success hasn't changed Stan Getz."

Zoot Sims said that Stan was "a whole bunch of interesting guys," and Bob Brookmeyer, when a rumor circulated that Stan had undergone open-heart surgery, said, "What did they do? Take one out or put one in?"

As previously noted, Jobim, Sergio Mendes, and I were all Aquarians. Stan Getz, with whose name Jobim's became so closely associated, was born February 2, 1927, eight days after Jobim. Once when Jobim was making a proud recitation of some of the great Aquarians in history, I reminded him: "Don't forget, Jobim, Stan Getz is also an Aquarian." There was a baleful pause, and then he said, "I think I'll change my sign."

As the spring came to New York, Creed Taylor planned an album to feature Jobim. He assigned Claus Ogerman as its arranger. I was horrified. I had never met Claus Ogerman, but I despised his writing. I had heard only his commercial work for people like Leslie Gore, and it was awful. He was giving Quincy Jones, then the a&r director of Mercury Records, the kind of crap that Quincy even then wanted. I had absolutely no idea that Claus Ogerman was the brilliant arranger he is.

Claus wrote the album mostly in taxis as he rushed about town, for his ability to turn out trash on command had made him one of the busiest arrangers in New York. The album was recorded on May 9 and 10, 1963, at the funky but effective old A&R studio, next door to Jim and Andy's, with Phil Ramone the engineer, and released with the title *Antonio Carlos Jobim: The Composer Plays.* This album too was a hit.

The music business being the exercise in unimpeded avarice that it was, and is, bossa nova was being ruthlessly exploited and corrupted in the United States. But Creed Taylor was treating the music with respect and dignity. Were it not for Creed Taylor, I am convinced, bossa nova and Brazilian music generally would, after the Carnegie Hall mockery, have retreated into itself, gone back to Brazil—or byack to Brazio, as the Brazilians pronounce it—and become a quaint parochial phenomenon interesting to tourists, instead of the worldwide music and the tremendous influence on jazz itself that it in fact became.

And Jobim would not have been the international celebrity he soon was to become. Brazil doesn't know what it owes Creed Taylor. He would record Walter Wanderley, Milton Nascimento, the Tamba Four, and others. The relationship between Claus Ogerman and Jobim evolved into a close, almost telepathic, communication, and over the years they would make a number of albums together, true works of art, classics transcending the term "popular music."

It was during this period that I had one of the bizarre experiences of my life. It's funny in retrospect but it wasn't at the time.

João Gilberto was having trouble with one hand. Jobim suggested it was psychosomatic. Gilberto went to a chiropractor who, Astrud told me, wanted money in advance for a course of treatments. Incredibly, they gave it to him, perhaps thinking that was the way things were done in this country. When the treatments did João no good, and he still could not easily play guitar, she asked me to go with them to ask for the return of the money, which they were severely short of at the time. She was afraid their English was not adequate to these negotiations.

I went with them to the man's office on the West Side. He turned out to be six-foot-three, a huge man. He looked like Rasputin. And he was blind. As I stood in front of him and explained the problem of my Brazilian acquaintances, the man went into a psychotic fury and grabbed me, with both hands, by the throat, screaming at me for daring to impugn his abilities. I tried to claw his hands away. And you can imagine the strength of his chiropractor's hands. I thought this was the end of it for me, and what a strange way to go: strangled by a blind chiropractor. Finally he released me. Whether the Gilbertos got all or any of their money back, I no longer recall.

Mulligan and I were still hovering, as it were, over Jobim, who seemed naive. In later years, I found he was anything but that. Nor were a number of the other Brazilians, as Claus Ogerman observed. For all their charming apparent innocence, some of them were quite cunning.

By now Jobim was attracting media attention, although whether the word "media" had come into its present currency, I don't know. One of the television networks wanted to do a news feature on Jobim. By now he had picked up quite a bit of English and they planned to interview him. They needed a place to shoot the interview. Gerry Mulligan at that time had a penthouse apartment near West 72nd Street and Central Park West. Gerry offered the use of the place, which had a piano that would permit Jobim to play a little. We took him up there, and the news people set up their equipment. At some point, Jobim and I walked out onto the terrace. It was a gray, rather bleak day, and chilly, in that spring of '63. Jobim did seem lost; twelve months before this, he had been completely unknown in North America, and only a year or two before that, for that matter, not that well known even in Brazil. Big gray-and-white birds were swinging through the air on still wings, riding the currents and crying. Jobim said, "How do you call these bird?"

"Sea gulls."

He repeated it, then said it again. He did this with new words you taught him, assimilating them. "Yes," he said. "We have those in Brazil." I never heard anyone sound more homesick. But they don't have that word in Portuguese. But they do have *saudade*, and he was filled with it.

Jobim was living in a small hotel that catered to Brazilians, just east of Times Square. And there were the Brazilian restaurants nearby, although he showed a peculiar liking for the food at Horn and Hardart's. "It's good, honest, plain food," he would say. I was with him in that hotel room one day as we worked on the song that he called *Vivo Sonhando* (I Live Dreaming) in Portuguese. He liked to do that: work face-to-face with me. He called it "working in the deep way." But I didn't like it. Lyrics take incredible patience to write, and therefore they take time, and composers become impatient. I like to work on lyrics in solitude, turning over ideas and abandoning them. I have often said that you don't write lyrics, you find them. You keep looking for the right ideas, the ones that give you that Eureka! click.

He was playing the chords on his guitar and singing the melody. At one point he looked up and said with a sly smile, "We're fooling them. They think we're writing popular music."

I couldn't find a thing. Finally I went home. I awoke the next morning with the English lyric complete in my head, wrote it down as fast as I could move the pencil, and took it to him. Fran Jeffries was one of the first singers to record it.

Sometimes he would come over to my basement apartment in a little brownstone on West End Avenue, between 70th and 71st Streets. It had a small courtyard, which kept one from claustrophobia. He would work on my guitar, one I had bought in La Paz, Bolivia, from the old man who made it. It was built therefore at an altitude of 11,000 feet and wasn't meant for the climate of New York City. But then, a lot of the Brazilians who stayed in New York had trouble with their guitars too. By their second winter there, they found that the city's steam heat was causing some of their instruments to break up. Mine already had a cracked back. "But it's a nice friendly little guitar," Jobim said.

By then, it seemed, all the drummers in New York were trying to get the hang of the eighth-note patterns of bossa nova, coupled with those off-center rim shots, and not getting them right. Gene Bertoncini was starting to get the guitar patterns, and later he became masterful at Brazilian music, as did Bucky Pizzarelli. And in later years, I found that one of the finest drummers for Brazilian music is Joey Baron. But American musicians just didn't have the feel for it in 1963 and '64.

At one point I had surgery at Roosevelt Hospital for a torn miniscus. Jobim wanted lyrics for *Samba do Avião*, and, as was usually the case, he wanted them right away, so he came to the hospital. I wrote the English lyrics for *Song of the Jet* as Jobim sat by my hospital bed playing guitar. Tony Bennett recorded it with Carlos Lyra on guitar and Al Cohn playing the tenor solo.

From that same time came *Someone to Light Up My Life*, which a number of singers have told me is their favorite of the songs I wrote with Jobim. In this case, the lyric in English has nothing to do with the Portuguese original, which means "If Everyone Were Like You." I daresay I couldn't make it work in English. (Some years later, when Debby Boone got a hit on a song called *You Light Up My Life*, Jobim phoned me and said in his best dark manner, "They have stolen our song.")

Late in his life, Jobim told an interviewer in Brazil, "I'm a guy who wakes up at 5 A.M. to write music. As you know, one of the jobs I'm working on right now is the revision of all my music, because the first publishers got everything wrong. They made mistakes in the melody, in the harmony and in the rhythm. And there's no point in leaving all of this music full of mistakes."

If mistakes were left in his music, it is at least in part his own fault. Howie Richmond and TRO had the sub-publishing rights to *Someone to Light Up My Life*. And Richmond was willing to give Jobim anything within reason that he wanted. What Howie wanted, in turn, was lead sheets on that and other tunes. Neither he (nor I) could ever get Jobim to write one. Finally, Howie turned to Alec Wilder for help. Alec studied one of the records and then harmonized the tune. The published harmonization of that song in North America is Alec's, although in subsequent recordings with Claus Ogerman and others Jobim got the harmonization he wanted.

Creed Taylor came to a dispute with MGM, which owned the Verve label. He disagreed on the count of his record sales, sued them, and won.

But he left Verve and established a relationship with his own CTI imprimatur on albums released by the A&M label, one of whose owners was Herb Alpert. Creed promptly signed Jobim and began to record him again. One of the resultant albums was *Wave*, recorded in 1967, again with charts by Claus Ogerman. Jobim was advancing, moving on from his bossa nova years. But those songs were far from abandoned.

That same year, 1967, I went out to Los Angeles to work on some songs for a film with Lalo Schifrin, by now an established movie composer. Claus and Jobim had alerted me that they were going to do an album with Frank Sinatra. I got in late one evening before the recording sessions and phoned Claus at the Beverly Hills Hotel. Jobim got on the phone and they insisted that I come over for a few drinks.

They had been put up by Reprise Records in two bungalows. Claus had a small nightclub piano, one of those, I believe, that is an octave short. Jobim had his guitar, and Claus was writing the charts at this late date! They were working on the arrangement for Irving Berlin's *Change Partners*. But neither of them knew the tune that well, and I did. So I sang it, Jobim played guitar, and Claus built that chart around me. It was fun, unforgettable fun.

They had already done the chart on *Quiet Nights of Quiet Stars*. Jobim was very pleased that Sinatra was going to record it. Sarah Vaughan, Marilyn Maye, and a few others had recorded it as I had written it. But with Sinatra's power, his record would go far to eradicate the other version of it.

I went to the studio with Claus and Jobim. They began to run down the tunes. Sonny Burke, the producer, was sitting with the engineer at the control table. In front of it was a sofa. I sat down and looked out through the double glass at the orchestra. Suddenly I felt behind me something akin to a shock wave. It wasn't that someone had opened a door; the door was already open. I simply knew that Sinatra had entered the room. I turned and saw him greeting Sonny Burke and others who had assembled. He had that kind of presence, which people find hard to believe. But it's true.

Sinatra went out into the studio. Jobim sat on a stool with his guitar. Claus ran the orchestra through the first chart, Sinatra joining them. The engineer asked Sinatra if they could move the microphone to put a little more distance between him and the orchestra. He said he was having trouble getting adequate separation. "That's *your* problem," Sinatra said. He liked to be near the orchestra, be part of it, and he absolutely refused to record with headphones. That was the nearest I saw Sinatra come to being imperious in the whole session. He was unfailingly courteous to everyone, quietly humorous, and consummately professional. He was, of course, and he was famous for this, impeccably dressed.

They got to *Quiet Nights of Quiet Stars.* He did several takes on it, each of them better than the one before. Finally Sonny Burke, the producer, said, "I think that does it, Frank. That's a good one."

Sinatra said, "I can get a better one." And he did.

Jobim continued to record with Creed Taylor. *Wave* was followed by *Tide.*

I too continued a cordial association with Creed, and because of Creed and Jobim, it seemed that my apartment in New York, by now a much larger one on West 86th Street, became a sort of landing pad for arriving Brazilians. The Tamba Four stayed there once while I was away, and only recently, Flora Purim reminded me that she and Airto Moreira, her future husband, stayed in that apartment when they too reached New York.

Most of the Brazilians, to be sure, continued to go home. Luiz Eça had a falling-out with the other members of the Tamba Four and left. Eventually they all went home. Like Sergio Mendes, Flora and Airto decided to stay and make their careers here.

Jobim, however, was spending more and more of his time in Brazil, although he maintained a small apartment on East 86th Street, walking distance from the Metropolitan Museum.

By now Creed had left A&M records to establish his own label. In six sessions during April and May, 1970, Jobim recorded *Stone Flower.* It contained a tune called *Children's Games,* a sort of samba in three, which Jobim had written for a film called *The Adventurers.* If *Stone Flower* was not the most successful of Jobim's albums, it was one of the best from that period of his life. It was Jobim's last album for Creed Taylor.

In 1974, I was again visiting Los Angeles, working on some project or another. Jobim had come up from Brazil. In those years we always remained more or less in touch. He was staying at the Sunset Marquis, a building of apartment suites in West Los Angeles on a sloping street south of Sunset Boulevard and just east of the Beverly Hills town line. Jobim wanted me to put English lyrics to the tune he had called *Children's Games* and had now renamed *Chovendo Na Roseiro,* which means Raining on the Roses. Because, he said, a double rainbow was a sign of luck, he wanted to call the song *Double Rainbow* in English. We worked very closely on that song and finally finished it.

When Jobim showed me the lyric to *Wave,* to which he had written English lyrics himself, I tried to dissuade him from ever using it, but he was convinced it was a good lyric. It isn't. Indeed, it's awkward and contains that ludicrous couplet, "When I saw you first, the time was half past three. When your eyes met mine, it was eternity." That's one of the worst lines since Larry Clinton wrote "Let's dispense with formality," in his adaptation of Debussy's *Reverie*. Fortunately, Jobim's music is so good that it overpowers the lyric's weaknesses.

Jobim signed a contract making Ray Gilbert his publisher. And thus Ray Gilbert, through Jobim, gained access to other Brazilian composers, including Marcus Valle. Jobim gave my lyric to *Bonita*, which I had written in New York, to Ray Gilbert, who altered a phrase or two and put his name on it. If you look at the credits on the back of the album titled *The Wonderful World of Antonio Carlos Jobim*, which has charts by Nelson Riddle, you'll find that the writer credit on *Bonita* reads Jobim/Gilbert.

Gilbert produced an album for Warner Brothers in which he again used the song, again taking credit for the lyric. He is seen in a photo on the back of the album. He was a small man with a neat goatee and a bald head, and he looked remarkably like Lenin.

I was furious about both records and took the matter up with the American Guild of Authors and Composers. A hearing was organized, with Sheldon Harnick as its chairman, and I presented the evidence of my authorship. The committee ruled that it was indeed my lyric, solely or largely.

I was not the only one to be fleeced by Ray Gilbert. Marcus Valle complained, almost with a broken heart, of what Gilbert had done to him. And, eventually, so did the late Aloysio de Oliveira, who was always called Luiz Oliveira in the United States.

The lyric credit on the recording of *Dindi* is shared between Gilbert and Luiz. But an exegetical examination suggests that it was not written by anyone whose native language was English. It has odd grammatical lapses, such as "say all the beautiful things that I see." You can describe them, tell of them, but you can't *say* them. That nuance would have been lost on Luiz. I have considered ways to fix that song, only to conclude that its anomalies, its slightly alien quality, are part of its peculiar charm. And Luiz Oliveira told me that the lyric was entirely his. These things, and others, are the reason I say Jobim could cause damage to the lives of his friends.

The contretemps over *Bonita* was one of the reasons I parted company with Jobim.

Ray Gilbert was married to actress Janis Paige. After his death, she asked Luiz and me to have a meeting with her. She wanted to do the right thing with Gilbert's publishing estate. I was impressed by this. She paid me royalties on *Bonita* from then on.

And then one day, by which time I had moved to California, I got a call from New York from Luiz Oliveira.

Warner Brothers wanted to do a new two-LP set of Jobim's material, and Ray Gilbert would *not* be the producer. Luiz was producing it, and Warner Brothers would pay all my expenses. The arranger was Claus Ogerman. I told Luiz that I wanted nothing to do with Jobim, ever. Luiz said, "We need you. We can't just record the old songs again. They have been recorded too many times." He said Jobim had some wonderful new melodies that needed English lyrics. I reminded Luiz of our mutual adventures with Ray Gilbert. He said Claus wanted to speak to me. Claus got on the phone. He said, "We all want you. Luiz wants you, I want you, and Antonio wants you." I told him, "Absolutely not." And finally Claus said, "Luiz and I will protect you."

I trusted Claus, and for that matter, Luiz as well. And so, with misgivings, I went to New York and checked into the hotel where Jobim, Claus, and Luiz were staying. Jobim was flattering.

He had left his wife of many years, Tereza, a woman I liked a great deal. Indeed, when last I had seen her, at the Sunset Marquis, she'd had a worried, frightened quality about her. She was entreating me to advise him against some business move he was about to make, but I could only tell her I had no influence over him. Perhaps the marriage was breaking even then.

And now Jobim had a new girl, many years his junior. They were not yet married. He had brought her and her mother to New York. Jobim said he had quit drinking, on doctor's orders.

His behavior became increasingly erratic. I would be up early and wanting to work. He would say he was tired, or that he didn't feel like it yet, we should wait until the afternoon. And I would sit with Luiz Oliveira or Claus and waste another day.

There was one song over which Jobim and I clashed badly. I no longer remember what it was, or what it became. But he was fixated on a symbolism he wanted used in the lyric, a play on words about a priest trying to climb a temple or a castle wall or some such; it was really about his desire for the girl. It was hopelessly obscure, and even if I could render it into English, it promised to be an even worse lyric than that of *Wave*— what Alan and Marilyn Bergman call physical discomfort lyrics.

And then the Heinekens began. At first it was a little of it, but then he was drinking more of it, and I could see the signs in the behavior. I didn't care if Warner Brothers was paying my expenses, I couldn't waste all this time. After a week or two nothing had been accomplished. Even the loyal Luiz Oliveira was talking of walking out on the project, and Claus, I knew, was seriously exasperated. Finally I said to Luiz, "This is crazy. I've had all I can handle. I am going home."

Luiz said, "I cannot blame you."

I packed my bags and left for the airport.

When the album came out, a two-LP set now on CD and titled *Tera Brasilis*, it was largely a recapitulation of songs we had written years before.

I would never work with Jobim again. I had lunch with him a few years later in Los Angeles. The past seemed far away, and the bad parts of it not worth remembering. He seemed saner now, and he was still creating superb music, explorative and very stirring. I never, even for a moment, lost the musical respect for him I had held since first hearing his songs.

For all that he was revered in Brazil, Jobim was criticized there, and he was not averse to criticizing back.

"Some Brazilians," one journalist wrote, "never forgave Jobim for being so extraordinarily successful. He has been described as someone who sold his soul to the United States."

I sometimes think those who most criticize a country are those who love it most, not the conspicuous posturing patriots. Those who truly love a country call on it to adhere to its highest ideals and aspire to even higher. And Jobim said, "I've never seen a more corrupt, more bureaucratic country than ours." I daresay that cost him a few friends. And he said, "We have this misery mania. Brazil cannot see anything that works. Brazil loves Garrincha"–a noted soccer player–"but it needs to learn to love Pele. He was a success and Garrincha died a pauper." (Jobim was a soccer fan.)

The remark was no doubt in response to the resentment of his success. But this attitude is endemic in the North American jazz world where success is seen as evidence of mediocrity, while failure, a miserable life, alcoholism, or an early drug death empower a certain kind of critic to bestow an essentially condescending praise. Cannonball Adderley, Dave Brubeck, and even Miles Davis have known the sting of this.

Jobim said, "I'm not the one who badmouths Brazil. Brazil badmouths Brazil."

He had even undergone criticism for his music itself, as superb as it is. He said, "The more my music is Brazilian, the more they call me Americanized."

And he said, "I've dedicated my life to Brazilian music, because you already have the French to write French music and Americans to write American music." For myself, I found his music becoming more deeply Brazilian as he grew older and explored a broad range of the musical materials of his country.

He said, "The praise comes from the people, the roguery from the intelligentsia."

There is one point about Jobim's work that I would like to clear up. After his death, I read a Brazilian piece about him that, for all the admiration in its tone, said that he wasn't much of a pianist or a singer. He indeed wasn't much of a singer, but he was a very fine pianist whose simplicity on records was deceptive. Listen to his performance on electric piano of Ary Barroso's *Brazil* on the *Stone Flower* album. And there are some very good examples of his piano on the *Wave* album.

But I have another reason to be aware of the scope of his playing. One day, looking for tape on which to record something, I was playing some cassettes that were without labels. I heard a pianist playing *Someone to Light Up My Life*. He was playing it beautifully, a little like Bill Evans and with plenty of technique. I could not decide who it was, until the ending, when I recognized three voices laughing and talking: Gerry Mulligan, Jobim, and me. I remembered an evening in my apartment, just after I had written that lyric. Jobim was demonstrating the song for Gerry. Having no rhythm section, no need to stay out of its way, he was using the full resources of the keyboard. And he was a formidable pianist.

Interviewing him in Brazil in 1990 for the introduction of the 1990 *Tom Jobim Songbook*, Almir Chediak, its editor and compiler, reminded him that Villa-Lobos had been severely criticized in Brazil.

"He sure was," Jobim responded. "His choices got pretty limited: either change his profession, shoot himself, or do what he did. Fortunately, he chose the best alternative: he faced up to all those people who had absolutely no understanding of what he was doing.... In defense, he put on vainglory, saying, 'I'm a genius,' and that was all. He just pretended to be vain. Eventually he had to leave Brazil. And if he hadn't left, I doubt whether he'd have reached the point of achieving world renown as a composer, which he quite deserves."

Chediak said, "You too."

"Maybe so," Jobim said. "If I'd stayed in Brazil, I wouldn't have made it past the corner bar, where I'd be sitting around drinking beer.... In the Northern Hemisphere, people take things more seriously. Up there it's cold and people stay indoors, all bundled up. Without anything else to do, they write or compose. And that's why all the great works were created in the Northern Hemisphere. In the tropics, the heat generates a search for water."

I am convinced that had Jobim not been a major star in the United States, he wouldn't have been one in Brazil either. But the very need of Brazilians for American endorsement produces a covert resentment of the United States. To succeed in New York City and, by extension, Hollywood, is to succeed in the world, and everyone knows it. In 1953, when the couturiere Coco Chanel came out of an eight-year retirement, the French critics destroyed her. Then her work was praised in *Women's Wear Daily*, Americans went wild about it, and *then* the French took her to their bosom.

So this phenomenon is not limited to Brazil, nor for that matter is it new. Otherwise you would not find in Matthew the sarcastic (and usually misquoted) observation: "The prophet is not without honor, save in his own country, and in his own house."

There is no question in my mind that Jobim was a Brazilian nationalist. But he was more than that, and of all the things he said, one remains particularly vibrant in my mind. It was a rejection of jingoism, of nationalism, of racism, of parochialism. It seemed to echo something Jesus said, speaking of his spiritual unity with the world: "Before Abraham was, I am."

Jobim said to me, and he said it in English, "I am prior to borders."

Jobim suffered from bladder cancer. In November of 1994, he flew to New York to undergo treatment at Mount Sinai Medical Center. He returned to Brazil, telling reporters there that he had undergone an angioplasty. His heart condition had been discovered during the cancer examination. None of this surprised his doctors, who for years had been warning him about his eating and drinking habits. Jobim had been trying to cut back on his alcohol intake, but some of his friends said he had to have a little Sco-watch at least once a day.

He returned to Mount Sinai, where he underwent surgery. He died on December 8, in the same hospital in which Bill Evans had died fourteen years earlier. A little over thirteen months later, Gerry Mulligan would also be gone.

His body arrived at the International Airport of Galeão at 10:15 a.m. the next day, Friday. A spontaneous demonstration materialized. A firetruck carried his coffin, covered with a Brazilian flag, through the city. This developed into a parade that lasted four hours as Cariocas poured into the streets to bid him farewell. Some sang his songs, some stood in silence. The truck passed in front of Churrascaria Plataforma, a restaurant he particularly liked. Its waiters and clients stood outside, some of them in tears. Its owner was already considering putting a plaque, perhaps bronze, on Jobim's favorite table.

There were hundreds of mourners at the Botanical Gardens, where he liked to walk and near which he had lived in recent years. His body was taken in the evening to São João Batista (Saint John the Baptist) Cemetery, from which you can see Corcovado, and laid in a tomb near the graves of friends such as Vinicius de Moraes. Also buried there is Carmen Miranda Francisco Alves.

The ways in which popular music reflect and affect the political climate of a country are fascinating. Nor, as we have noted, is this phenomenon limited to popular music, as witness the predominance of serialism and its derivatives in postwar Germany, and, given Germany's historical musical prestige, in other countries as well. But popular music is ubiquitous, all but inescapable in our electronic age, and it is very powerful.

As I said, it is not, I think, a coincidence that an exquisite sunburst of great popular music occurred in Brazil during the time of optimism generated there by the Kubitschek administration. After that, the generals. Nor is it coincidence that this bossa nova music took hold in the United States during the Kennedy administration, which in its early days inspired a mood of aspiration and optimism, whether justified or not. After Kennedy's assassination, there arose a general unarticulated sense that something had gone terribly historically wrong. And the shriek of distorted guitars and the moral pomposities of Bob Dylan were heard in the land. The popular music of the United States began an accelerating decline into ugliness and illiteracy that has not ended yet.

The day after Jobim's death, the governor of the state of Rio de Janeiro announced a three-day period of mourning.

That night, in the bars, most of the talk was of Jobim. Waiters remembered his heavy drinking. He was said to have given up Scotch, his *uisquinho*, but not beer. A waiter at the bar named Garota de Ipanema— the girl from Ipanema—in honor of the song said that in the past Jobim would have ten glasses of beer a day, then come back the next day to pay his bill. Really? Then he was doing well. Sergio Mendes and I remember when he arrived in California to stay at Sergio's house in Sherman Oaks for a few days. Knowing Jobim's habits, Sergio had filled the refrigerator with Heinekens. By that night, Jobim had gone through all of it.

The next day, Saturday, the mayor of Rio announced that Avenida Vieira Souto, the boulevard along the Ipanema oceanfront named after a famous engineer, would be renamed Avenida Tom Jobim. Jobim liked to sit on a bench there and watch the girls go by. Jobim said, "I'm already at that age to watch the girls from afar. The bad part is the older you get the prettier the girls become." Indeed, it was there that he saw the gorgeous adolescent who inspired the song that, more than any other, launched the career that made him a millionaire. How Jobim would have felt about this is of course unknown, but we can make a guess: when a street was named after Vinicius de Moraes, he said, "Look what they have done with Vinicius. He has become a street. Now the cars roll over him and the dogs come and pee over him."

The plates bearing Jobim's name went up in January. Residents along this street of luxurious tall apartment buildings immediately complained. They prepared to file a lawsuit against the city government. Helio Cabal, who once was Brazil's ambassador to the United States and, retired now, lived on the street, said, "Can you imagine if the mayor of New York–what's his name, Giuliani?–decided to change the name of Park Avenue to Frank Sinatra Avenue?"

At a more practical level, residents and businessmen along the *avenida* worried about the cost of changing their stationery, business cards, invoices, advertising, even drivers' licenses.

The mayor recanted and the new signs were taken down, the old ones restored. But the battle was not ended. A number of politicians came up with the idea that Rio's Galeão (it means galleon) airport should be named after Jobim. This drove travel agents and aviation executives wild: this would necessitate changing computer and ticketing procedures all over the world.

On this issue, I think I can speak for Jobim: in both the Portuguese lyrics and my lyrics to *Samba do Avião* (Song of the Jet), we wrote of arriving at the airport of Galeão. How can I change that to arriving at Tom Jobim International Airport? It doesn't have the same ring, and anyway, it cannot possibly be made to fit the music in either language.

Someone else came up with the idea of naming the road from the airport into the city after Jobim. I think he would find all this very funny. After all, as far as I know, they haven't got around to naming anything after Dorival Caymmi or Ary Barroso, two of Jobim's friends and certainly his idols.

"Dorival Caymmi," he told me in 1974, "is a very important Brazilian composer. He is from Bahia, so he has a different background from me. He is one of the pillars. He came when he was about twenty-something to Rio de Janeiro, and then back and forth for a period of time, and then he moved permanently to Rio. He tried to live in Bahia, but by now it is a touristic resort. Not only foreigners, but also the Brazilians themselves. He had a house there, but it was like a museum. The bus would stop with the tourists. I think Dorival will never return to Bahia. In the big city he is anonymous. In his beautiful penthouse in a high building, he can fix his hammock. He can have the guitar and think about Bahia as it used to be. Bahia is a painting on the wall.

"Caymmi met Ary Barroso, who wrote *Bahia* and *Brazil*. He did very well with Walt Disney. Barroso was the most famous composer in Brazil. He was a very good friend of mine. He got cirrhosis. He called me. He said, 'Antonio, ain't you gonna visit me?' I said, 'Sure. I read in the newspaper that you were a little sick and I didn't want to disturb you.' He said, 'What do you mean, a little sick? I'm dying, man. You come here *now*. I want to see you.'

"I rushed to his house. He had a beautiful house on a hill. You could see the sea. He had a grand piano. He called Dorival Caymmi too. We got together there. He said, 'Well, my friends, I'm gonna die.' Naturally we said, 'No, come on.' Dorival said, 'No. You have to change your life. You can't go on drinking as you used to do.' He was in his sixties. Dorival convinced him that he was not gonna die. Then he would say, 'No, I'm gonna die.' He was very nice. He said, 'Even if I don't die, what kind of life? I will go to a square to read the newspaper.' Because he always liked to be with the orchestra, drinking Scotch. He liked to live.

"Ary was born in Minas Gerais." It is one of the large states of Brazil. It is north of Rio de Janeiro. Its name means General Mines. "It had such tremendous, beautiful forests, with wild life. Everything was gone. He went there. Tried to get back to the old place. The place is not there any more. The same thing that happened with Dorival. And sometimes now I find myself thinking about Ipanema, like the paradise that I knew, the strip of sand with the lagoon on one side, the sea on the other side, and the blue transparent water, the sun and the surfing. And the fish! The incredible amount of fish. If you would drop a line in the water, you could catch pompano, double A class fish, bluefish, snook. Everything. For nothing. Within half an hour, you would give fish to your friends.

"And Guanabara Bay, that was such a paradise. All that is gone. It's oily. You can see the sewage going to the sea, the industrial things. The fish started to die in the lagoon. They used to come, all kinds of fish, shrimp, they used to come to the lagoon to spawn. The beach was white with this fine, singing sand, that you run, you listen *cling cling cling*. It was so fine that it sings when you run. Now, naturally, Brazil is booming industrially, and all this is gone. The freeway came, and industry pollutes the sea and the air."

About the time Jobim had gone back to Brazil, I had gone back to Canada, or more precisely to a picture in my mind of the days of my youth. And like Jobim's Rio, it had all changed. Now you couldn't swim in Lake Ontario. The glorious orchards of the Niagara Peninsula were disappearing, like those of Michigan. In the nineteenth century, the railways came to transport the food. The towns sprang up along the railways. The doctors diminished death, or rather postponed it. The populations grew. Then came the automobile, and the highways to connect those towns, and the big transport trucks, endless flows of traffic day and night, not only leaving their emissions, but, which everyone forgets, devouring the very oxygen out of the air at the same time we are cutting down the great forests that produce it. At last the shopping malls and the parking lots. I had been as shocked by what was happening to Canada as he was by conditions in Brazil. I told him I had written and recorded a song about it, *What in the World?*:

> This is a place where the pines used to stand.
> What in the world are they doing to the land?
>
> This was a field that my dog used to roam.
> What in the world are they doing to my home?
>
> This was once a place to watch the silent clouds.
> Now the neon screams at frightened rushing crowds.
>
> This is a beach that was lonely and free.
> What in the world are the doing to the sea?
>
> This was once a place to watch the herons fly.
> What's become of them? What's happened to the sky?
>
> The hands on the clock read a quarter to twelve
> What in the world are we doing to ourselves?

The process of recording has changed our perceptions beyond imagination. The dead don't die. If you play back the raw tapes of old record dates, you hear the small talk, the ghosts of old laughter and conversations. Listening to the tape of Jobim and me talking, it is hard for me to believe that he grew old—well, almost old—and is gone. I still see the young man opening the door to me on that rainy night in Rio.

"I agree," Jobim said after I finished the song. "I used to go to the mountains, to what they call the virgin forest that had these huge trees that take four centuries to grow. They're all gone.

"The song we just wrote ..." He was referring to *Double Rainbow*, which we had finished that very morning. "It's about the rain," he said, "it's about the forest, about the fox. I love nature, you know. I hope she loves me. And naturally, we don't like to see things being destroyed. Now, for instance, they are opening the trans-Amazon highway, these tremendous roads. And the wood will be gone, those big trees, mahogany, precious woods. And the animals will vanish. And yet at the same time they need the land to plant, to grow food, and roads to transport it.

"We are quite a mean animal, an ingenious, destructive animal. We are building a desert."

And then, to throw off the mood, he said, "Let's sing our song."

Double Rainbow has had quite a number of recordings in the years since that conversation, by Stan Getz (with our friend Oscar Castro-Neves on

guitar) and others. But in my mind's ear, it remains as it was on the day
we wrote it and were full of that curious pride and stillness, a vague
amazement that you have been able to do it yet again, that come with
completing a song, and it was still fragile and new and naive, and we
sang it, accompanied only by Jobim's guitar.

> Listen!
> The rain is falling on the roses.
> The fragrance drifts across the garden,
> like the scent of some forgotten melody.
>
> This melody belongs to you,
> belongs to me,
> belongs to no one.
>
> See the way crimson petals
> scatter when the wind blows.
> Ah, the secret sigh of love that,
> suddenly, the heart knows.
>
> See now!
> A robin's there among the puddles,
> and, hopping through the misty raindrops,
> has come to tell us that it's spring.
>
> Look at the double rainbow!
> The rain is silver in the sunlight.
> A baby fox is in the garden.
>
> O rain, sweet loving mother rain
> that soaks the earth,
> that swells the streams
> and cleans the sky,
> that drains the blue.
>
> See now,
> the jasmine vines are all in blossom.
> A little brook of clever waters
> flows into a vast river. . . .

It was the last song we would ever write together. Like his little brook
of clever waters, Jobim has flowed into the river of history.